MANX CHURCH
ORIGINS

Also published by Llanerch:

FOLK LORE OF THE ISLE OF MAN
A W Moore

SYMBOLISM OF THE CELTIC CROSS
Derek Bryce

THE PHYNODDERREE
AND OTHER LEGENDS
OF THE ISLE OF MAN
Edward Callow

CELTIC FOLK TALES
FROM ARMORICA
F.M.Luzel

THE CELTIC LEGEND
OF THE BEYOND
Anatole LeBraz

THE AGE OF THE SAINTS
IN THE EARLY CELTIC CHURCH
Nora Chadwick

SAINTS OF CORNWALL
G.H. Doble (vols. 1-4 & 6)

For a complete list write to
LLANERCH PUBLISHERS
Felinfach, Lampeter, Ceredigion,
Wales SA48 8PJ

MANX CHURCH ORIGINS

D.S.DUGDALE

First published in 1998,
Llanerch Publishers,
Felinfach.

ISBN 1 86143 067 1

CONTENTS

Illustrations, etc.

See centre pages of book

Preface

The present line of enquiry deals chiefly with written sources, although archaeological reports provide essential evidence for discriminating between alternative propositions. However, it is not enough to attach labels saying whether each piece of information is right or wrong according to the latest assessment. Beliefs that have been widely held for a long time have an intrinsic value and invite an investigation of where they came from. Further, the work of past generations of serious scholars should not be ignored on the grounds that it is not quite in tune with the latest thinking. This would cause confusion in the minds of many people, who expect explanations to be given when any change is proposed to the scenario with which they are familiar.

Undoubtedly, the Norse invasion of the Isle of Man was a catastrophic event. Many have entertained hopes that the new settlers merely modified what they found when they arrived. It might be better to assume that what went before was so heavily overwritten that little of it is now visible. This proposition has to be examined from all angles.

It is recognized that students have a paramount need to know where each piece of information comes from, if the text is to be of any value. Close attention has therefore been given to referencing. At the same time, I have tried to follow a style that does not needlessly fatigue the reader. If the result falls short of the intent, apologies are offered, especially for the numbers of dates that seem to be needed for showing the sequence of events.

I was originally encouraged to pursue these enquiries by the late Archdeacon Edward B. Glass. I am grateful to the Mansk-Svenska Publishing Company for permission to use a translation by G.V.C.Young. An extract from the translation of the Book of Armagh by L.Beiler is reproduced by kind permission of the

Governing Board of the School of Celtic Studies of the Dublin Institute for Advanced studies. An extract from the translation of Bede's 'History' by L.Shirley-Price is reproduced by kind permission of Penguin U.K. Quotations from the books of A.W.Moore and D.Craine are reproduced by kind permission of Manx National Heritage. I am also indebted to the Manx Museum for giving me access to Swift's edition of Jocelin's 'Life of Patrick'. My thanks also go to Dr. Peter Davey for drawing attention to recent studies, also to friends who have offered helpful advice, including Dr Fenella Bazin of the Centre for Manx Studies and Dr Neville Flavell of Sheffield.

Sheffield,
1998.

Chapter 1
CHRISTIANITY IN ROMAN BRITAIN

Christianity obviously came from Palestine. It was carried west-wards by traders along the Mediterranean. Details of how it was transmitted need not be given here, but notice may be taken of the early dioceses of Vienne and Lyons in the south of Roman Gaul. To fix a point in time, Irenaeus, the bishop of Lyons died in the year 202. Already, there were a few Christians in Britain. Christianity as an overt practice was not yet allowed in the Roman Empire, as its adherents were not willing to acknowledge the divine status of the Emperor. After various emperors had carried out massacres of Christians, Constantine issued his Edict of Milan in 313. This recognised Christianity as one of the approved religions of the Roman Empire, so churches could then be built.

1.1 Churches in Gaul

The Roman province of Gaul included modern France and extended up to the Rhine. Christianity was propagated within the Roman Empire by establishing territorial bishoprics in the centres of Roman administration. One of the early bishops was Martin, who was born around 320 in Pannonia, modern Hungary, where his father served in the Roman army. Martin himself joined the army at an early age, but was attracted by Christian precepts. In the year 360, the bishop of Poitiers gave Martin a piece of ground for a monastery. Although Martin was not an outstanding scholar, his straightforward character won him popular support. On this account, he was elected in 372 as bishop of Tours on the River Loire. Nearby at Marmoutier, he set up a monastery to accommodate eighty monks, giving practical expression to ideas that were then in circulation in North Africa.

While Emperor Constantine's 'Peace of the Church' permitted Christianity, it offered no hindrance to other religions. Pagan temples continued to flourish in Gaul. Martin energetically destroyed these temples to extend Christianity into rural districts. He died in 397, his festival day being November 11. A biography of Martin written by Sulpicius Severus received wide circulation.

Two notable achievements of Martin can be discerned. From his establishments at Tours, monastic ideals radiated northwards over the next century. More immediately, his policies promoted the development of a homogeneous Christian culture in Gaul through the medium of the provincial Latin language. This culture was strong enough to hold out against the later Frankish military conquest. The story in England was to be rather different.

1.2 The Romano-British Church

In what follows, the term `British' will be used to refer to the Celtic inhabitants of Britain to distinguish them from the Anglo-Saxons who came later. The British people spoke the British or Brythonic language, akin to Welsh, which was different from the Gaelic or Goidelic language of the Irish. Although Christianity was not particularly associated with the Roman army in Britain, it first appeared among clandestine groups in the garrison towns. One of the early martyrs in this country was Alban. According to the writer Gildas, he lived at Verulamium, now St Albans. Current opinion dates this incident to around 250. Promptly after Constantine's edict had brought religious toleration, British bishops attended the Council of Arles in Gaul in 314. These bishops were from London and York and possibly Colchester. British bishops also attended the Council of Rimini in Italy in 359.

One of the religions of this period was Mithraism, which required moral discipline and which had adherents among the soldiers. Also, many temples were devoted to Roman gods such as Jupiter, Mercury, and Mars. Further temples were devoted to local deities who were often the personified spirits of the sun or of wells or rivers. Temples not only remained in use through the fourth century, but new ones were built. An example is the temple erected around 367 at Lydney in Gloucestershire to serve the Celtic god Nodens (1). It was not until 391 that Emperor Theodosius ordered that Christianity should be the official religion of the Roman Empire and that pagan temples should be closed.

The British Church was kept under observation by bishops in Gaul. Victricius, bishop of Rouen, a former pupil of Martin, came to Britain in 396. This relationship with Gaul continued after the Roman forces withdrew from Britain, as shown by the visit of Germanus, whose career can now be outlined. He was born in 378 at Auxerre, eighty miles south-east of Paris. Germanus studied law in Rome and then became Roman governor in the north of Gaul. He relinquished this position to become a monk at Auxerre. In 418, Germanus was persuaded to become the new bishop there. He died in 448, his festival day being July 31.

When Germanus came to Britain in 429, he was accompanied by Lupus, who was bishop of Troyes, a town a hundred miles south-east of Paris. These high-ranking officials were sent by Pope Celestine to suppress the heresy of Pelagianism. This theological outlook was not in keeping with the doctrine officially accepted by the Western Church. Constantius, a monk of Lyons, produced a biography of Germanus around 480. This was the source used by later writers such as the Venerable Bede, who described how Germanus visited the shrine of St Alban (2).

Bede gave a colourful account of how Germanus assisted the British army, when they raised the battle-cry `Alleluia'. Later writers located the battlefield at Maes Garmon, near Mold, Flintshire, but such details are now considered to be fictitious.

Bede continued to describe how Germanus paid a further visit to Britain in 447. While details of this second visit have been disputed, it may be reasonable to assume that up to a time around 440, an active church organisation existed in Britain. This organisation was managed by about twenty-five territorial bishops supervised by three or four metropolitan bishops.

When Germanus baptised British soldiers, he had to erect a temporary church. This implies that Christianity had not spread effectively into the countryside. Although the British Church

9

maintained a presence in the Roman towns and was supported by at least some of the wealthy proprietors of the Roman villas, it did not gain a strong hold on the rural population. Archaeologists have been able to discover only trivial remains of the churches of this time (3).

1.3 Post-Roman Britain

During the fourth century or earlier, there was an aggressive advance of tribes in Ireland from their homelands in Ulster and Connacht. As a result, displaced peoples of the Deisi tribe of central Ireland moved southwards into Waterford and some crossed to Menevia (Dyfed) in South Wales while people of the Laighin tribe of north Leinster migrated to the Lleyn peninsula in North Wales and also to the Isle of Man. This migration occurred during the period 350 to 400, as estimated by John Davies (4). Irish immigrants set up kingdoms in South Wales, including one at Narberth in Dyfed and another at Brecon.

In 367, a major attack on Lowland Britain was launched by the Picts and by the Irish who were then called Scots. When peace was restored, defensive measures were renewed by the Roman governor Magnus Maximus. He entered into agreements with chieftains on the perimeter of Lowland Britain, including the Irish princes who were already established in Wales. One of these was Brychan Brycheiniog who ruled at Brecon. Welsh tradition strongly asserts that both Magnus and Brychan were Christians, so it it perhaps permissible to assume that Magnus sent priests to the Irish princes in Wales.

Having made these arrangements for defence, Magnus Maximus left Britain in 383. Welsh sources preserved his name as *Macsen Wledig*. Wade-Evans mentioned a rather dubious tradition that Macsen left his sons in Britain, including Antonius or Anthun in the Isle of Man (5). Macsen was the supposed ancestor of a line of princes in Galloway.

In post-Roman Britain, the chief king was Vortigern who had his

10

base in Powys. According to Laing, he flourished from 425 until his death in 461 (6). Vortigen had the task of holding out against Pictish incursions from the north and Irish raiders from the west. Cunedda was a soldier who was invited to come to North Wales to control the Irish immigrants there. The chronicler Nennius stated that Cunedda came from Manau Gododdin, the territory of the British Gododdin tribe on the south bank of the Firth of Forth (7). Nora Chadwick and others now believe that this move took place within the period 430 to 450 (8). If so, the arrangements were probably made by Vortigern.

1.4 The Anglo-Saxon Invasion

Under Roman government, considerable numbers of Germanic soldiers had been stationed in Britain. Vortigern made use of them for resisting attacks of the Picts and Irish. At a date soon after 440, these so-called Saxons asserted their independence. From about 450, further numbers of Teutonic people arrived in England. These people had not been subjected to Romanising influences, and brought their own heathen religion with them. In the territories they colonised, all traces of churches and ecclesiastical organisation were obliterated.

Two primary reasons why this happened can be put forward. Many Saxon settlers arrived with their wives, thus providing a cultural core that withstood pressures exerted by the native population. Further, they found the native tribes in a state of disarray, both in a military and a religious sense. The British Church, by neglecting to strike a decisive blow against the pagan temples, had failed to secure any religious or cultural uniformity among the indigenous peoples, as mentioned by Frend (9). The British language soon withered away in the newly colonised territories.

From about 460, the advance of the Saxons from the east side of England was opposed by the forces of Ambrosius Aurelianus. Very likely, he was sponsored by citizens of the Roman towns. Eventually, the British forces won a victory at Mount Badon, a place somewhere in south-west quarter of England, the date being around

11

495. At this stage, the Saxons occupied England east of a line that might be roughly drawn from the Isle of Wight to Berwick-on-Tweed. North and west of this line, the country was still in British hands and communication with Gaul could be maintained. It was fifty years or so before the Saxons started to advance again.

Decay of the Roman towns was not primarily due to them being burnt down, but was due to a gradual economic decline of the whole country, which began before the end of direct Roman rule. Further, the Saxon farmers had no use for these towns. The British Church may have continued to function in York up to around 450, but the post-Roman historical record there is quite blank.

1.5 Sub-Roman Monuments

In Britain, the typical funerary monument of the pagan Romans consisted of a dressed block of stone carrying an inscription in capital letters. Often this opened with a formula such as *Diis Manibus*, `To the Underworld Deities'. This was followed by the name and official position of the deceased. This custom appealed to Celtic tribesmen on the fringe of Roman Britain, to whom genealogy was a matter of importance. The simplest form of memorial they used had an inscription in Roman letters incised in horizontal lines on a slab, without any decoration. Such a monument can be placed in a Christian context only if the wording reveals this. Some examples follow.

It might be supposed that the British Church exerted some influence in the western territories controlled by the British princes. The `Annals of Ulster' recorded the death of Docco, a British bishop, in 473. He has been associated with Llandough on the south side of Cardiff (10). During the period 450 to 500, the British Church may have continued in some form in Dumnonia (Devon and Cornwall) and to the west of a line drawn from Gloucester to York, serving the Romanised communities in both South and North Wales.

Leslie Alcock has described a stone at Llanerfyl, a village thirty miles west of Shrewsbury (11). The Latin inscription reads: "Here

12

in the tomb lies Rustica daughter of Paterninus, aged thirteen. In Peace". The estimated date is early in the fifth century, and the formula "In peace" shows that it was erected by a Christian community.

1.6 The Early Phase of British Whithorn

The Roman fort at Carlisle, under the name of *Luguvalium*, developed into a significant provincial capital around 250. According to Charles Thomas, the Carlisle area shows distinct traces of fourth-century Christianity (12). From Carlisle, Christianity was propagated north of Hadrian's Wall. When the Northumbrian bishop Pechthelm took up his post at Whithorn just prior to 731, he gathered information about St Ninian and communicated it to Bede, who recorded it in his `History' (2):

"The Southern Picts who live on this side of the mountains... accepted the true Faith through the preaching of Bishop Nynia... a man of the British race, who had been regularly instructed... in Rome. Nynia's own episcopal see, named after Saint Martin and famous for its stately church, is now held by the English, and it is here that his body and those of many saints rest. The place, which is in the kingdom of Bernicia... is commonly known as Candida Casa, the White House, because he built the church of stone, which was unusual among the Britons."

The reliability of this report has not been questioned, apart from the reference to Rome. Earlier, it was believed that as Martin had died in 397, the church at Whithorn might have been set up by Ninian at this time. Recent writers consider that Ninian arrived rather later, between 420 and 450. It is now thought that the dedication to St Martin was bestowed at a time not much earlier than the time of Bede's report, and not in Ninian's time (13).

Aildred, a monk from Rievaulx Abbey wrote his `Life of St Ninian' around 1160. He mentioned a miracle performed by Ninian for the benefit of Tudwal, king of Galloway. Welsh genealogies suggest that Tudwal may have been a great grandson of Macsen Wledig

13

(14). This leads to an estimated date for Tudwal's death of around 470, so it is possible that he was a contemporary of Ninian. The kings of this family are of interest as they figured in Manx affairs in later times.

A further document that can be considered is the letter written by St Patrick to the soldiers of Coroticus, king of Strathclyde (15). These soldiers had carried off people whom Patrick had baptised and had sold them "as slaves of the utterly iniquitous, evil and apostate Picts". This letter has been dated 460 but Thomas proposed a slightly later date of 470 (16). The Christianity that the Picts had cast aside must have been carried to them at some earlier time, perhaps by Ninian's mission.

The presence of a church at Whithorn at an early date is attested by at least one monument. This has an inscription beginning with the words TE DOMINUM LAUDAMUS and commemorates a man called LATINUS. This writing, in capital letters, is arranged in horizontal lines, and the stone does not carry any monogram. Dr Ralegh Radford dated this stone to the mid-fifth century, and most writers agree (12).

Ninian's field of activity extended northwards from Whithorn to the Clyde-Forth line. Daphne Brooke accepted that Ninian founded a church at the village of Eccles, now called St Ninians a mile south of Stirling (17). This place was just within Pictish territory. Over fifty other churches were named after Ninian, as far afield as Cumbria and the north of Scotland, but it is likely that most or all of these were so named at times much later than Ninian's lifetime (12).

Monuments inscribed with a cross or monogram appeared slightly later than those having a simple Latin inscription. The early representations of a cross were in the form of a Greek cross having equal vertical and horizontal arms, often enclosed in a circle. According to Nora Chadwick, the Latin cross with an elongated lower limb came into popularity rather later, perhaps during the late 6th century (13). If an inscription is present, the style of the lettering aids in dating the monument.

Kirkmadrine is in the Rinns of Galloway, a mile or two west of Sandhead. Here, three memorial slabs have been found, all having the same monogram, which consists of a Greek cross within a circle, the upper limb having a small Rho symbol attached to it. The first of these slabs has an inscription in Roman letters: HIC IACENT SANCTI ET PRAECIPUI SACERDOTES ID EST VIVENTIUS ET MAVORIUS, `Here lie the holy and eminent priests Viventius and Mavorius'. The term *sacerdos* does not necessarily mean a bishop. Above the incised cross are the Greek letters Alpha and Omega. The second of these slabs commemorates FLORENTIUS, while the third bears the words INITIUM ET FINIS, `beginning and end'. Collingwood assigned the first two slabs to the sixth century, the third being slightly later (18). However, the more recent opinion of Charles Thomas is that the date should be taken as the late 5th century (19).

Thomas has suggested that Ninian was sent from Carlisle as a bishop within an episcopal form of church organization, and that the priests at Kirkmadrine were sent from the same place. He further suggested that there are no indications of a monastic organization at Whithorn until the late sixth century, but other writers prefer an earlier date. To give approximate dates, the episcopal phase of Whithorn may have extended over the century 430 to 530.

To summarize, the British Church developed under the watchful eye of the bishops in Gaul. It flourished during the period 350 to 450, but by the end of this period it had already gone into a decline, together with the Roman towns on which it was based. The legacy it left included churches that continued to flourish in Wales and at Whithorn and it provided the Christian environment from which St Patrick came.

References for Chapter 1

(1) C.A.Ralegh Radford, *The Early Church in Strathclyde and Galloway*, Medieval Archaeology, Vol.11, 1967, p.105
(2) Leo Sherley-Price, *Bede: A History of the English Church and People*, Penguin Books, 1968, Chap.18, p.61
(3) Dorothy Watts, *Christians and Pagans in Roman Britain*,

Routledge, London, 1991

(4) John Davies, *A History of Wales,* Penguin Books, 1994, p.52

(5) A.W.Wade-Evans, *Prolegomena to a Study of the Lowlands,* Trans. Dumfr. & Gall. Nat. Hist. & Ant. Soc., Series 3, Vol.XXVII, 1950, p.54

(6) Lloyd Laing, *Celtic Britain,* Routledge and Kegan Paul, London, 1979, p.133

(7) John Morris, *Nennius, British History and the Welsh Annals,* Phillimore, London, 1980, Cap.62, p.37

(8) Nora K.Chadwick, `Early Culture and Learning in North Wales', in *Studies in the Early Britishn Church,* (authors: N.K.Chadwick, K.Hughes, C.Brooke & K.Jackson), Cambridge Univ.Press, 1958, p.34

(9) W. H. C. Frend, `Romano-British Christianity and the West: Comparison and Contrast', in *The Early Church in Western Britain and Ireland,* British Archaeological Reports, British Series, No.102, 1982, p.5

(10) Gilbert H. Doble, *The Saints of Cornwall,* Part 5, Holywell Press, Oxford, 1970, p.90.

(11) Leslie Alcock, *Arthur's Britain,* Allen Lane, The Penguin Press, London, 1971, pp.240, 242, 238

(12) A. C. Thomas, `The Evidence from North Britain', in *Christianity in Britain, 300-700',* (editors: M. W. Barley & R. P. C. Hanson), Leicester Univ. Press, 1968, p.99

(13) N. K. Chadwick, *St Ninian: A Preliminary Study of Sources,* Trans. Dumfr. & Gall. Nat. Hist. & Ant. Soc., Series 3, Vol.XXVII, 1950, p.9

(14) C. A. Ralegh Radford, *Excavations at Whithorn,* Trans. Dumfr. & Gall. Nat. Hist .& Ant. Soc., Series 3, Vol.XXVII, 1950, p.85

(15) A. B. E. Hood, *St Patrick, his Writings and Muirchu's Life,* Phillimore, London, 1978, p.58

(16) Charles Thomas, *Christianity in Roman Britain to A.D.500,* B.A.Batsford, London, 1981, p.342

(17) Daphne Brooke, *St Ninian and the Southern Picts,* Trans. Dumfr. & Gall. Nat. Hist. & Ant. Soc., Ser.3, Vol.LXIV, 1989, p.21

(18) W. G. Collingwood, *Northumbrian Crosses of the pre-Norman Age,* 1927, reprinted by Llanerch Publications, Lampeter, 1989, p.2

(19) Charles Thomas, *The Early Christian Archaeology of North Britain,* Oxford Univ. Press, 1971, pp.14-22

16

Chapter 2.
IN PATRICK'S TIME

A reliable document states that in 431, Pope Celestine sent Palladius to be the first bishop of the Irish (1). Palladius landed at Wicklow and established three churches in Leinster which had the names Cell Fine, Tech na Roman and Domnach Airte (2). He left Ireland after about a year, and was followed by Patrick.

2.1 St Patrick

Patrick was born at some place on the west coast of Britain, probably near Carlisle. He belonged to a prosperous Romanised British family, his father being a deacon and his grandfather a priest. As a youth, Patrick was captured by pirates and taken to Ireland. After six years he escaped and returned home. After training as a priest, he decided to go on a mission to the Irish. The most reliable information comes from Patrick's *Confessio*. This is a letter he wrote in his later years protesting that his arduous work in Ireland had received little recognition from the bishops of the British Church.

He also said that while he was working in Ireland he often had a wish to visit his kinsfolk (3). He did not do so, and stayed in Ireland for the rest of his life. It has usually been accepted that Patrick arrived in Ireland in 432 and died there in 461. These dates are based on biographies of Patrick written two centuries after his death. Present-day scholars are not completely satisfied with these dates and some would prefer to fix them twenty years later (4).

After reaching the coast of Ireland, Patrick sailed northwards to Strangford Lough and set up his first church at Sabhal or Saul near Downpatrick. His main field of activity was in Ulster. He addressed himself to the tribal rulers and built a church in each tribal territory. While his achievements cannot be doubted, the task of bringing Christianity to the mass of the people could not be accomplished immediately.

17

Adamnan in his *Vita Columbae* written around 690 made only one passing reference to Patrick, and the Venerable Bede who wrote his Ecclesiastical History in 731 did not mention him at all. The historian James Kenney has said: "Patricius was not entirely forgotten, but such evidence as we have regarding the two hundred years following his death seems to show that his memory had slipped into the backgound of old and far-off things" (5).

2.2 Early Irish Churches

Patrick and his contemporaries aimed at setting up an organisation of the kind found in the Roman Empire, in which dioceses were supervised by bishops. This scheme was not well suited to Ireland where no towns existed. The country was ruled by about a hundred and fifty chieftains who formed only temporary alliances with five or six provincial kings.

Some of the saints who worked during Patrick's lifetime are named in the *Annals of Ulster* and elsewhere. It has to be remembered that very few fifth-century dates in Irish annals are completely trustworthy, as contemporary records were not kept until the middle of the sixth century. Benignus (died 467) was an assistant to Patrick and succeeded him. Three more bishops were sent around 439, possibly from Gaul. Secundinus, who died in 447 at the age of 75 had his church at Domnach Sechnall, now Dunshaughlin, twenty miles north-west of Dublin. Auxilius had his church at Killashee, near Naas, Co Kildare. He died in 459. Iserninus had his church at Kilcullen, also in Kildare. He died in 468. Mention may also be made of the church at Nendrum on Mahee Island in Strangford Lough, founded by Mochoe, who died 496.

Declan was the patron saint of the Deisi tribe and had his church at Ardmore, Co. Waterford. It is said that he came from Wales, but in fact, little is known of him. Later, a monastery flourished at Ardmore, as shown by buildings which can still be seen. Another early bishop was Ibar who founded a church at Begerin Island in Wexford Harbour, his death being dated 499.

18

Bridget may be mentioned here, as the church at Kildare was said to have been founded around 490. It was initially under the supervision of Bishop Conlaed. Bridget was born near Dundalk and died in 524. Her principal biographer was Cogitosus, who wrote around 640, but his account gives little useful information. Bridget was portrayed as the guardian of domestic affairs. To some extent, she may have provided a replacement for a pagan goddess of the same name. Bridget's festival day was put at February 1, this being the pagan Celtic festival of Imbolc, celebrating the return of the sun after winter.

2.3 Ogham Inscriptions

During the late 4th century, a form of writing came into use which represented Gaelic speech in terms of the phonetic values of Roman letters. New characters were devised, consisting of groups of one to five straight strokes set above, across or below a base line, with five more characters consisting of oblique strokes (6). This ogham alphabet was convenient for cutting letters with a knife on a length of wood which had a square edge representing the base line.

For funerary monuments, the symbols were transferred to the corner of a stone slab of rectangular section, so that when the slab was set in the ground, the message could be read from the bottom upwards. More than three hundred inscriptions in ogham have been found in Ireland, nearly all in the counties of Kerry, Cork and Waterford. Most of these stones can be dated to the 5th and 6th centuries. The use of this script spread to the Irish colonies in Wales and the Isle of Man. About forty ogham inscriptions have been found in Wales, nearly all of these being in Pembrokeshire. Concerning the Irish colonies in Britain, Kenneth Jackson has written (7):

"The distribution of the Ogams agrees closely with what is known about thes colonies. There was a dynasty of Irish kings established in south-west Wales, where most of the Ogam inscriptions are concentrated, apparently from the end of the third century..... There is reason to think that they kept in touch with their homeland until at least the eighth century. These settlers had come from the Irish petty kingdom of the Deisi of Co. Waterford, a branch of the people called Erainn who were widely scattered across southern Ireland in the counties of Kerry, Cork and Waterford, the very districts where the Ogam inscriptions are thickest."

The custom of remembering and reciting the parentage and tribal connections of a dead person comes from a pre-Christian Irish background. The typical inscription is very simple, commemorating "N son of M". Of the six ogham inscriptions found in the Isle of Man, one is of special interest. This stone (Manx Museum No.2) is from Ballaqueeney in Rushen parish, east of Port Erin. The inscription, as given by Cubbon, reads (8): BIVAIDONAS MAQI MUCOI CUNAVA, which is translated: "(the stone) of Bivaidu, son of the tribe of Cunavali". The Conailli were a tribe of north Louth and Co. Down. This stone has been dated late fifth century.

The Bivadu Stone, with another similar stone had been re-used for making a lintel grave (9). A lintel grave is one made of slabs of stone set on edge and covered with similar slabs. However, these ogham stones were re-used at a date much later than the date of the stones themselves. So it cannot be deduced that the ogham stones are necesarily monuments from a Christian environment, or that a church existed at Ballaqueeney at a date as early as that of the stones. However, it can be said that the Manx ogham stones of the late 5th century are suggestive of cultural links with Ireland or Wales but not with Whithorn.

2.4 Irish churches called *Domnach*

When Christianity first came to Ireland, the Latin word *dominicum* was taken into the Irish language as *domnach*, meaning Sunday, but it also had the meaning of "church". Early records show about sixty of these church names in Ireland. As many are found in Tirechan's biography of St Patrick, it has often been assumed that the churches of this name were set up by Patrick, but they extend into the south of Ireland beyond the range of Patrick's mission. Deirdre Flanagan estimated that Domnach names were given to churches within the period 430 to 550 (10). The name is not known in Scotland or Wales.

The relationship between ogham inscriptions and Domnach names in Ireland can now be examined. Useful distribution maps have been prepared by Mytum from the data of other investigators (11). A plot of 150 ogham inscriptions shows a concentration in south-west Ireland, where they have a coastal and riverine distribution. A plot of about 50 Domnach names shows that more than half of them are confined to a band stretching from the Dublin region northwards into Ulster. There seems to be no correlation between these two distributions and they are almost mutually exclusive.

Literary evidence leaves no doubt that the Domnach churches were set up by St Patrick in Ulster and by his contemporaries in Leinster. This phase started at a fairly well-defined date of around 430 and may have continued until 500. It represents the work of missionary bishops sent from the British Church and probably also from Gaul, as they made their way to the more densely populated areas on the eastern side of Ireland. While these bishops agreed to the use of the Irish name *Domnach* for their churches, they did nothing to encourage the use of ogham-inscribed monuments.

Distribution maps have lumped together ogham inscriptions of various ages. Some may be pre-Christian. Some may relate to the episcopal phase of missionary activity, but it has been seen that there is no strong support for this idea. Many ogham inscriptions in south-west Ireland occur on slabs that stand at the sites of monasteries. The likely date-range for this monastic phase is 550 to 650. The use of ogham inscriptions in south-west Ireland is strongly associated with a similar usage in Dyfed, and suggests that these communities kept in communication by sea from the late 4th century onwards. However, a proliferation of ogham inscriptions in south-west Ireland may represent a late continuation of this practice by the numerous small monastic churches there. Some discussion of this question has been given by Ann Hamlin (12).

2.5 Manx *Doonee* sites

In modern Manx Gaelic, *Jedoonee* means Sunday, but at some early time, the word *doonee* must have acquired the meaning of `church'. Place-names in the Isle of Man containing this element are now examined. An early reference to Knock-y-dooney in the parish of Andreas occurs in a list of the stations for Watch and Ward for the year 1627. The outline of a keeill can still be seen there, but of course, this need not be the outline of the original building.

Also, there is a hill called Cronk-y-dooney on the land of Ballakilpheric in the parish of Rushen. Mr Kneen has stated that the church at this hill was called Keeill Pharic (13). Kermode stated that stone pillars once stood on either side of the doorway of Keeill Pharic, though nothing is now left of the keeill (9). According to the Manorial Roll of 1511, the keeill stood in the treen or land division of "Kyrke Patryk".

Mr Kneen reported a local legend that this was the first church that St Patrick erected in the Isle of Man (13). It would be expected that the original `Doonee' name would have had a descriptive part, which has been lost long ago. It is likely that the chapel was rebuilt and renamed after St Patrick during Norse times. It appears that the treen in which the chapel stood then took its name from the chapel. In the spoken language, the term `Doonee' ceased to have the meaning of `church' before historical times, and in recent years, attempts to translate the above two `Cronk-y-doonee' names have produced `Sunday Hill'.

A further site was reported by Kermode, this being the graveyard situated in the north of Malew parish, having the name Rullic y Doonee. He says (9): "This name proclaims the site of a church of early date, and many lintel graves have been found". Lintel graves were used over a long period between the 9th and 12th centuries. However, the name of the place suggests that the site was in use some centuries before the date of the lintel graves.

Thus, the Isle of Man provides three Doonee place-names, each associated with a former church. It seems to be accepted that the Manx name `Doonee' is a form of the Irish term `Domnach', and Mr Kneen directly translated the term `doonee' as `church' (13). Therefore, it is suggested that the Manx Doonee churches were analogues of the Irish Domnach churches. In view of the extensive use of Domnach names in Ireland, it is assumed that the usage evolved there and spread to the Isle of Man. As the Irish name `Domnach' is associated with the first phase of church-building under an episcopal organisation, the implication is that the Manx `Doonee' churches were also established by missionary bishops, at a time somewhere around the year 500.

2.6 Latin Inscriptions in Wales

Early monuments have been found at Penmachno, Caernarvonshire. One of these reads: "Cantior lies here, citizen of Gwynedd", while the other side of the stone mentions his cousin, a magistrate. This stone is dated to the late 5th or early 6th century. On the evidence of this stone and others, Davies has remarked (14): "Christianity in some form or another was the accepted religion of a stable kind of society in north west Wales towards the end of the fifth century, and intrusive elements need play little part in it".

Further attention is now given to gravestones in Wales bearing the formula *Hic iacit*, 'Here lies'. This formula has not been found in Ireland, the nearest approach to it being *Hic dormit* inscribed on a stone at Innismurray, Sligo (15). Charles Thomas, quoting the work of Bu'lock, has mapped over forty stones with the formula *Hic* iacit in the Conway Valley, the Lleyn peninsula and Anglesey (16). One of these is at Llansadwrn in south-west Anglesey, commemorating SATURNINUS (17). It is believed that he founded the church there and died around 520. It seems that use of the *Hic iacit* formula was rooted in the British Church but does not, by itself, provide accurate dating since its use was prolonged into later times.

In Ireland, inscriptions on early Christian monuments are found to be written in Gaelic using ogham letters, but bilingual inscriptions are practically unknown. On the other hand, in those parts of Britain where Irishmen settled, and where fifty-seven ogham inscriptions have been found, forty-four of these are bilingual. For example, Leslie Alcock described the stone at Castell Dwyran, Carmarthenshire (18). This gives the Latin: MEMORIA VOTOPORIGIS PROTICTORIS, this being the Brythonic form of the name, while the ogham version reads: VOTECORIGAS, this being the Irish form, as explained by John Rhys (19). This person is thought to be Vortipor, tyrant of Demetia (Dyfed), whose behaviour was criticized by Gildas. This monument may be dated around 550, and may have followed a style that had already been in use for some time.

An explanation for the occurrence of bilingual inscriptions in Wales has been offered by Kenneth Jackson (20). Irishmen in Ireland had not been greatly influenced by Roman culture. They understood Gaelic written in ogham, but as Latin was a strange language to them, they had no motive for writing memorials in Latin. On the other hand, Irish colonists in Britain came into closer contact with the culture of the Roman Empire and wished to emulate the Romans by writing in Latin. As they wished the inscription to be understood by Gaelic speakers, they duplicated it in ogham script.

2.7 Latin Inscriptions in the Isle of Man

About two hundred Latin inscriptions from a Celtic background are known in the British Isles. Many have dates from the 5th century to the 7th. Four Latin inscriptions have been found in the Isle of Man, and two of these have attracted much attention. An epitaph slab was found in 1911 at the chapel site at Knock-e-dooney, Kirk Andreas (21). On the face of the slab is written in capital letters: AMMECATI FILIUS ROCATI HIC IACIT, while the edge of the slab has Gaelic in ogham characters: AMBICATOS MAQI ROCATOS. Jackson has discussed the linguistic aspects of these names (20). Imchadh and Rochadh are Irish names, and are the names of warriors. Jackson gave the date of this stone as late 5th or early 6th century (21). Trench-Jellicoe considered that the best date

24

was early sixth century (23).

A further Latin inscription occurs on a stone that was found at Santan when the parish church was being rebuilt in 1774. The stone was found deeply buried. In later times, such stones may have been regarded with suspicion and buried in a consecrated place where they could do no harm. This long thin slab bears the words: AVITI MONOMENTI, `Monument of Avitus'. The final `i' of each word was written as a stroke parallel to the line of writing. This peculiarity is also found on monuments in south-west Wales and Cornwall. Mr A.M.Cubbon has given the date of the Santan stone as 5th or 6th century (24). Trench-Jellicoe favoured the second half of the 6th century (23). During this period, the name Avitus was a common one in Gaul (25).

Around the year 500, inhabitants of the Isle of Man were predominantly of Irish stock, having arrived during the previous century or so. They would be well aware that churches in Ireland were, at this time, quite commonly called `Domnach'. So when they called their churches in the Isle of Man by the name `Doonee', this need not imply that the moving force was provided by missionaries from Ireland, as Irish missionary activity had not yet started. The bilingual inscription on the Knock-e-dooney stone has no affinity with Irish monuments but has a strong affinity with those of North Wales. Therefore, it is suggested that the chapel at Knock-e-dooney came into existence soon after 500 as an extension of the strongly established Romano-British Church in the Conway Valley.

By implication, the other Doonee churches that have no monuments are of the same provenance, and also the chapel which provided the Santan slab. Originally, all of these chapels may have been attached to forts of local chieftains, but there is no indication that any of them developed into a monastic church or were influenced by the monastic movement. One might speculate that a chief church was located somewhere on the south side of the Isle of Man.

References for Chapter 2

(1)   Judith McClure and Roger Collins, *Bede: The Ecclesiastical History of the English People,* Oxford Univ. Press, 1994, Cap.13, p.25

(2)   Michael Richter, *Medieval Ireland, the Enduring áTradition,* Gill & Macmillan, Dublin, 1988, p.43

(3)   A.B.E. Hood, *St Patrick, his Writings and Muirchu's Life,* Phillimore, London, 1978, p.50

(4)   Charles Thomas, *Christianity in Roman Britain to AD 500,* B.T.Batsford, London, 1981, pp.306-346

(5)   J.F.Kenney, *The Early History of Ireland - Ecclesiastical,* Irish Univ. Press, Dublin, 1929, p.324.

(6)   Charles Thomas, *The Early Christian Archaeology of North Britain,* Oxford Univ. Press, 1971, p.95

(7)   K.Jackson, *Language and History in Early Britain,* Edinburgh Univ.Press, 1953, pp.154-5

(8)   A.M.Cubbon, *The Art of the Manx Crosses,* Manx Museum, 1977, p.5

(9)   P.M.C.Kermode, *List of Manx Antiquities,* L.Meyer, Douglas, 1930, pp.85, 84.

(10)   Deirdre Flanagan, `The Christian Impact on Early Ireland: Place-names Evidence', in *Irland und Europa,* (editors: Proinseas Ni Chattain & M. Richter), Klett-Cotta, Stuttgart, 1984, p.25

(11)   Harold Mytum, *The Origins of Early Christian Ireland,* Routledge, London, 1992, pp32-39

(12)   Ann Hamlin, `Early Irish Stone Carving: Content and Context', in *The Early Church in Western Britain and Ireland* (editor: Susan M.Pearce), British Archaeological Reports, British Series, No.102, 1982, p.283

(13)   J.J.Kneen, *Place Names of the Isle of Man,* Manx Gaelic Soc., Douglas, 1925, pp.13, 30

(14)   W.H.Davies, `The Church in Wales', in *Christianity in Britain 300 - 700,* (editors: M.W.Barley & R.P.C.Hanson), Leicester Univ.Press, 1968, p.137

(15)   J.G.Higgins, *The Early Christian Cross Slabs of County Galway,* British Archaeological Reports, Internat.Series, No.375, 1987, p.157

26

(16) Charles Thomas, 'East and West: Tintagel, Mediterranean Imports and the Early Insular Church' in *The Early Church in Western Britain and Ireland*, (editor: Susan M.Pearce), British Archaeological Reports, British Series, No.102, 1982, p.17

(17) Royal Commission on the Ancient and Historical Monuments of Wales and Monmouthshire, *An Inventory of the Ancient Monuments of Anglesey*, HMSO, London, 1937, p.cix

(18) Leslie Alcock, *Arthur's Britain*, Allen Lane: The Penguin Press, 1971, pp.243-8

(19) John Rhys, *Celtic Britain*, SPCK, London, 1904, republished by Senate, London, 1996, p.324

(20) K.Jackson, *Language and History in Early Britain*, Edinburgh Univ.Press, 1953. pp.173-4

(21) P.M.C.Kermode, *Notes on the Ogham and Latin Inscriptions from the Isle of Man*, Proc.Soc.Antiquaries of Scotland, 4th Ser., Vol.IX, 1911, p.437

(22) K.Jackson, 'Notes on the Ogham Inscriptions of Southern Britain' in *The Early Cultures of North-Western Europe*, (editors: C.Fox & B.Dickins), Cambridge Univ.Press, 1950, p.199 (see p.209)

(23) R.Trench-Jellicoe, *A Re-definition and Stylistic Analysis of P.M.C.Kermode's pre-Scandinavian Series of Manx Sculptured Monuments*, Univ. of Lancaster, Ph.D. Thesis, 1985

(24) A.M.Cubbon, *The Art of the Manx Crosses*, Manx Museum, 1977, p.5

(25) Nora K.Chadwick, *Studies in Early British History*, Cambridge Univ.Press, 1951, p.220

Chapter 3
CELTIC MONASTERIES

The British Church had been organised in territiorial divisions managed by bishops. After the Romans left, Christianity continued to spread into territories on the periphery of Roman Britain. In these territories, a monastic form of church organization proved to be more effective. On setting up a new monastery, a priest would request the local ruler to provide a site. However, the priest did not then submit to control by a central hierarchy, but became an autonomous abbot.

A conspicuous example of devotion to religious ideals was presented by St Anthony, who lived in the Egyptian desert. Before he died in 356, his colleagues such as Pachomius demonstrated how practical communities of monks could be organized. Their concepts were transmitted to Gaul, where Martin, before his death in 397, inaugurated monasteries at Poitiers and Tours. However, monastic ideals were slow to reach Britain, and archaeologists now insist that there were no proper monasteries in the British Isles until the late fifth century (1). This chapter sketches the way in which the monastic movement spread through the western districts of the British Isles.

3.1 Events in Gaul

Withdrawal of the Roman legions from their bases at Trier and Cologne left the way clear for Teutonic tribes of Franks to move southwards into Belgium, where they became established around 430. When the Roman governor Syagrius arrived in Gaul in 463, he had control over the northern districts, but the southern districts were already overrun by Visigoths. In 485, Clovis or Chlodovech, king of the Franks was ready to move his army westwards and soon occupied Paris and Rouen. Clovis, at the prompting of his wife Clotilde, received baptism from Archbishop Remigius at Rheims in 496. In 511, Clovis presided over a synod of thirty-two Gaulish bishops at Orleans. So it appears that the Gallican Church had not suffered extensive damage. The kingdom of Clovis was eventually taken over by his son Childebert, who died in his capital city of Paris in 558.

Westward movement of the Franks in Gaul brought them to the border of the former Roman province of Armorica. Meanwhile, the westward advance of the Saxons in Britain persuaded many British chiefs and their followers to migrate across the English Channel. Two migrations can be distinguished, one around 450 from southern England and another around 575 from Devon and Cornwall. Armorica received so many British refugees that it gained the name of Lesser Britain or Brittany. No doubt, these settlements helped to maintain communication between the western seaboard of Britain and the Continent.

The earliest monasteries in Britain are to be looked for in Cornwall and South Wales, where they were set up from 475 onwards. It was formerly thought that an early monastery was located at Tintagel in Cornwall, but this not now accepted (2). The new missionary movement was emanating from Gaul, particularly from Martin's foundations at Tours, and was not necessarily interrupted by the arrival of the Franks in Gaul.

3.2 Schools in Wales

One of the pioneers in Britain was Illtyd, who was a Breton by birth. During the last decades of the fifth century he set up a monastery at Caerworgern, which came to be known as Llanilltyd and is now Llantwit Major in Glamorgan. At his school, monastic ideals from Gaul were combined with a classical syllabus to provide education of a high standard. The date of Illtyd's death may have been as late as 535.

Five miles east of this place, another monastery was set up by Cadoc, also in the closing years of the fifth century. This was at Nantcarvan, later called Llancarvan. In the decades following 500, Cadoc lived in some style as the head of a large establishment (3). These two monasteries served the immediate purpose of training a new generation of monastic founders, but they continued to flourish until Norman times.

One of the earliest pupils at these monasteries was David. He took over a church in Demetia, now St David's, Pembrokeshire, and became renowned for his austere life-style. David's death may by placed around 600. A further saint, Dyfrig or Dubricius, had his main church at Hentland in Archenfield, west of Ross-on-Wye. In this district there were many Roman roads and villas, so it is possible that he inherited property formerly belonging to the British Church (4). As the date of Dyfrig's death is now placed at 612, he properly belonged to the age of monastic abbots. Later, he was adopted as a patron saint of Llandaff Cathedral.

Another pupil in the South Wales schools was Gildas, who was born at Strathclyde around the year 500. He was best known for his book *De Excidio et Conquestu Britanniae,* The destruction of Britain', written around 545. In this book he condemned the moral shortcomings of the British princes of his day. As texts about Britain in the Dark Ages are so scarce, this one is valuable. Gildas probably visited Ireland around 565. Ryan expressed the opinion that Gildas was the ablest teacher of the Celtic peoples in the sixth century (5).

Support for this opinion is provided by the *Catalogus Sanctorum Hiberniae,* an Irish document written in the 9th century (6). It stated that the monastic founders of Ireland received a mass-book "from bishop David and Gillas and Docus, who were Britons." These saints can be identified with David, Gildas and possibly Cadoc. Although the monastic movement in Ireland was already developing while David was still in his youth, the above document may rightly imply that the Irish monasteries received inspiration from those in South Wales.

3.3 Further Events in Wales

The literary record of ecclesiastical developments in Wales is scanty, but valuable confirmation can be derived from gravestones. It has been observed that there are concentrations of memorial stones in north-west Wales and in Pembrokeshire. There are very few along the Welsh border, even though the border territory remained in British hands until after the battle of Deorham in 577 when the Saxons advanced to Gloucester. This distribution of monuments can be associated with areas of Irish settlement. The Irish brought to these places a custom of recording parentage and tribal status which they retained after accepting Christianity.

Around 480, Cadwallon Llawhir, a reputed grandson of Cunedda won a victory over the Irish colonists at Trefdraeth in south-west Anglesey. In the settled period that followed, there may have been a fusion of cultures. Traditions of the British Church were modified by the Irish settlers, who, in turn, were influenced by the arrival of the monastic movement. This process is illustrated by the stones at Aberdaron in Lleyn, carrying the inscriptions: VERACIUS PBR HIC IACET and SENACUS PRSB HIC IACIT CUM MULTITUDINEM FRATRUM. The abbreviations PBR and PRSB show that the people commemorated were presbyters. Leslie Alcock suggested that they belonged to a brotherhood or monastery (8). These stones are dated to the late 5th or early 6th century. It appears that the monastic movement, already established in South Wales from around 480, had reached North Wales by the turn of the century.

Cadwallon Llawhir was followed by his son Maelgwn. Information about him has been provided by Gildas (8). Maelgwn Gwynedd was educated by "the most refined master of almost all Britain", which points to Illtyd or Cadoc. Gildas referred to Maelgwn by the name Maglocunos, and called him *Insularis draco*, by which he probably meant 'Dragon of the Island of Britain'. In spite of the despotic character which Gildas gave him, Maelgwn is reputed to have been generous in supporting churches. According to Welsh tradition, he gave an old Roman fort to Cybi, a Cornishman, and this place became Caergybi, later Holyhead (9). Maelgwn died of the plague in 547 at his fortress at Deganwy. The Isle of Man was within Maelgwn's sphere of influence, but it is uncertain whether he actively intervened there.

Tradition says that Cybi had a colleague Seiriol who founded the monastery of Penmon on the eastern extremity of Anglesey. The picture that emerges here is that while churches may have existed in Anglesey in the late fifth century, they were reinforced during the period 500 to 550 through the activities of saints who were imbued with monastic ideals and who were advancing northwards. St Deiniol, whose death occurred in 584, belonged to a later period. He was said to be of Cumbrian parentage and is credited with founding the monastery of Bangor in Caernarvonshire.

3.4 Irish Monasteries

In Celtic lands, monasticism reached its fullest state of development in Ireland. When a monastery was established, the founder had ownership rights. On his death the property passsed to his nominee, usually a relative, who was then named as the *coarb* or successor of the founder. A later abbot was not necessarily a bishop or even a priest, and he procured the services of a bishop when one was needed. The abbot was not answerable to anyone for the conduct of affairs in his monastery. A hundred or more independent houses sprang up in Ireland, and perhaps a dozen amassed considerable wealth.

Biographies of Irish saints contain many contrived accounts of pupil-teacher relationships, but it is possible to distinguish a few of the principal figures in the propagation of monasticism in Ireland. One of these was Enda. In his younger days, Enda was a rampaging

31

chieftain, but was persuaded to go to Rosnat to study under the abbot Maucennus. Rosnat was formerly equated with Whithorn, but it is now believed that this place may have been somewhere in south-west Britain, as discussed by Wilson (10). Enda returned around 500 to set up his school on the island of Aran Mor in Galway Bay, and died around 530. Perhaps the most significant of the early teachers in Ireland was Finnian. He was born in Leinster and spent some years in South Wales at the school of Cadoc. He returned to Ireland to teach, and eventually transformed an old church at Clonard into a monastery, at a date probably between 520 and 530. Clonard is about thirty miles west of Dublin on the southern boundary of Meath. Finnian died in the plague of 549, his feast day being December 12. In his lifetime he taught a number of outstanding men, who in turn established their own monasteries in Ireland. Clonard reached the peak of its prosperity in the tenth century and continued as one of the principal churches of Meath until decline set in soon after 1200. No monastic buildings now remain. At the risk of oversimplifying a complex situation, a couple of the later monasteries will now be briefly mentioned. Ciaran the Younger was taught by Enda or Finnian of Clonard or by both. Around 544 he set up his own monastery at Clonmacnois on the east bank of the Shannon, eight miles south of Athlone. He died in the plague of 549 at the age of thirty-two, his festival day being September 9. Capable abbots built up this monastery until it became the largest in Ireland. It had the stamina to recover from numerous raids and survived until the sixteenth century.

Another prominent Irish saint was Comgall or Congallus, who was born near Larne in 517. He founded his monastery at Bangor on Belfast Lough in 558 and died in 600, his festival day being May 10. This monastery sent missionaries to the Pictish territories of Scotland and farther afield. After the Vikings had raided Bangor in 823, a steady decline set in. By around 950 the last of the scribes and lecturers had died. The monastery became a deserted ruin until it was rebuilt by Malachy in 1125. A selection of the leading Irish monasteries of the 6th century might include Armagh, Clonmacnoise, Kildare, Clonard and Bangor.

3.5 The Scots of Argyll

The early inhabitants of Scotland were Picts. Their language had some affinity with the Brythonic dialects such as Welsh. By contrast, the Irish spoke a Goidelic or Gaelic language. Irishmen from the northern part of Antrim had been settling in Kintyre before the year 500, but at about this time a new migration occurred under the leadership of Fergus Mor. These Irishmen, then called Scots, occupied Argyll, which included Islay, Kintyre, Arran and Cowal, and their colony took the name of Dalriada.

In 560, the Picts under Brude mac Maelchon attacked the Scots colony and killed its leader Gabran mac Domangart. The new king was Conall mac Comgall, whose fortress was at Dunadd in Knapdale, and he requested Columba to negotiate with the Northern Picts. More will be said about Columba. When Conall died in 573 he was followed as king by Aedan mac Gabran.

The Annals of Ulster recorded that in 581, Aedan mac Gabran won the battle of Manand or Manonn (11). Formerly, certain writers took this place to be the Isle of Man, but there is now a consensus that the actual location of the battle was at Slamannan in Central Scotland. However, it appears that Baetan mac Cairill, who was king of Antrim 572 to 581, kept a force of soldiers in the Isle of Man. Under the year 578, the Annals of Ulster recorded "The return of the Ulidians from Eumania", though the reason why they were there is not clear.

3.6 Brendan the Navigator

Brendan was born in Tralee in 484. In his younger days, he probably visited South Wales and Brittany. Around 545 he conducted a mission to the Western Isles of Scotland. Chapels named after him can be found on the islands of Mull, Tiree and Islay, also at Seil in the Firth of Lorn. Later, around 559, he set up a monastery at Clonfert in Lough Corrib in the east of Co. Galway, where he died in 577, his festival day being May 16. An excerpt from the `Brussels Copy' of the `Lives of Saints', quoted by Plummer, may be translated (12):

'Then after a while he (Brendan) said to his brethren "We must go into the regions of the Mananei, for that land has work for us. Perhaps there our remains may rest.'

As pointed out by Plummer, the district referred to here is in the neighbourhood of the town of Roscommon, and is not the Isle of Man as some have supposed. Clonfert continued to flourish through the 10th and 11th centuries.

In the past, some writers have gathered place-names from maps and have used them to construct a narrative about the supposed journeys of a founder-saint. Care is needed here, as shown by the following two sites, the first being Skipness Castle in Kintyre. According to Graham and Collingwood, the first castle was erected around 1220, together with a chapel of St Columba just outside its walls (13). When a larger castle was built around 1280, its walls enclosed this chapel. Therefore, the Kilbrannan Chapel, named after Brendan, was built three hundred yards away. Its walls still stand. No monuments of an earlier date have been found that might cast doubt on these dates of construction (14).

As another example, Mackinlay mentioned a chapel built in the 12th century in Glenlyon, Perthshire (15). It was built by a man who came from Lorn in Argyll, and he dedicated his chapel to St Brendan, the patron saint of his homeland. These are rare examples where ruined chapels can be dated fairly accurately, and it is seen that both literary references and archaeological reports must be examined together.

Although no remains of buildings of the 6th century can now be found, it has not been disputed that Brendan did conduct a mission to the Western Isles. This proposition is supported by the name *Ailech*, mentioned in Brendan's biographies, which has been equated with Eileach an Naoimh, one of the Garvellach Islands, south of Mull, where the remains of a later monastery still exist.

Brendan's reputation outside of Ireland was much enhanced by the appearance of the book *Navigatio Brendani*. This work of fiction was written during the ninth century by an Irish monk living in the Rhineland. It received a wide circulation and was translated into many European languages, including Old Norse. The form taken by the Brendan legend through the Middle Ages is well expressed by John of Fordun, who wrote around 1370 and said (16):

"St Brendan flourished in Scotland... Moreover, he went a seven years' voyage in quest of the Fortunate Isles and saw many things worthy of wonder. Saint Machutes, also called Macloveus, who was baptized and regularly educated by him and accompanied him on his voyage, lived in Britain, renowned for his miracles and holiness."

As the best date for the death of Machutus is 621, he was much younger than Brendan and they may or may not have met in South Wales.

3.7 Further Irish Missionaries in Scotland

In the past, it has been supposed that various Irish and Scottish saints gave their names to churches in the Isle of Man, so it might be useful to provide biographical information about some of these saints.

Columba or Columcille was born in 518, his father Fedlimid being a member of a ruling family in Donegal. After receiving a broad education, and after working in Ireland for some years, Columba set out for Scotland in 563. On arriving, his first task was to make peace with the Pictish king Brude mac Maelcon at his fortress at Inverness. Columba then took over a church on Iona, which was to be his base. On the death of Conall in 574, Columba nominated Aidan mac Gabran as the next king. Columba died in 597, his feast day being June 9. Through his personal vigour, the community at Iona was set on a course that was to have widespread consequences.

Another notable missionary in Scotland was Lugaidh, also called Luoc, Molocus or Moluag. He went from Bangor to Scotland around 562 and set up his main church on the island of Lismore in the Firth of Lorn. Moluag was a contemporary and rival of Columba, as mentioned in Adamnan's book. Moluag gave his name to churches in Kintyre and on the islands of Tiree, Mull and Skye and possibly in Harris. He died in 593, his festival day being June 25. The monastery at Lismore continued up to or after 750. When the diocese of Argyll was established in 1185, a cathedral church was built on this site. A parish church still stands there.

Two more saints may be mentioned, the first being Blane or Blaanus. He was a Briton, born in Bute. His uncle Catan sent him to Bangor for training. When he returned, he founded a monastery at Kingarth around 574. He is credited with setting up churches in Dumfriesshire and Kintyre as well as at Dunblane. Blane died a little after 600, his feast day being August 10. The names of abbots of Kingarth have been recorded, one of these being Ronan, who died in 737. The last known abbot died in 790, and soon afterwards, Kingarth together with other churches in Bute were destroyed by the Vikings. After a long blank in the history of the site, a fine stone church was erected in the 12th century, the walls of which still stand.

According to Irish records, Donnan, whose name was also spelt Donan, came from Ireland. Churches attributed to him include Kildonan and Chapel Donnan in the Rhins of Galloway, with two more in Ayrshire. Further churches were on the islands of Skye,

Lewis and South Uist. His main church was on the island of Eigg just south of Skye. There he perished at the hands of pirates in 617. The names of later abbots have been recorded up to 725. Although the monastery did not survive through Viking times, Donnan's festival was celebrated until recently by the people of Eigg on April 17.

From the above notes it can be seen that from about 550 onwards, several highly motivated men set out from Ireland, notably from Bangor, on missionary expeditions to the west coast of Scotland. Historical records confirm that quite a few churches are still named after their founders. However, it is unlikely that any of the above-named saints visited the Isle of Man in person.

During the next century, Adamnan had an important part to play in Scottish affairs. He was born in 624 and was related to Columba through his father Ronan, a chieftain in Donegal. In 679, Adamnan became abbot of Iona and head of the Columban churches. In 686 he acted as emissary to Northumbria where his former pupil Aldfrith was king. On a second visit in 688 he spent a year at the monastery of Jarrow. Adamnan became convinced that the Celtic Church should conform with the practice of the Roman Church, but during his lifetime, his colleagues at Iona were unwilling to agree. Adamnan's outstanding literary contribution was his `Life of Columba', written around 690. He died in 704, his feast day being September 23.

3.8 The British Monastery at Whithorn

It is assumed that at some time after the year 500, the British Church was no longer able to send bishops to Whithorn, and that the church then came under the control of an abbot. Some support for this assumption comes from Irish sources. For example, the *Liber Hymnorum* contains the `Hymn of Mugint', and the preface to this hymn states that "Mugint composed this hymn in Futerna". This preface was written or copied in the 11th century when `Futerna' was an Irish version of the name Whithorn.

This account described how Finnian of Moville and his colleagues Talmach and Rioc studied under Abbot Mugint. A further pupil was Drusticc, daughter of Drust, king of the Picts, and she fell in love with Talmach. As Finnian died at an advanced age in 579, the date of the above incident may have been between 510 and 530. Confirmation is supplied by Pictish king-lists which gave two kings named Drust within this period. The above story has been

36

examined in detail by Wilson (10). His conclusion was that Finnian of Moville and his associates may have spent some time at Whithorn. The implication is that a monastery existed there, with Irish connections.

In order to estimate the likely life-span of the monastery at Whithorn, it may be useful to consider the political situation in the north of England and south of Scotland. During the 6th century, these regions were occupied by a number of small British kingdoms, as mentioned by Chadwick (17). Rivalry between rulers culminated in the battle of Arthuret in 573. This battleground was near Longtown, north of Carlisle. As a result of the changed balance of power, two strong kings emerged. Rhydderch Hen became king of Strathclyde in his fortress at Dumbarton Rock while Urien rose to power in Rheged and gained control of Carlisle (see Figure 1). Rhydderch and Urien together made attacks on the Anglian chiefs Hussa and Theodoric who had their fortress at Lindisfarne.

Urien was killed around 590, when he was succeeded by his son Rhun. It is usually acknowledged that a township persisted at Carlisle, though nothing is heard of any church there. When Rhydderch had established himself at Dumbarton, he brought Kentigern to be his bishop there. It is no longer accepted that Kentigern previously worked at Hoddom near Ecclefechan, as there is no evidence that a church existed there prior to Anglian times, as pointed out by Nora Chadwick (18). Both Rhydderch and Kentigern died around 612.

After the Northumbrian victory at the battle of Degsastan in 603, the power of the British princes was broken, and it seems likely that a state of anarchy existed in the lands extending from Carlisle along the coast of south-west Scotland until Northumbrian control was confirmed later. Therefore, the period envisaged for the British monastic phase at Whithorn is very approximately the century 530 to 630. This has significance in relation to the monastery at Maughold, to be considered next.

References for Chapter 3

(1) A.C.Thomas, `The Evidence from North Britain', in *Christianity in Britain, 300-700*, (editors: M.W.Barley & R.P.C.Hanson), Leicester Univ.Press, 1968, p.96
(2) Charles Thomas, `East and West: Tintagel, Mediterranean Imports and the Early Insular Church', in *The Early Church in*

Western Britain and Ireland (editor: Susan M.Pearce), British Archaeological Reports, British Series, No.102, 1982, p.17

(3)   Christopher Brooke, `St Peter of Gloucester and St Cadoc of Llancarvan', in *Celt and Saxon: Studies in the Early British Border* (authors: K.Jackson *et al*), Cambridge Univ.Press, 1963, p.258

(4)   Kathleen Hughes, *The Early Church in Irish Society*, Methuen, London, 1966, p.29

(5)   J. Ryan, *Irish Monasticism*, 1931, reprinted by Irish Univ.Press, Shannon, 1972, p.113

(6)   Nora K.Chadwick, *The Age of the Saints in the Early Celtic Church*, Llanerch Publishers, Lampeter, 1997, p.71

(7)   Leslie   Alcock, *Arthur's Britain*, Allen Lane: The Penguin Press, 1971, pp.248, 243

(8)   M.Winterbottom, *Gildas: The Ruin of Britain and Other Works*, Phillimore, London, 1978, pp.31-35

(9)   Gilbert H.Doble, *The Saints of Cornwall*, Part 3, Holywell Press, Oxford, 1964, p.125 (There is a Llanerch reprint, 1998)

(10) P.A.Wilson, *St Ninian and Candida Casa: Literary Evidence from Ireland*, Trans.Dumfr.& Gall.Nat.Hist.& Ant.Soc., 3rd Ser., Vol. XLI, 1964, p.156

(11) A.O.Anderson, *Early Sources of Scottish History*, Vol.1, Cambridge Univ.Press, 1954, p.90

(12) Charles Plummer, *Vitae Sanctorum Hiberniae*, Clarendon Press, Oxford, 1910, Vol.1, p.144, Vol.2, p.335

(13) Angus Graham and R.G.Collingwood, *Skipness Castle*, Proc.Soc.Antiquaries of Scotland, Vol.LVII, 1923, p.226

(14) Royal Commission on the Ancient & Historical Monuments of Scotland, *Argyll, Vol.1, Kintyre*, HMSO, Glasgow, 1971.

(15) J.M.Mackinlay, *Ancient Church Dedications of Scotland*, David Douglas, Edinburgh, 1910, p.69

(16) W.F.Skene, *John of Fordun's Chronicle of the Scottish Nation*, Edmonston & Douglas, Edinburgh, 1872, pp.100, 39. (There is also a Llanerch reprint, 1993)

(17) H.M.Chadwick, *Early Scotland*, Cambridge Univ.Press, 1949, p.142

(18) N.K.Chadwick, *St Ninian: A Preliminary Study of the Sources*, Trans.Dumfr.& Gall.Nat.Hist.& Ant.Soc., 3rd Ser., Vol.XXVII, 1950, p.9

Chapter 4.
CELTIC MAUGHOLD AND THE EARLY KEEILLS

When all the original buildings of a Celtic monastery have vanished, it may still be possible to trace parts of the enclosing fence, as for example, at Iona. The wall of Maughold churchyard now encloses almost five acres and parts of it may coincide with the original fence (1). In the absence of documents, the history of the monastery has to be put together from a study of the engraved stones. The earliest of these are dated a little after the year 600. A review of this site has been given by Basil Megaw (2).

4.1 Maltese Crosses and Marigolds

As seen in the previous chapter, there were churches in the Isle of Man early in the 6th century. However, the site at Maughold has not revealed any monuments having ogham or bilingual inscriptions that might be dated to this early period. It is noted that at the sites of monasteries founded in Ireland during the second half of the 6th century, ogham stones have not usually been found, as this practice was then being discontinued (3).

One of the earliest monuments at Maughold is the incised fragment marked No.41 by the Manx Museum. Enough of the monogram remains to show that it consisted of a Maltese cross enclosed in a double circle. Although most of the upper arm of the cross has been broken off, a distinct portion of a Rho can be seen in the position where a Chi-Rho symbol would be expected. At the upper right-hand position outside the cross, a worn Omega can be traced, this being in the position where an Alpha-Omega symbol would be expected. Although the cross was found in 1900, the above details have only recently been described by Trench-Jellicoe, who dated the slab to the early 7th century (3).

By way of comparison, two slabs may be considered from Raasay Island off the coast of Skye, as reported by Galbraith (5). Each has a Maltese cross formed from intersecting semicircles and has a Chi-

39

Rho symbol, but the cross is enclosed in an incised square, and Pictish ornamentation appears below the monogram. Another stone has been reported from Iona, having the inscription: LAPIS ECHODI. This consists of an incised Maltese cross with the arms terminated by straight horizontal and vertical lines, the upper arm bearing a Chi-Rho symbol. The Royal Commission dated the lettering on this stone to the 7th century (5).

Dr Trench-Jellicoe concluded that the crosses at Raasay and Iona are significantly different from the one at Maughold. He also pointed out a striking resemblance between the Maughold fragment and the St Peter Stone at Whithorn, which has an identical monogram, including Alpha-Omega symbols. It will be argued in the next chapter that although the St Peter Stone may have been erected during the Anglian phase of Whithorn, its style belongs to the early 7th century.

Another of the earliest monuments at Maughold is Cross Slab No.46. This has an incised Maltese cross formed from compass-drawn arcs. The arms of the cross are closed at the outside by concave arcs, the whole being enclosed within a double circle. Below this figure is a further compass-drawn hexafoil or marigold, but there is no lettering present. The date has been set around 650 by Mr A.M.Cubbon (6). A further example of a Maltese cross enclosed within a double circle appears on an `altar-front', found at Ronaldsway near Castletown (1). The above Maltese crosses may be compared with an identical cross incised on a slab at at Ballyvourney, west of Macroom in County Cork, this slab being dated by Curle to the early 7th century (7).

A more developed sculptural technique appears on the cross-slab at the burial ground of Cladh A'Bhile at Ellary on the north shore of Loch Killisport in Knapdale. This has a deeply cut six-pointed marigold at the top of the slab with a Maltese cross below it. The Royal Commission gave it a date in the first half of the 8th century (8). A further example is the cross-slab at Carndonagh cemetery in the Inishowan Peninsula, Donegal. This has a seven-pointed marigold in an upper position with a Maltese cross below it. Harbison suggested a date in the first half of the 9th century (9).

Perhaps these relief carvings of rather late date are not very relevant to the simpler incised crosses at Maughold.

The most informative of the Maughold slabs of this period is the Irneit Cross, No.47. It was found in 1900 beneath the floor of the church (10). The main feature is a compass-drawn hexafoil figure surrounded by an annulus in which lettering is cut. The inscription is in abbreviated Latin, written with some of the letters in Greek form. A translation given in 1925 was "In Christ's name, Itspli, bishop of God in the Isle, abbot". This and other interpretations should now be set aside in favour of one given in 1982 by Mr A.M.Cubbon (11): "Of Christ, Irneit, Holy Priest, Holy Bishop of God..." The inscription is extremely difficult to interpret, and perhaps finality has not yet been reached.

Nothing is known of Irneit from literary sources. On this slab, beneath the hexafoil, two small Latin crosses have been cut. Each cross has four expanded terminal points. An unusual feature is that each cross has a small Rho carved at the top of the upper limb. This is illustrated in Figure 2. Inscriptions adjacent to these small crosses have been interpreted: "In the name of Jesus Christ", and "In the image of the cross of Christ". These two small crosses may be compared with the cross on a slab at Kilshannig in the Dingle peninsula, reported by Ann Hamlin (13). The lettering on the Irneit Cross at Maughold suggests a date of just before 700 or slightly later (6).

It is seen that the art-forms of incised Maltese crosses and hexafoil marigolds appeared over the period 600 to 750. In Ireland, these slabs tend to be found in coastal districts extending from Kerry to Donegal, suggesting that these places maintained communication by sea with south-western Britain and Gaul.

As designs using compass-drawn figures and Chi-Rho symbols continued in use over a long period, accurate dating is difficult. It is known that from 550 onwards, missionaries from Ulster vigorously directed their efforts towards the west of Scotland. However, the Irish annals of this time do not make any reference to the Isle of Man, and the Maughold monuments do not clearly indicate links

41

with Ulster. The art-forms at Maughold are rather non-specific and are common to the western coasts of the British Isles.

The early phase of the monastery at Maughold, as revealed by the monuments, appears to fall within the century 620 to 720. The art-forms have points in common with those at Whithorn. However, the monastery at Maughold could not have had strong support from the churches at Carlisle and Whithorn for the reason that through this period, these churches were in a state of disarray. It is more likely that at Maughold, there was an influx of monks who had come from Whithorn on account of unsettled conditions there. In the next chapter, it will be seen that the Isle of Man came under the domination of the Northumbrians through much of the 7th century, but there is no sign that they interfered with the Celtic monastery at Maughold during this time.

4.2 Early Keeills

A keeill is a disused church of any date, but it may not be easy to establish its date. Hardly any stone building in Ireland can be dated with certainty to before the year 900, though soon after this date, many stone buildings started to appear. The earliest stone chapels in Ireland were rectangular buildings with inside measurements about 15 by 10 feet, but sometimes smaller. Early keeills in the Isle of Man were of a similar size. Boulders were laid in a foundation course and drystone walls three feet thick were built on top. It may be impossible to date a structure on the basis of such primitive architecture. Nevertheless, other considerations suggest that some of these structures rest on foundations laid during the 7th and 8th centuries. Reasons for believing this are now considered.

The monuments at Maughold seem to give the first positive indication of the successful functioning of a monastic establishment. It is suggested that the spread of Christianity to the people of the countryside had to wait for the arrival of effective monastic churches.

When missionaries set to work in the Isle of Man, they found religious practices which might be loosely called Druidical. Religious and social activities were centred on sites characterised by sacred mounds, sometimes encircled by standing stones, these sites being also used as cemeteries. It is known that cremation was practised in the British Isles during the 2nd and 3rd centuries, that is, prior to the arrival of Christianity. Former religious practices would not be in keeping with Christian principles, so the missionaries saw an urgent need to reform these practices by taking possession of the sacred mounds.

This was done by building a chapel directly on top of the mound, which was first levelled to some extent. Mr A.W.Moore noticed that many keeills were built on top of a platform of earth (13). Canon Kermode stated that twenty-four keeills were situated in this way, but this number may be slightly higher (14). Other chapels may have been located near a sacred well, so as to ensure that well-worship was discontinued. These small buildings were symbolic, declaring that Christianity had replaced Druidism. They primarily contained an altar on which the priest prepared the sacrament.

Some examples of a keeill built on a platform could now be reviewed. One is at the Corrody, at Tholt y Will, Lezayre. A well nearby is said to have the name of Chibbyr Karrin, but the keeill itself seems to have no authentic name. The foundations still remain and indicate internal dimensions 15 by 8 feet (4.5 by 2.5 m). Slabs standing on end mark part of the inside of the wall, while the outside was built up with sods. This building was erected on a platform of earth about 18 inches high. The outer edge of this platform was marked by standing stones, set in a circle of 42 feet diameter, and half a dozen of these stones still remain. Excavation has revealed a cinerary urn under the floor, assigned by Kermode to the Bronze Age. This shows that the platform of earth was not constructed at the time when the building was erected, but existed previously.

Another nameless keeill is at Ballashimmin, near Little London in the north of the parish of German. The foundations that can now be seen indicate internal dimensions 15 by 9 feet (4.5 x 2.7 m). The foundations are on a platform 30 to 40 feet in diameter standing six feet above the level of the field. Excavations by Kermode produced a portion of an urn, but whether this indicates a cremation burial has been questioned. A further keeill that may be mentioned is at Ballacamain in Kirk Bride. This has the name Cabbal ny Cooilley, `Chapel in the corner', referring to its situation in a three-sided corner of a field. The mound on which the keeill stood is four to six feet high and 50 feet in diameter, but the outline of the former building is now poorly defined.

A theory put forward by Charles Thomas is that the first evidence of the arrival of Christianity should be looked for in the form of Christian interments (1). A little later, a church might be built adjacent to the cemetery, so that the site became a "developed cemetery". To some extent, this idea may be correct, but it seems to underestimate the organisational aspect. The large number of chapels built on platforms leaves the impression that this work was directed by a central authority. Although some sites of keeills have both a platform and cremated remains, some platforms show no signs of cremation while some sites have cremated remains but no platform. Many details of the Manx keeills have been described by Christopher Lowe (15).

Some guidance as to the appearance of a typical church in Ireland has been given by Kenney (16):

"Every important Irish church was a monastic church, that is, it was the church of a little walled village whose dwellers were monks or nuns living under ecclesiastical discipline and ministering to the spiritual needs of the surrounding people.

This suggests that the Manx keeills were looked after by an itinerant priest from a monastery.

4.3 Developments at Armagh

Irish literature appeared in the late 7th century which has been understood to have a bearing on churches in the Isle of Man. At this time the monastery at Maughold had already existed for almost a century, so this literature is best discussed here.

When St Patrick established a church at Armagh around 444, this church did not have any special status. A century later it developed into a monastery. When monasteries sprang up in Ireland, many did not remain in close communication with the Church of Rome. Differences in points of practice arose, such as method used for calculating the date of Easter. At Magh Lena, a place near Durrow in Offaly, a synod met in 629 and recommended alignment with Roman practice, but agreement was not complete (17). In the ensuing debate, those favouring the Roman viewpoint used the name of Patrick as a rallying cry.

An important book, Muirchu's `Life of St Patrick' was finished around 695. Muirchu was sponsored by Bishop Aed of Sletty in County Laois, who belonged to the party that wished to Romanise the Irish Church. At the Synod of Birr in 697, Adamnan proposed a uniform acceptance of Roman practice throughout Ireland. It is necessary to keep these circumstances in mind when reading the ancient biographies of Patrick. Muirchu's account is widely recognised as being a restrained compilation of the information available when he wrote.

An independent biography of Patrick was provided around 680 by Bishop Tirechan, who came from Connacht. Tirechan stated that Patrick made a tour of Connacht followed by a tour of Leinster, and that he founded forty-two principal churches, including a number having the name `Domnach'. Tirechan's method was to obtain local information about the founder of a church and then to devise a story of how he had been baptized and commissioned by Patrick. Tirechan revealed his motives when he wrote: "If the heir of Patrick were to demand his diocese, he could recover to him almost the whole island, for God gave him the whole island."

Around 734, the Book of the Angel was produced at Armagh. This made a forthright claim that an angel had addressed Patrick, telling him he had jurisdiction over all the churches that were not already attached to a monastic house. Particularly included were all the churches called `Domnach', these being churches that existed before the monasteries became dominant. Certain notes called *Additamenta* have been regarded as part of Tirechan's memoir, although they were probably written at Armagh around 750. These notes include an account of how Lomman, an assistant of Patrick, founded the church at Trim in Meath.

A collection of biograghical writings about Patrick was prepared on the instructions of Torbach, abbot of Armagh, and became known as the Book of Armagh, the date of compilation being 807. This composite book incorporated Patrick's *Confessio*, the memoirs of Muirchu and Tirechan and the Book of the Angel, and is the source from which these separate parts have been obtained. A further book, the `Tripartite Life of Patrick' was written around 900, this being largely a paraphrase of the Book of Armagh. The `Tripartite Life' was again paraphrased by John Colgan in his *Triadis Thaumaturgae*, written in Louvain, Belgium in 1647.

The abbots of Armagh insisted that their establishment held a premier position, claiming that Patrick, their founder, had been the first regularly appointed bishop in Ireland. Patrick's star began to rise around the year 700, and by 900 he had reached the height of his popularity in Ireland.

4.4 The Legend of Mac Cuill

The only document that might possibly have a bearing on the Manx Church in Early Christian times is the one to be considered here, so it must be examined in detail. The text of this legend originally appeared in Muirchu's `Life of St Patrick'. An extract is given here from Bieler's translation (18):

"There was a man in the territory of the Ulaid in Patrick's time, Macc Cuill moccu Greccae. He was a fierce and wicked ruler... they set a trap for the holy man... And after this, Macc Cuill said further "I confess to you my holy lord Patrick that I had planned to kill you " ... And Patrick said "you now go down to the seashore unarmed, and leave this part of Ireland." ... And Macc Cuill left ...

46

and went to the sea south of Mag Inis ... and put to sea in a small boat, and the north wind blew in his rear and took him southwards and landed him at an island called Euonia.

There he found two admirable men ... who had been the first to preach the word of God and baptism in Euonia, and by their teaching, the inhabitants of that island had been converted to the catholic faith. The names of the two men are Conindrus and Rumilus. Having found spiritual fathers in the place given to him by God, he trained his body and soul according to their rule and spent all the time of his life there with those two holy bishops until he became their successor in the episcopate."

Ulaid is an older name of County Down and Mag Inis is the Lecale Peninsula. To be exact, the Isle of Man is due east of this place and not to the south, but the name `Euonia' can be accepted as meaning the Isle of Man. This is confirmed in the writings of Nennius, who, in 829, applied the name *Eubonia, id est Manau* to the Isle of Man (19). Muirchu's account has received attention from many scholars. The historian J.B.Bury gave his opinion (20):

"Some old legend connecting Man with the coast of Dalaradia seems to have been hooked on to Patrick, and perhaps Mac Cuill, of Cyclopean type, may be the mythical Mac Cuill, `son of hazel', husband of Banba."

Mac Cuill, a chieftain of the Tuatha De Danann was, indeed, a character from Irish mythology. If the name was borrowed from this source, it follows that Muirchu was not pointing a finger at any person in the Isle of Man who was known to him by name. So it is futile to look for a person called Mac Cuill in the Isle of Man. It has to be accepted that the story is basically a work of fiction, but some factual elements may be woven into it.

A Welsh tradition mentioned the clerics Kynan and Run, said to be descendants of Brychan, king of Brycheiniog, that is, Brecknock in Wales. These clerics were said to have lived in *Manan* or *Mannia*. This probably means the Isle of Man, although Watson thought that it might alternatively mean Manau Gododdin (21). There is some

47

doubt about whether the Welsh writer gave an independent account or whether he utilized the names Conindrus and Rumilus from Muirchu's account. This difficult question is not pursued here, but deserves further attention. Meanwhile, it is observed that the bishops appear to be Romano-British rather than Irish.

The concluding sentence of Muirchu's account, as transcribed by Stokes is (22):

Hic est `Maccuil diMane', episcopus et antestes Arddae Huimnonn.

Scholars have had some difficulty in translating this sentence. Stokes suggested that `diMane' might be a mistake in copying *de mare*, giving `Mac Cuill from the sea'. Ludwig Bieler gave: `This is Macc Cuill, bishop of Mane and prelate of Arde Huimnonn (the Isle of Man)' (18). Alan Hood gave: `This man is Macuil *dimane*, bishop and prelate of Ardd Huimnonn' (23). It is not satisfactory to render either *Mane* or Ardd Huimnonn as `Isle of Man', as Euonia is previously given in this account as being the specific name of the Isle of Man. The Gaelic *Ard* or *Aird* conveys the meaning of either a high place or a promontory. By the year 700, a monastery existed at Maughold and there may have been another significant church at Peel. However, it remains uncertain whether the names mentioned by Muirchu were intended to refer to particular churches.

Muirchu's story appears to be an attempt to draw the Manx churches into the orbit of Armagh. Muirchu knew that Patrick had not personally established churches there, but he claimed that an intermediary called Mac Cuill went at Patrick's bidding, and that the Isle of Man had been given to Mac Cuill by God. Muirchu did not mention any place called Maughold. There is no essential connection between the names Mac Cuill and Maughold. A reconstruction of this kind was devised only in the 12th century, as will be discussed later.

48

References for Chapter 4

(1) Charles Thomas, *The Early Christian Archaeology of North Britain*, Oxford Univ.Press, 1971, pp.41-2, 48, 188

(2) B.R.S.Megaw, *The Monastery of St.Maughold*, Isle of Man Nat. Hist. & Ant. Soc., Vol.(NS) V, No.11, 1950, p.169

(3) R.Trench-Jellicoe, *A New Chi-Rho from Maughold, Isle of Man*, Medieval Archaeology, Vol.24, 1980, p.202

(4) J.J.Galbraith, *The Chi-Rho Crosses on Raasay: Their Importance and Chronological Relationships*, Proc.Soc.Antiquaries of Scotland, Vol.LXVII, 1933, pp.318, 63

(5) Royal Commission on the Ancient and Historical Monuments of Scotland, *Argyll, Vol.4, Iona*, HMSO, Edinburgh, 1982, p.182

(6) A.M.Cubbon, *The Art of the Manx Crosses*, Manx Museum, 1977, pp.6, 7

(7) C.L.Curle, *The Chronology of the Early Christian Monuments of Scotland*, Proc.Soc.Antiquaries of Scotland, Vol.LXXIV, 1939, p.60

(8) Royal Commission on the Ancient and Historical Monuments of Scotland, *Argyll, Vol.7*, HMSO, Edinburgh, 1992, p.55

(9) Peter Harbison, `A Group of Early Christian Carved Stone Monuments in County Donegal', in *Early Medieval Sculpture in Britain and Ireland*, (editor: John Higgitt), British Archaeological Reports, British Series, No.152, 1986, p.49

(10) William and Constance Radcliffe, *A History of Kirk Maughold*, Manx Museum, 1979, p.25

(11) A.M.Cubbon, `The Early Church in the Isle of Man', in *The Early Church in Western Britain and Ireland*, (editor: Susan M.Pearce), British Archaeological Reports, British Series, No.102, 1982, p.257

(12) Ann Hamlin, *Early Irish Stone Carving: Content and Context*, British Archaeological Reports, British Series No.102, 1982, p.283

(13) A.W.Moore, *A History of the Isle of Man*, T.Fisher Unwin, London, 1900, p.76

(14) R.D.Kermode, *The Annals of Kirk Christ Lezayre*, Norris Modern Press, Douglas, 1954, p.15

(15) C.E.Lowe, *Early Ecclesiastical Sites in the Northern Isles and Isle of Man: An Archaeological Survey*, Univ.of Durham, Ph.D. Thesis, 1987

(16) J.F.Kenney, *The Early History of Ireland: Ecclesiastical*, Irish Univ.Press, Dublin, 1929, p.291

(17) James MacCaffrey, *History of the Catholic Church*, M.H.Gill, Dublin, 1912, p.70

(18) Ludwig Bieler, *The Patrician Texts in the Book of Armagh*, Dublin Inst. for Advanced Studies, 1979, p.107

(19) John Morris, *Nennius: British History and the Welsh Annals*, Phillimore, London, 1980, p.59

(20) J.B.Bury, *Life of St Patrick*, Macmillan, London, 1905, p.267

(21) W.J.Watson, *History of the Celtic Place Names of Scotland*, Blackwood, Edinburgh, 1926, p.163

(22) Whitley Stokes, *The Tripartite Life of Patrick*, HMSO, London, 1887, p.286

(23) A.B.E.Hood, *St Patrick, his Writings and Muirchu's Life*, Phillimore, London, 1978, p.94

Chapter 5
NORTHUMBRIA AND ANGLIAN MAUGHOLD

First, a wider view has to be taken of affairs in Europe subsequent to the decline of the Roman Empire. English peoples who knew nothing of Roman civilization had become established in Britain. The problem of introducing these inhabitants to Christianity was addressed by Pope Gregory. He had spent his earlier years as an administrator in Rome, but he then became a monk and was chosen as pope in 590. For the next fourteen years, Gregory applied his exceptional abilities to unifying the Roman Church in Western Europe. He sent a mission to England headed by Augustine, about whom more will be said.

Among the English kingdoms, Northumbria advanced to a position of leadership over the century 600 to 700. A sequence of six notable kings encouraged cultural progress and extended Northumbrian influence to the eastern shores of the Irish Sea.

5.1 The English Church

When Augustine arrived in 597 he was received by Ethelbert, king of Kent at his capital town of Canterbury. Augustine had been told by Pope Gregory that he was to have authority over all the bishops in Britain, so he arranged meetings with them. On one occasion he met seven British bishops led by Dinooth, abbot of Bangor Iscoed near Wrexham. However, the outcome was that these bishops were not prepared to bring their practices into line with those of the Roman Church and were not eager to co-operate in preaching to the Saxons, who were their long-standing enemies.

Augustine had been authorized to establish provinces centred on London and York, each served by an archbishop and twelve bishops, but this scheme did not reach maturity. In 604, Augustine was able to appoint bishops at London and Rochester, but he died in the same year, leaving an organisation of restricted coverage. When Theodore arrived as archbishop in 668, he proceeded to organise dioceses in a practical way by subdividing the territories of the existing English kingdoms. Meanwhile, much had happened in Northumbria.

5.2 Northumbrian Kings

Aethelfrith was an outstanding leader of a powerful army. In 593 he became king of Bernicia, the region between the River Tweed and the Forth. Within a few years he gained control of Deira, the region north of the Humber, and then ruled a united kingdom of Northumbria. In 603, he inflicted a crushing defeat on Aedan mac Gabran, king of the Dalriadic Scots, at the battle of Degsastan in south-west Scotland.

Aethelfrith then drove back the Britons of Wales at the battle of Chester in 614. Near the battlefield, he killed a number of monks who had come from Bangor Iscoed. This victory secured the safety of Anglian settlers in Lancashire who, over the following decades, continued to take possession of this territory (1). Aethelfrith was killed in 616 in a battle near Retford against King Raedwald of East Anglia.

Edwin son of Aella then returned from exile to become king of Northumbria. In 625, Edwin assembled a fleet and sent it to take control of Anglesey and the Isle of Man. The text of the Venerable Bede reads: *Mevanias Brettonum insulas*, which means `the Mevanian islands of the Britons' (2). Anglesey belonged to Gwynedd, but the Isle of Man may have belonged to the Britons of Rheged. In a further statement Bede said (3):

"He (Edwin) even brought the islands of Anglesey and Man under his power... The former of these, which is to the south, is larger in size and more fruitful, containing 960 hides... while the latter has more than 300."

A hide is a little over a hundred acres, enough to support one household. A possible motive for this expedition was to evict rebels from Wales or Galloway who were sheltering there.

In 625, Edwin married Ethelburga, daughter of the king of Kent. She brought her chaplain Paulinus, who was then made a bishop. At his hands, Edwin received baptism in 627. Edwin was killed in 632 at Hatfield Chase near Doncaster in a fight against the combined forces of Penda of Mercia and Cadwallon of Gwynedd. Paulinus then returned to Kent, and at this point, only a limited amount of progress had been made in bringing Christianity to the Northumbrians.

Then Oswald son of Aethelfrith returned from exile in Dalriada. In 635, he established himself in Northumbria by defeating the Welsh king Cadwallon at Heavenfield near Hexham. He brought the monk Aidan from Iona, who set up a monastery on the Columban pattern at Lindisfarne. The sequence of bishops there was: Aidan 635-51; Finan 651-61; Colman 661-64. Oswald died in a battle with Penda of Mercia at Oswestry in 642. He was designated Saint Oswald in recognition of his efforts to introduce Christianity.

Oswald's place was taken by his brother Oswy. After suffering harassment from the Mercians, Oswy succeeded in defeating Penda at the battle of Winwaed near Leeds in 655. Before long, Oswy ruled Northumbria with undisputed authority. By one of his marriages, Oswy had a son Aldfrith, the mother of whom was Fina, daughter of an Irish king. A little later, around 643, Oswy married Eanfled, daughter of the late King Edwin, and they had a son Ecgfrith. The careers of Oswy's sons will be followed up in a moment.

5.3 The Synod of Whitby

Members of the Celtic Church adhered to what they thought was the correct method for calculating the proper date of Easter in each year. On the other hand, the Roman Church had already adopted revised tables calculated by Dionysius Exiguus in 525. Queen Eanfled, who had been brought up in Kent, was concerned that the movable feasts celebrated at her court by the Celtic priests fell at times different from those recognised by the Roman Church. King Oswy called a synod at Whitby in 664. Colman, abbot of Lindisfarne presented the older opinions while Roman practice was advocated by the priest Wilfred. The point at issue was whether Northumbria should accept the authority of the Roman Church, and it was decided that this should be so.

Wilfred, after being a student at Lindisfarne, made a journey to Rome where he was impressed with what he saw of church architecture and decoration. On his return he gave a considerable impetus to building in stone. The church of St Peter at Ripon was built of mortared stone in 671 and the church of St Andrew at Hexham was built in 674. The original crypts of these churches can still be seen. After a turbulent career, Bishop Wilfred died in 709.

Cuthbert was a contemporary of Wilfred, but of a very different nature. As a boy he entered the monastery of Melrose on the River Tweed. He then worked at Lindisfarne, implementing the decisions taken at the Synod of Whitby. During this time he pursued missionary work in the Northumbrian territories beteen the Humber and the Firth of Forth. He was made bishop of Lindisfarne in 685, but died in 687.

King Oswy died in 670 and was followed by Ecgfrith, who drove his half-brother Aldfrith into exile. He soon proceeded to impose his rule on the old British kingdom of Rheged. Ecgfrith may have been involved with an event entered in the Annals of Ulster under the year 681, this entry being *Jugulatio Muirmin in Mano* (4). Muirmin can be identified with Merfyn Mawr, whose name appeared in a genealogy of Galloway princes as being tenth in descent from the Roman governor Macsen Wledig (5). Most scholars take this report to mean that Mervyn was killed in the Isle of Man. While no explanation of this incident has been given, it might be guessed that Merfyn posed a threat to King Ecgfrith, who secured his assassination.

In 684, Ecgfrith sent a force to Ireland to ravage in County Meath. He may have wished to punish Galwegians who had been assisting his enemies and who were taking refuge in Ireland. Soon afterwards, Ecgfrith was killed while fighting Brude mac Bile, king of the Picts, at Nechtansmere, now Dunnichen near Forfar in 685. After this disaster, Northumbrian control of the peripheral British territories was relaxed.

Church organisation in Northumbria was strengthened during the reigns of Oswy and Ecgfrith. At this time, work on monastic buildings was promoted by Benedict Biscop. King Ecgfrith was impressed by books that Benedict had acquired during a visit to Rome, and granted land at the mouth of the River Wear, near present-day Sunderland. Benedict, who was on friendly terms with Archbishop Theodore, brought stone masons from Gaul to build in the continental style, and the monastery at Monkwearmouth with its church of St Peter was founded in 674.

King Ecgfrith was again impressed and granted more land to Benedict at Jarrow on the Tyne estuary. The church of St Paul was dedicated there in 685. So the period 671 to 685 saw the building of stone churches by Benedict Biscop and Bishop Wilfred. These dates set a base-line for the development of the distinctive sculptural styles which developed in Northumbria during the next century.

King Ecgfrith was followed by his half-brother Aldfrith, who had been educated at Malmesbury and had lived for some years in Ireland. He stands out as a patron of learning. One of the visitors at his court was Adamnan, abbot of Iona. Upon Aldfrith's death in

704, he was followed by three rather insignificant kings until Ceolwulf ruled 729 to 737.

A prominent figure of Ceolwulf's reign was the Venerable Bede. As a youth he entered the monastery at Jarrow, where he spent the rest of his life. By using the library there, which was the best in England, and by engaging in correspondence with the scholars of his day, Bede compiled his `Ecclesiastical History of the English People', and finished it in 731.

In Northumbria, political confusion was then caused by usurpers belonging to various families. The story of the Northumbrian kings is picked up again after the nine-year reign of Alhred, who was displaced in 774 by Ethelred. In 788, Osred son of Alhred made a bid for power but was soon driven out. When Osred returned from *Eufania* in 792, he was killed by Ethelred. This report comes from the `History of the Kings of England' written in 1129 by Simeon of Durham (6).

No doubt, the kings of Northumbria regarded the Isle of Man as a source of trouble. It has been seen that Edwin sent an invading force in 625 and that Merfyn was killed there in 681. Ecgfrith sent his punitive expedition to Ireland in 684, and a century later in 792, Osred took refuge in the Isle of Man. Over this long period the Isle of Man may have sheltered fugitives from the kingdom of Rheged as well as Northumbrian rebels, but apparently, neither of these groups wished to plant a permanent colony there.

5.4 Anglian monasteries

The eighth century saw the golden age of Northumbrian culture. Sculptors from the Continent demonstrated their refined techniques of relief carving. One of the new Anglian monasteries was at Hoddom, a mile south of Ecclefechan, Dumfries. Possibly, this was the home of the sculptors who created the magnificent high cross at Ruthwell, between Annan and Dumfries, also the Bewcastle Cross at Shopford, north-east of Carlisle. These crosses with inscriptions in Anglian runes are dated 740 to 750.

The Anglo-Saxon Church in England was based on monasteries, each serving quite a large district. The local ruler granted a charter which assigned farm lands and required the monks to perform pastoral duties. The main church or minster was dedicated to a biblical saint such as Peter, Paul, Andrew or the Virgin Mary. Church services were regularly conducted at outlying places, often in the open air.

Although a few of the leading monasteries such as that at Jarrow had stone buildings, most Anglian monsteries initially had wooden buildings. Anglian stone monuments were usually associated with monasteries, in contrast to the later Norse monuments which were commissioned by particular landowners. Notable minsters were founded at Whithorn and Hoddom, while others to the south of Carlisle were at Dacre, Heversham and Lancaster. In the twelfth century when diocesan bishops appeared, the districts of the minsters became subdivided into parishes, each with its own priest, but old endowments sometimes persisted into later times.

5.5 Anglian Carlisle and Whithorn

On the death of Urien around 590, his kingdom of Rheged probably disintegrated, the part north of the Solway becoming attached to the kingdom of Strathclyde. Anglian settlers travelling westwards had possibly reached the Eden Valley by 590. After the Northumbrian victory at Degsastan in 603, the British princes in south-west Scotland held little authority, so Anglian settlers were free to proceed westwards. Archaeologists have examined the Mote of Mark, on the Urr estuary south of Dalbeattie. They found signs that this British fortress had been captured by the Angles early in the 7th century (7).

What was left of the kingdom of Rheged passed to Urien's son Rhun who was followed by his son Royth. One of the wives of Oswy, king of Northumbria was Rhiainfellt or Riemmelth, daughter of Royth. The date of this marriage was about 638, the date favoured by Kirby (8). This marriage could be seen as a political move to justify the Northumbrian occupation of Rheged, which had already taken place. It appears that by 650, the entire coastline from Lancashire to the Solway and along to Galloway was in the hands of heathen Anglian settlers.

Ecgfrith was able to make good his father's claim to Rheged, as he granted a large area of land around Carlisle for the building of a new monastery (9). In 685, Cuthbert, in his capacity as bishop of Lindisfarne, went to Carlisle to view this property. At the prompting of Cuthbert or otherwise, missionaries reached out to the Anglian settlers in south-west Scotland during the latter part of the 7th century. When they reached Candida Casa, they found the remains of the British monastery, to which they gave the Anglo-Saxon name *Hwit-aern*, 'White House', so that it became known as Whithorn.

After the battle of Nechtansmere in 685, relations between Picts and Northumbrians gradually improved. At some time around 710, Nechtan mac Derile, king of the Picts of Angus approached Ceolfrith, abbot of Jarrow and asked his advice on ecclesiastical matters. Nechtan wished to build a new stone church in the Roman fashion, dedicated to St Peter, as recorded by Bede. A few years later in 717, Nechtan expelled the Columban monks from his territories. It appears that he was trying to Romanize his churches in the face of opposition from the Columban Church.

The first notice about the Anglian bishopric at Whithorn was provided by Bede (3):

"At the present time (731), there are four bishops in the kingdom of Northumbria... Pehthelm in the place called Whithorn where the number of believers has so increased that it has lately become an episcopal see with Pehthelm as its first bishop. The Picts now have a treaty of peace with the English and now rejoice to share in the catholic peace and truth of the Church universal."

Apparently, an Anglian church already existed at Whithorn, but exactly when it was founded is not known with certainty. Some writers have seen the founding of this bishopric as part of a Northumbrian policy to appease the Picts by pre-empting the Columban Church in this part of Scotland.

An important monument has been found by the road leading from the town of Whithorn to the Isle of Whithorn, this being the St Peter Cross. This has an incised Maltese cross of compass-drawn arcs extending out to an enclosing double circle. A small open Rho is attached to the upper arm of the cross. The stone carries the inscription: LOCI PETRI APUSTOLI, 'the place of St Peter', showing that it marked a preaching place or cemetery.

Collingwood, writing in 1927, believed that the reference to St Peter implied a date subsequent to the Synod of Whitby, and that the stone was contemporary with King Ecgbert and St Cuthbert (10). He argued that when the stone was carved, an archaic style was copied from existing monuments. Professor Simpson disagreed and gave an earlier date (11). On the basis of the lettering, which has accentuated serifs, Ralegh Radford believed that the inscription belonged to the British period at the beginning of the 7th century (12). Despite these further opinions, Collingwood's argument has not been refuted.

The coast of Galloway remained under Northumbrian control. King Eadbert of Northumbria conquered Kyle in south-west Scotland in 750. A few years later, in alliance with the Picts, he attacked the headquarters of the Strathclyde Britons at Dumbarton. Anglian bishops continued at Whithorn, the succession being Pechthelm until 735; Frithwald 735 to 763; Pechtwin 763 to 776; Ethelbert 777 to 789; Badulf 790 to 803. The name of Heathored, said to have been bishop around 833, has been added by writers such as Oram (13). It is to be expected that at this time, the Anglian monastery at Whithorn was working under the threat of Viking raids while Northumbrian military power had already declined.

Relative to eighth-century Maughold, a cultural background was provided by the Anglian monastery which existed at Carlisle from 685 and from those at Hoddom and Whithorn which may have existed from a similar date. These monasteries continued in the Anglian tradition until a rather uncertain date some years after 800, when they may have been exposed to new influences.

5.6 Galloway and Gwynedd

A family tree of the princes of Galloway has been reproduced by Ralegh Radford (5). Merfyn Mawr, who was killed in the Isle of Man, had a son Anarawd, who was followed by his son Tutagual. Cenelion, daughter of Tutagual married Sandef, a chieftain who was descended from the ruling house of Rheged and who may have lived in the vicinity of Carlisle. Sandef and Cenelion had a son Elidyr, who was the father of Gwriad of the Isle of Man.

We turn now to the descendants of Cunedda who ruled in Gwynedd. There, Idwal Iwrch was followed in 720 by Rhodri Molwynog, who fought vigorously against the Saxons until his death in 755. His sons were Hywel and Cynan. The death in 818 of Hywel, king of Gwynedd marked the end of the male line of Cunedda. Cynan's daughter Esyllt married Gwriad of the Isle of Man, who, as we have seen, had his roots in Galloway and Rheged. Their son was Merfyn Frych.

Merfyn left the Isle of Man to take over Anglesey, and by 825 he had gained control of the rest of Gwynedd. However, the career of Merfyn Frych need not be followed any further here. When he departed from the Isle of Man in 818, he left the way open for Scandinavian settlers.

It is possible that the kings of Gwynedd collected tribute from the

Isle of Man during the eighth century. However, cultural links during this time were not with Gwynedd, but with Galloway and Northumbria.

5.7 Monuments at Maughold

During the seventh century, the monastery at Maughold had been the recipient of cultural debris from the disintegrating British monasteries. From roughly the year 700, new cultural influences were emanating from the Anglian monasteries built around the opposite coast of Britain. During the eighth century, Irish annalists kept silent about the Isle of Man, probably because the churches there were not affiliated with Irish houses. Eighth-century monuments at Maughold show points of similarity with the monuments of the new Anglian monastery at Whithorn. This is illustrated by the cross-slabs that will now be described, though none exhibit the finesse of the best Anglian workmanship.

Blakman's Cross is a simple slab with an incised Maltese cross. On the arms of this cross are lightly incised triquetae, or three-cornered knots, sometimes considered to be of Irish origin. This figure is surrounded by an annulus containing the name Blakman, written in Anglian runes. This personal name is Northumbrian, and the date of the slab is a year or two before 800. The next three crosses show more elaborate styles.

Branhui's Cross was found in Maughold churchyard in 1948. It has an incised cross with four deepened pockets in the corners of the cross. A square panel at the centre of the cross contains an inscription. Mr A.M.Cubbon's reading of this is: IHS XPS BRANHUI HUC AQUA DIRIVAVIT, `Jesus Saviour: Christ: Branhui led water to this place' (14). Mr Basil Megaw believed that the name Branhui was Irish (15). Mrs Nora Chadwick took this name to be Welsh (16). Mr Cubbon considered that his name was British (14). The miniscule lettering suggests a date possibly as late as 820.

Guriat's Cross is a large rectangular slab, the surface of which has been carved away to leave a central boss and four others standing in relief. Incised circles surround this group of bosses. This ar-rangement of bosses resembles that found on the slabs at Whithorn which have been described by Collingwood (17). However, that the Guriat Cross lacks the plaited ornamentation of the Whithorn crosses. This cross was found at a keeill site about a mile from Maughold Church along the road to Ramsey. An inscription in

Roman letters, *Crux Guriat* is cut on one edge of the slab. Estimates of the date of this monument vary from the second half of the eighth century to a little after 800.

Wade-Evans suggested that this cross commemorated Gwriad, father of Merfyn Frych of Gwynedd (18). However, historians are not completely convinced about this. The monuments mentioned above tend to show that communication was maintained between Maughold and the Anglian monastery at Whithorn during the eighth and early ninth centuries.

5.8 The Monks Cross

From around 670, scupltors in Northumbria turned their attention to free-standing crosses. These were intended to stand outside a church as a decorative feature, an example being the Ruthwell Cross in Dumfriesshire, dated around 750.

This cross has free arms. If a cross of this kind had sharp armpits, that is, right-angled corners between the arms, there would be a danger that the arms might break off. So the angles between the arms were hollowed out into smooth curves to make the arms less brittle. A further strengthening effect could be obtained by leaving an integral ring of stone to support the arms. This kind of ringed cross has come to be called a Celtic Cross (See Figure 2). An early and well-developed example is the South Cross at Ahenny, Co. Tipperary, dated by Seabourne to the period 700 to 750 (19). A further early example is the St Martin Cross at Iona, dated 750 to 800.

A kind of "poor man's Celtic cross" can be made by carving the outline of a ringed cross on the flat surface of a rectangular slab. Here the ring serves no practical purpose and has become an artistic motif. The Monks Cross at Maughold (No.96) is a rectangular slab, the surface of which has been cut away to leave two main features. The ring extends out to the extremities of the cross and round pockets have been formed at the four armpits. Further, two figures have been carved in relief, positioned symmetrically on either side of the shaft. These figures have been identified with Paul and Anthony, hermit-monks in the Egyptian desert. A few monuments of similar design are now considered.

Through the 8th century the Pictish kingdom was dominant in Scotland, and monumental art developed to a high degree. Two slabs having ringed crosses are the Aldbar stone in Brechin

Cathedral and the Fowlis Wester stone located four miles east of Crieff, mentioned by Sutherland (20). The second of these crosses has figures seated on either side of the shaft, taken to be Paul and Anthony. A further stone is the "Mourning Angels" stone at the roadside at Aberlemno five miles south-west of Brechin (20). This is a large rectangular slab with the cross carved quite deeply in relief and with the figure of an angel positioned on each side of the shaft.

The theme of Paul and Anthony was a widely used during the late 8th and early 9th centuries. It occurs on the Ruthwell Cross, already mentioned. Further examples have been given by Seaborne (19). These include panels on a cross-slab at Nigg, Cromarty Firth, on the shaft of a cross at Penmon Priory, Anglesey, on the South Cross at Castledermot, Co. Kildare and on the high cross at Moone near Castledermot, the last two being dated to around 800. A further example is at Nash, Glamorgan.

The cross slabs at Iona were reviewed by the Royal Commission (21). About twenty of these show a ringed cross, either incised or in low relief. Most of these have rounded armpits and some have a ring with beaded rims. Those that have lettering have been dated on the basis of this lettering to the 8th century. None of these crosses have ornamentation at the sides of the vertical shaft. For this reason, it cannot be claimed that the Monks Cross at Maughold was directly inspired by monuments at Iona.

Collingwood pointed out that no representation of a ringed cross cut in relief on a rectangular slab is known within the Northumbrian region (9). It is seen that the nearest parallels to the Monks Cross at Maughold occur in Pictland. However, the significance of this observation tends to be diminished by two considerations. By the opening of the 9th century, Pictish monumental art of a high standard set an example for sculptors to follow. Also, at that time, the theme of 'Paul and Anthony in the Desert' was popular all round the British Isles.

The amicable relationship between Whithorn and the Pictish kingdom has already been mentioned. If it is admitted that art-forms seen on the Monks Cross at Maughold show Pictish influence, this lends weight to the proposition that communication was maintained between Maughold and Whithorn, but does not speak for any connection between Maughold and Iona. Trench-Jellicoe classified the Monks Cross as being pre-Norse (22). It is fairly certainly dated to the 9th century, and most likely belongs to the first half of this century.

It appears that the church at Maughold was patronised by displaced people from Galloway and Northumbria. The diversity of the monuments there suggests that itinerant Anglian stone-masons were engaged to carve them. Here, the eighth-century monastery has been called "Anglian Maughold" because it was clearly within the Northumbrian sphere of influence, but this does not imply an organisational link, which is a question that is left open.

Stone monuments at Maughold and its dependent chapels must have been carved while settled life was still possible. Around 850, it would be expected that Norse settlers would tighten their grip on the monastic lands, and it is likely that the monks then took flight. All written records were lost and the very name of the monastery at Maughold is not now known.

5.9 Subsidiary Chapels

It is accepted that Maughold was the principal monastery in the Isle of Man, but possibly there was another on Peel Island. When the cathedral was built on Peel Island, its walls encroached on a cemetery having graves of the 7th or 8th century, as reported by Dr Freke (23). In the land grant made to Rushen Abbey in 1134, a passing reference was made to a monastery of St Leoc, but its existence is not otherwise confirmed.

One of the few keeills that can be dated by means of its monuments is that at Ballavarkish, Bride. A slab found there (Manx Museum No.52) carries the incised outline of a ringed cross, as described by Kermode (24). This slab has been described as an altar front of eighth century date. The cross has been called *Crux Lugri* from a name scratched on it at a later date. The keeill at which it was found has been called *Keeill Varkys*, `Church of St Mark', but this name is of doubtful authenticity, as pointed out by Gill (25). There is no reason to believe that the keeill had such a name in the 8th century. It is reasonable to assume that this keeill was a subsidiary chapel of Maughold, and that this chapel and similar ones were served by monks from Maughold.

A few cells existed at remote places, and must have been occupied by hermits. Perhaps the most refined piece of art-work of this period is the Crucifixion Cross, dated to the late 8th century. This altar panel belonged to a chapel on the Calf of Man which has now been demolished. Romily-Allen described this art as being distinctly Irish in character (26). The chapel on the Calf of Man was either an outpost of a monastery at Peel or it was a hermitage having Irish connections. The keeill at the remote situation of Lag ny Keeilley in the parish of Patrick was fairly certainly a hermitage. Slabs bearing simple crosses suggest that this site was in use during the 8th century.

References for Chapter 5

(1) F.T.Wainwright, *Scandinavian England*, Phillimore, Chichester, 1975, p.23

(2) Carolus Plummer, *Venerabilis Baedae Historiam Ecclesiasticam Gentis Anglorum*, Vol.1, Clarendon Press, Oxford, 1896, p.89, 97

(3) Judith McClure and Roger Collins, *Bede: The Ecclesiastical History of the English People*, Oxford Univ.Press, 1994, Bk.II, Cap.9, p.84; Bk.V, Cap.23, p.289

(4) Wm.M.Hennessy, *Annals of Ulster*, HMSO, Dublin, 1887

(5) C.A.Ralegh Radford, *Excavations at Whithorn*, Trans.Dumfr.& Gall.Nat.Hist.& Ant.Soc., Vol.XXVII, 1950, p.85

(6) J.Stevenson, *Simeon of Durham: A History of the Kings of England*, 1858, reprinted by Llanerch Publishers, Lampeter, 1987, p.42

(7) Lloyd and Jennifer Laing, *Celtic Britain and Ireland, AD 200-800*, Irish Academic Press, Dublin, 1990, p.58

(8) D.P.Kirby, *Strathclyde and Cumbria: a Survey of Historical Development to 1092*, Trans.Cumb.& Westm.Ant.& Arch.Soc., Vol.LXII, 1962, p.77

(9) T.H.B.Graham and W.G.Collingwood, *Patron Saints of the Diocese of Carlisle*, Trans.Cumb.& Westm.Ant.& Arch.Soc., (NS) Vol.XXV, p.1

(10) W.G.Collingwood, *Northumbrian Crosses of the Pre-Norman Age*, 1927, reprinted by Llanerch Publishers, Lampeter, 1989, pp.2-4, 22, 82

(11) W.D.Simpson, *The Celtic Church in Scotland*, Aberdeen Univ.Press, 1935, p.50

(12) C.A.Ralegh Radford, *Excavations at Whithorn*, Trans.Dumfr.& Gall.Nat.Hist.& Ant.Soc., 3rd Ser. Vol.XXXIV, 1957, p.131

(13) Richard D.Oram, `Scandinavian Settlement in South-west Scotland', in *Scandinavian Settlement in Northern Britain*, (editor: Barbara E. Crawford), Leicester Univ. Press, 1995, p.127

(14) A.M.Cubbon, `The Early Church in the Isle of Man', in *The Early Church in Western Britain and Ireland*, (editor: Susan M.Pearce), British Archaelogical Reports, British Series 102, 1982, p.257

(15) B.R.S.Megaw, *The Monastery at Maughold*, Isle of Man Nat.Hist.& Ant.Soc., Vol.V, No.11, 1950, p.169

(16) N.K.Chadwick, *Celtic Britain*, Thames & Hudson, London, l963, p.227

(17) W.G.Collingwood, *The Early Crosses of Galloway*, Trans.Dumf.& Gall.Nat.Hist.& Ant.Soc., Vol.X, l925, p.205

(18) A.W.Wade-Evans, *Prolegomena to a Study of the Lowlands*, Trans.Dumf.& Gall.Nat.Hist.& Ant.Soc., Vol.XXVII, l950, p.54

(19) Malcolm Seaborne, *Celtic Crosses of Britain and Ireland*, Shire Publications, Aylesbury, 1994, p.46

(20) Elizabeth Sutherland, *In Search of the Picts*, Constable, London, 1994, pp.127, 160, 152

(21) Royal Commission on the Ancient and Historical Monuments of Scotland, *Argyll, Vol.4, Iona*, pp.183-6

(22) R.Trench-Jellicoe, *A Re-Definition and Stylistic Analysis of P.M.C.Kermode's "Pre-Scandiavian" series of Manx Sculptural Monuments*, University of Lancaster Ph.D. Thesis, l985

(23) D.Freke, *The Peel Castle Dig*, Manx Museum, l995, p.11

(24) P.M.C.Kermode, *Cross Slabs recently discovered in the Isle of Man*, Proc.Soc.Ant.Scot., Vol.xlvi, 1912, p.53

(25) W.W.Gill, *A Manx Scrapbook*, Vol.1, Arrowsmith, London, 1929, p.68

(26) J.Romily Allen, *The High Crosses of Ireland*, Llanerch Publishers, Lampeter, l992, p.144.

Chapter 6
NORSEMEN AT HOME AND ABROAD

There may have been various reasons for the upsurge of activity of the Vikings. Their homelands were under increasing pressure of population. They had the means of travel as they were a seafaring people who could build ships of a high standard of seaworthiness. The earlier phase of activity consisted of raiding, organised by local leaders. To go "a-viking" was to set off on a sea cruise for gain, either by robbery or by trade. Raiding started soon after 790. Favourite targets were churches on the coast or on rivers accessible to their ships of small draught. In Scotland and Ireland, those churches that were firmly established were able to make a recovery when the raiders left, but some had to be abandoned.

Soon after raiding started, the Norsemen showed a hunger for new lands in which to settle. This movement started before the year 800 in the Orkney and Shetland Isles. One of the leaders who arrived in the Hebrides was Ketil Flatnose. He came from Norway soon after 830, which may be taken as the time when colonizing started in the Isle of Man (1).

6.1 Scandinavian culture

Norse settlers arriving through the 9th century brought their own pagan culture from their home country and lived with this culture on new shores after driving off the natives. Their three principal gods were Thor, the sky god who governed the weather, Odin the giver of victory in battle and Frey the god of fertility. Boat-burials in lands where Scandinavians settled imply a belief that the dead person embarked on a journey to an other-world destination. Articles that might be needed in the next world were put in the grave. A warrior might need a horse and weapons, a smith his hammer and tongs and a woman her personal ornaments.

In Scandinavia, civil administration was conducted through a *Thing*, or assembly of freemen. The local Thing served a community called a *herad*, consisting of something like a hundred families. Whenever Scandinavians settled in a new land, they quickly established a *Thing-volar*, or meeting field. This was used not only for purposes of government but also served social and religious purposes. One of the features of the meeting field was an artificially raised mound. The senior men sat in conference on this Thing-mound in the open air.

As part of the ceremonial opening of an assembly, a sacrifice or *blot,* was offered at the temple or *hof.* This temple was a wooden structure containing wooden images of the gods and also an altar. Of course, no trace can now be found of the temples or their contents, but written descriptions have been preserved in Scandinavia. On the altar was kept a sacred ring, also a vessel in which to collect blood from the sacrificial animal. Various animals were sacrificed, including horses, bulls and dogs. Adjacent to the sacrificial site was a grove of trees. The body of the victim was suspended on a tree until it decayed.

On special occasions, a human sacrifice was offered. The victim, often a slave, was killed on the sacrificial stone or was drowned in the sacred well or *blot-kelda.* There were no full-time priests, so the sacrifice was conducted by a *godi,* chosen from the leading landowners. A sacrifice was offered at Thing assemblies and also at the mid-winter festival of Yule and at the spring equinox. The Thing-field site also included a cemetery and a nearby place for hanging criminals. A famous temple and royal burial ground was that at Old Uppsala in Sweden.

When Christianity arrived, it was necessary to build a church at the site of each temple. On this point, Axel Olrik has written (2):

"Many churches in Scandinavia were erected on pagan sacrificial sites. The grove or the spring was often preserved into a later age."

Thing-field sites are marked by place-names in many of the lands colonized by Scandinavians. Examples are at Thingvellir east of Reykjavik in Iceland and at Tinganes in the Faroes. Also at Tingwall parish north of Lerwick in the Shetlands, at the town of

Dingwall on Cromarty Firth, at Tinwald north of Dumfries, at Thingwall in the parish of Woodchurch, Wirral, and at Thingwall in the district of Knotty Ash, Liverpool, and at other places.

6.2 Christianity in Norway

The Archdiocese of Bremen was set up in 849 and had responsibilty for the Scandinavian kingdoms. This had little effect until King Harald Bluetooth declared himself a Christian in 965, as recorded on his epitaph at Jelling in Denmark. Each of the `herred' districts in Norway had a Thing-field with its temple, and additionally the more important landowners maintained private temples. Norway was ruled by Harald Fairhair until his death in 945. His son Haakon had been brought up in the Christian court of King Athelstan in England. He returned with priests from England, but they made little progress. Haakon died in 960 and was followed by Harald Greycloak, son of Eric Bloodaxe.

A little later, Olaf Trygvason, when he came to reside at Nidaros in 995, made a new attempt to bring Christianity to Norway. He had been baptized during a visit he paid in the previous year to the English court of Ethelred the Unready. Olaf destroyed the temple of Frey at Nidaros and proceeded to build a church there with assistance from his bishop Sigurd and priests from England. However, Olaf Trygvason's policies aroused resentment in Norway, leading to his downfall in 1002, when control of the country passed to Denmark.

The boy Olaf Haraldson, called Olaf the Thick or Stout on account of his strong stature, grew up and went abroad in search of adventure, until he resolved to liberate Norway. He accomplished this in 1015, and then he promoted Christianity with assistance of bishops of Scandinavian nationality trained in England. His policy was to use force. In the words of the *Heimskringla* (3):

"He...laid great penalties upon them, if there were people who would not give up their heathen ways. He drove some away from the land, some he caused to be maimed either in hand or foot, or to

67

have their eyes plucked out, and some he caused to be hanged or beheaded; and no one he let go unpunished who would not serve God."

Olaf alienated himself from factions in Norway and was killed by the Danes at the battle of Stiklestad in 1030. His good intentions were recognized some years later when he was named Saint Olavus. Norwegians had already developed a national identity in conjunction with worship of their own gods, and they resisted change, while Scandinavians who went abroad responded more readily to new ideas.

The next kings in Norway were Magnus the Good and Harald Hardrada (the Ruthless). The latter met his end at Stamford Bridge, Yorkshire. From 1066, Olaf Kyrre (the Quiet or Peaceful) reigned in Norway. At this stage, bishops were attached to the king's court. In 1077, Olaf built a cathedral at Nidaros to replace the older wooden church, and this became the seat of a resident bishop. This church was called Christ-church, a name which Scandinavians reserved for a bishop's church. In organising churches he was assisted by monks from Durham, where a monastery had existed from 995. Under Olaf's rule, conversion of Norway was completed. The dioceses had parishes which were largely based on the districts previously served by temples.

From 1093 the king of Norway was Olaf's son Magnus Barelegs. During his reign he made an expedition to reassert his authority in the Hebrides and the Isle of Man, when he fortified Peel Island. He was killed in Ireland in 1103.

Up to this time, churches in the Scandinavian countries were supervised by the Archbishop of Hamburg-Bremen, but in 1104, they were attached to a new Archdiocese of Lund, this place being in the south of present-day Sweden. King Sigurd (1103 to 1130) introduced tithes in Norway. The Norwegians finally acquired their own archbishop at Nidaros in 1153. Generally, ecclesiastical developments in the Isle of Man followed an earlier time-table and were not much affected by happenings in distant Norway.

6.3 Settlement in the Northern Isles.

We now look at the Northern Isles, these being the Isles of Orkney and Shetland. Perhaps as early as 780, Norwegians started to arrive, and soon after 800, a mass migration was under way. These immigrants brought their wives, so their families grew up speaking Norn, a dialect of Old Norse, which continued in use as late as 1750. The change in place-names brought about by the colonists was total.

In order to explain these facts, it is not sufficient to assume that the culture of the previous Pictish inhabitants was merely degraded, but it is necessary to suppose that the Picts themselves were killed or deported as slaves. Nothing quite so drastic occurred in the Hebrides and the Isle of Man, where it must be supposed that a considerable number of the original inhabitants survived to intermarry with the newcomers.

Wherever Scandinavian colonists settled, their conduct was governed by the ingrained notions that they brought from their homeland. The earldom of Orkney remained a colony of Norway, subject to taxation by the king of Norway. Settled land in Orkney was divided into six *husaby* districts, as described by Loyn (4). Each husaby was divided into thirty-six urislands, eyrislands or ouncelands. Each ounceland was divided into four scattlands. A scattland was a portion of land sufficient for the support of a family. The ounceland, or group of four farms, took its name from the annual tax of one ounce of silver, which in most districts was equivalent to twenty pence. If the land was less fertile, the allocation was of larger extent, so that the tax remained the same.

Tax was collected by the head-man of the husaby and was forwarded to the earl, who forwarded an apportionment to the king of Norway. This scheme of tax collection was probably introduced at the time when settlers first arrived. Land divisions may have been based, to some extent, on divisions previously used by the dispossessed Picts. Every freeman in Norse lands was expected to attach himself to a temple. For this reason, it might be expected that each husaby would have its own temple. It is likely that colonising in the Hebrides and the Isle of Man proceeded in a similar way.

About 980, Sigurd the Stout, son of Hlodver, became Earl of
Orkney. His mother Eithne (Edna) was a daughter of Kjarrall or
Cearball, an Irish king, but he was not brought up as a Christian. In
982, Sigurd made an expedition to the Isle of Man and left Earl Gilli
in charge of the Sudreys. Around 995, King Olaf Trygvason of
Norway paid a visit to Sigurd in the Orkneys and exerted pressure
on him to accept baptism. It is unlikely that this had any effect on
Sigurd's personal behaviour, though it possibly marked a more
positive official attitude towards Christianity in the Orkneys.
Sigurd was killed at the battle of Clontarf at Dublin in 1014.

Among the original Pictish inhabitants were monks whom the Norse
called *papar*. In Orkney, one of their monasteries was on the
Brough of Birsay at the north-west corner of Mainland. Dr
Wainwright believed that Christianity in the Northern Isles survived
the impact of Scandinavian settlement and that the process of
conversion occurred much earlier that the sagas indicated (5). This
view has not been accepted by other writers, and Barbara Crawford
pointed out that several pagan graves in the Northern Isles are now
dated to the tenth century (6). The Orkneyingers' Saga clearly says
that the *papar* abandoned their cells when the Norsemen arrived (7).

6.4 The Earls of Orkney

Earl Sigurd had three sons from his first marriage, one of these
being Brusi. Sigurd also had a son Thorfinn from a later marriage
to a daughter of King Malcolm II of Scotland. Thorfinn was only
five years old when his father died, and was brought up at the court
of his grandfather in Scotland. Brusi eventually possessed the
Orkney Isles and had a son Rognvald Brusason. On the death of
Brusi in 1035, King Magnus the Good of Norway ordered that the
Orkney earldom should be divided between Rognvald and Thorfinn.
After Rognvald's death, Thorfinn became the sole ruler.

Meanwhile, Earl Gilli, who had been holding the Isle of Man for
Earl Sigurd, died in 1025. In 1040, Thorfinn went on an expedition

to the Isle of Man to assert his authority there. Thorfinn, now known as 'The Mighty', left Kalf Arnesson as his deputy in the Isle of Man. Kalf was the uncle of Thorfinn's wife Ingebjorg.

Thorfinn went to Norway in 1046 to obtain recognition of his position as ruler of both the Orkneys and the Sudreys. In 1048, he felt sufficiently secure to go on a pilgrimage to Rome. While he was there he asked for a bishop to be sent to him. On his return he started to build a Christ-kirk by his palace at Birsay. As his deputy in the Sudreys, Thorfinn appointed Sitric Reginaldson, son of Reginald Olafson.

At this time, the Scandinavian countries still came under the care of the archdiocese of Hamburg-Bremen. The archbishop there from 1043 to 1073 was Adalbert. One of the bishops he sent to Earl Thorfinn was Thorolf. According to Haddan and Stubbs, Thorolf arrived in 1055 (8). He was attached to the court of the Earl and usually travelled with him. The bishop had authority in all the Earl's territories, although at that time, no diocesan structure had been set up. Thorolf has been identified with Roolwer, the bishop mentioned in the *Chronicon Manniae*. Sitric Reginaldson continued as king of the Sudreys until both he and his overlord Thorfinn died in 1065.

In the Orkney Isles, chapels were built on private estates. Some may have existed before the dramatic conversion of Earl Sigurd in 995, but more probably followed this event. At this stage, chapels were not yet supervised by a bishop. When parishes were formed, the most prominent chapel in each parish district was turned into a parish church, as mentioned by Bailey (9). This did not happen in the Isle of Man, where parish churches are not associated with large estates and in general, they did not start life as private chapels.

An interesting development in the Northern Isles was the building of ounceland chapels. The remains of these can be recognised at 140 or more sites in Orkney and a similar number in Shetland. From the large number of these chapels and their association with ounceland divisions, it may be suspected that this project was the result of a political directive. Studies by Ralegh Radford and Hugh

71

Marwick suggested a date of construction late in the 11th or early in the 12th century (10). A slightly earlier date was favoured by Barbara Crawford who proposed that the scheme was initiated by Earl Thorfinn in 1050 when he returned from his pilgrimage (6). Martin, writing in 1716, reported that in Orkney, "There are thirty-one churches and about one hundred chapels in the country, the whole make up about eighteen parishes" (11). He did not say that the chapels were ruinous, so presumably they were still in use.

Thorfinn was followed in the Orkneys by his sons Paul and Erlend, who continued until 1098 when they were deposed by Magnus Barelegs, king of Norway. Their place was taken by Hakon son of Paul and Magnus son of Erlend. Eventually, Hakon demanded exclusive rights in Orkney, and in 1116 he killed his cousin Magnus, who was buried at Birsay. In 1136, Magnus was declared to be a saint and his remains were removed to Kirkwall. Meanwhile, Bishop William had been appointed as the first resident bishop at Birsay in 1102. From 1135 he lived at Egilsay where a church of St Magnus had been built. This church had a prominent round tower, and the ruin of it still exists.

Building of the cathedral of St Magnus at Kirkwall was started in 1137 by Earl Reginald Kolson. His mother Gunnhilda was a sister of the late St Magnus. For this work, he brought masons from Durham. This project continued for many years and put Reginald under some financial strain, until he died in 1158.
Meanwhile, Bishop William moved from Egilsay to Kirkwall, and in 1153, the diocese of Orkney became one of ten that were taken into the new archdiocese of Nidaros. William the Old, as he was called, died in 1168 after serving as bishop for the remarkable period of sixty-six years. It is seen that the people of the Orkneys were later than those of the Isle of Man in turning towards Christianity, but earlier in building a cathedral.

6.5 Colonisation of Iceland

Colonists started to arrive at a late date, around 874. They found a mere handful of previous inhabitants, whom they swept aside. The social order of noblemen, free-men and serfs resembled that of Norway, although a small number of the immigrants had brought wives from the western isles of Scotland. The colonists set up 'godords', which were groupings of estates, each under the leadership of a 'godi'. By 930, colonisation was fairly complete, and in that year a supreme court or Althing was founded. Iceland was initially divided into twelve districts, each having its local *heradsthing*, while each of these districts sent three representatives to the Althing. An analogous scheme was adopted in the Isle of Man, to be discussed later.

All the freemen in the land had to be attached to a temple and had to pay a toll for upkeep of the temple. This toll was collected by the *godi*, who was a *udaller*, that is, a recognised freeholder. The temple played an important part in the ritual of the assembly, as the sacred armlet or *baugr* was kept there. This was a ring of silver or copper, weighing about a pound. It was often slightly oval and was sometimes penannular. The 'godi' wore the ring on his arm while he sacrificed an animal, when the ring became smeared with blood (12). A person who had to take an oath did this while he touched the ring.

An important consequence of this procedure was that the official religion of the country had to be homogeneously heathen. Any person refusing to take an oath or to confess his belief in the heathen gods was debarred from taking part in the proceedings of the assembly and from pleading his legal rights before the court of the assembly. Christianity was not permitted, or it was practised only by dissident or servile groups. Eventually, this state of affairs brought Iceland to the verge of civil war.

Although the commonwealth of Iceland was not directly ruled from Norway, Olaf Trygvason, the king of Norway gave his support to the party in Iceland that favoured the adoption of Christianity. In the year 1000, the Althing agreed that Christianity would be the official religion of Iceland, and that the old gods would cease to be venerated on all public occasions. Here, a passage may be quoted from Jon Johannesson (12):

73

"After the conversion, the temples (*hof* and *horgar*) were no longer maintained ... Churches replaced the temples and in the period of transition, it appears that the temple priests (*godar*) were responsible for the construction of these churches ... Later on, farmers who wielded influence in their communities took it upon themselves to build churches on their farms. There is no indication that temples were ever converted into churches, but our sources mention that a temple was pulled down and then the timber was used for the building of a church. In the early years the churches were built outside the fence of the homefield to prevent church-goers from trampling on the field. Heathen idols were replaced by statues of Christ and the saints."

In Iceland, there were three categories of priest (12). A priest might own his church, thus continuing, for a while, the duties of the *godi*. Also, regular professional priests were appointed and paid by the bishop to serve one or more parish churches. Such priests were brought from England or Germany. Finally, landowners might provide education for a subordinate class of attendants who were then equipped to serve in private chapels. The first bishop in Iceland was Isleif, appointed in 1056. Payment of tithe was required by legislation of 1097.

From 1104, Iceland came under the jurisdiction of the Archbishop of Lund. By 1106, Jon Ogmundarson, one of the two bishops in Iceland, was able to demand that everyone in his territory should attend church regularly. From 1153, the Icelandic dioceses were taken under the jurisdiction of Nidaros. The Commonwealth of Iceland continued until 1264, when, due to the spread of disorder, the country was taken under the direct control of Norway. Thus it is seen that Iceland progressed from being a heathen state to become a Christian state under the supervision of the national Althing.

In both Iceland and the Isle of Man, the pattern of initial land settlement was the same and was such that all land of any value came into the hands of the colonists. These colonists recognised no laws other than those made by their own Thing courts. Possibly, a central or national assembly existed in the Orkney Isles and another in the Isle of Man, but in both of these places it probably functioned

74

under close control of the ruler.

6.6 The Initial Impact of the Norsemen

There is no written record of the Norse invasion of the Isle of Man, as local records were destroyed by the illiterate invaders, and the Isle of Man was outside the range of interest of Irish annalists. The first generation of settlers in the Isle of Man continued in their old way of life. This is shown by the boat-burials at Balladoole on the south-side and at Knock-y-Dooney on the north-side and the burial with a human sacrifice at Ballateare, Jurby, all dated 850 to 900.

A mound in Jurby churchyard is considered to be a pagan Norse *haugr*, or burial mound (13). There is no evidence that a Christian church or burial ground existed at Jurby prior to the mound being erected, so the mound was set up on a new site. This mound was one of a series of six built on quarterland farms along the Jurby coast. These mounds show that the first Norse occupants of these farms were buried on their own land (14).

The second generation used regional cemeteries, Jurby churchyard being one of them, but burials were still accompanied by pagan grave-goods. Further graves containing weapons have been found in enclosures that later became parish churchyards in the parishes of Michael, Maughold, Braddan and Malew, also at Tynwald Hill, St Johns.

Norse cross-slabs in the Isle of Man sometimes commemorated people with Celtic names. For example, a slab at Kirk Michael carved by Gaut Bjornson around 950 had the inscription "Mail-Brikti son of Athakan, smith, raised this cross..." These are Celtic names. Maelbrighde was a name widely used in Ireland at that time. Mr A.M.Cubbon remarked that this expensive monument shows that a complex social structure had already developed (13). However, this came a century after the beginning of the land-taking and after the arrival of Christianity. Such evidence still leaves open the possibility that none of the original colonists were converted to Christianity, and that during their life-span, they set up political and

75

religious systems modelled on those of their homeland.

The adoption of Christianity by the Norse residents in the Isle of Man may have run a course roughly parallel with events in Iceland, but earlier in time. Initially, it is likely that freemen were bound to pay respect to the Norse gods. Later, the pagan temples were replaced by churches. The array of churches that is seen today in the Isle of Man is largely the end-product of this process. What happened in adjacent countries will be traced in the chapters that follow.

References for Chapter 6

(1) G.V.C.Young, *The History of the Isle of Man under the Norse*, Mansk-Svenska Publ.Co., Peel, 1981, p.15
(2) Axel Olrik, *Viking Civilization*, Geo.Allen & Unwin, London, 1930, p.145
(3) Snorre Sturlason, *Heimskringla, or The Lives of the Norse Kings*, (editor: Erling Monson), W.Heffer & Sons, Cambridge, 1932, p.275
(4) Henry Loyn, *The Vikings in Britain*, Blackwell, Oxford, 1994, p.108
(5) F.T.Wainwright, *The Northern Isles*, Thos.Nelson, Edinburgh, 1962, p.162
(6) B.E.Crawford, *Scandinavian Scotland*, Leicester Univ.Press, 1987, pp.68, 169
(7) G.W.Dasent, *The Orkneyingers' Saga*, HMSO, London, 1894, p.xix
(8) A.W.Haddan and W.Stubbs, *Councils and Ecclesiastical Documents*, Vol.2, Part 1, Clarendon Press, Oxford, 1873, p.153
(9) Patrick Bailey, *Orkney*, David and Charles, Newton Abbot, 1985, pp.87, 109
(10) C.A.Ralegh Radford, `Art and Architecture: Celtic and Norse', in *The Northern Isles*, (editor: W.T.Wainwright), Thos.Nelson, Edinburgh, 1962, pp.174, 181
(11) Martin Martin, *A Description of the Western Isles of Scotland*, 1716, reprinted by James Thin, Mercat Press, Edinburgh, 1976, p.361

76

(12) Jon Johannesson, *A History of the Old Icelandic Commonwealth*, Univ. of Manitoba Press, 1974, p.139

(13) A.M.Cubbon, *The Early Church in the Isle of Man*, British Archaeological Reports, British Series, No. 102, 1982, p.257 (see pp. 271, 273)

(14) Basil and Eleanor Megaw, `The Norse Heritage in the Isle of Man', in *The Early Cultures of North-West Europe*, (editors: C.Fox & B.Dickins), p.143 (see p.146)

Chapter 7
AFFAIRS IN DUBLIN

Scandinavians came to Dublin to use this place as a port and a commercial centre rather than to take over land, though they eventually occupied much of County Dublin. The purpose of this chapter is to assess the political and cultural status attained by this settlement, particularly during the tenth century, when Norsemen living at places around the Irish Sea became receptive to Christianity.

This is not an easy task. If Dublin people kept any records, none have survived. Irish annalists called these people "foreigners" and took no notice of their domestic affairs.

7.1 Celtic Dublin

The River Poddle formerly entered the Liffey estuary by way of a tidal basin near the south-east corner of the present Dublin Castle. Although this basin has now been filled in, it gave rise to the name *Dubh-Linn*, 'black pool'. The ridge running along the south bank of the Liffey provided a convenient place for crossing this river, at *Ath-cliath*, 'ford of wattles'.

A Celtic monastery extended along the eastern bank of the River Poddle, as far as 600 metres south of the pool. Irish records mentioned by Clarke gave names of bishops of Dublin (1). These were Livinus, who died in 633, followed by Rumoldus and by Abbot Beraid who died in 650 and Abbot Siadal who died in 790. However, Gwynn and Hadcock commented that these names were not recorded earlier than the 17th century and are plainly unhistorical (2). Within the area of the supposed monastery there were five churches carrying the names St Brigit, St Peter, St Mac Tail, St Patrick and St Coemgen (Kevin).

On the ridge along the south bank of the Liffey there were churches of St Colum Cille, St Mo Lua, and St Martin. These names of

78

churches come from records dated no earlier than the Anglo-Norman invasion of 1169. The area in which these sites lie was eventually enclosed by the wall of the Norse town. However, excavation has not provided any evidence of pre-Norse occupation of this area.

Stokes envisaged that along the banks of the Poddle, a Celtic village existed at the same time as the Norse town, and contained the churches of St Bride, St Patrick and St Kevin (3). This idea is not very firmly founded. While there may have been a Celtic village or monastery here in pre-Norse times, the churches did not necessarily have these names during that period. By the time the churches had these names, they need not have belonged to a Celtic village. When the Norse people came to Dublin in 917, it is unlikely that they would permit the native Irish to live in the vicinity of their citadel.

On the other hand, there are trustworthy records of several Celtic monasteries in the vicinity of Dublin. Clondalkin, about six miles to the west of Dublin was founded by St Mochua in the 7th century. Tallaght, six miles south-west of Dublin was founded by Maelruain in 769. The monastery of Glendalough, twenty-five miles to the south of Dublin, was founded by St Kevin, who died in 618. These monasteries continued to flourish through the period of Norse occupation of Dublin.

7.2 Settlement in Dublin

The Norsemen established a base for ships at Dublin in 841. From 853, the leaders there were Olaf the White and his brother Ivar the Boneless. Eventually, in 902, a coalition of Irish kings attacked and destroyed the Norse settlement. Displaced people took refuge in various places around the Irish Sea, such as the Isle of Man and the Wirral.

In 917, Ragnald Ivarson, a grandson of Ivar the Boneless, with his brother Sitric Gale, established a new colony. Two years later, Sitric Gale defeated the Irish forces in a battle on the south side of Dublin, making the new settlement secure. Their fort was where

Dublin Castle now stands. A walled town was built on ground extending about 600 metres to the west of the fort on the south bank of the River Liffey. From this time Dublin gained economic strength through manufacturing and maritime trade.

The immigrants in Dublin brought with them their pagan Scandinavian institutions and customs. Four hundred metres east of the fort they built the Thingmount, a conical mound twenty-four metres in diameter and twelve metres high. The exact date when it was built is uncertain. The intervening ground was used as a cemetery and named Hoggen Green from the grave mounds (*haugar*), and later became College Green. The Thingmount was demolished in 1685. East of this site was a rocky hill, now quarried away, where a gallows was located. There would have been a temple near the Thingmount, but no evidence can now be found to prove this.

Excavations in Dublin, especially those made since 1962 in the area between Fishamble Street and Winetavern Street, have revealed much about the people who lived there in the later tenth century. The walled town was densely filled with dwellings and workshops. Some of the houses were built of wattle, that is, of posts connected by basketwork. The people earned their living by making articles of leather, horn and metal, and by sea-borne trade. They spoke Norse and used the runic alphabet for every-day purposes, but they have not left any documents.

7.3 Kings of Dublin

After the new colony was founded in 917 and during the next thirty years, the kings in Dublin were ready to take up residence in York whenever an opportunity occurred. Their aspirations in York will be followed in another place. Sitric Gale went to York in 920 leaving his brother Godred Ivarson in Dublin. Godred also went to York, but returned to Dublin in 927 where he remained until his death in 934. The Irish regarded Godred as an unprincipled brigand.

80

Godred was followed as king of Dublin by his son Olaf Godredson. His intersts lay in leading an army against King Athelstan of England, and during the period 939 to 945, Dublin was left in the care of Olaf's brother Blakari.

The next king in Dublin was Olaf son of Sitric Gale, called Olaf Cuaran or Anlaf. With short periods in York, he was king in Dublin over the long period 945 to 980. Olaf controlled a considerable area around Dublin, from Skerries in the north to Wicklow in the south, extending westwards to Leixlip (Figure 3).

The Dublin kings formed opportunistic alliances with Irish kings for engaging in pillaging expeditions. There was a ready market in Dublin for slaves. This violence prompted the construction of round towers for protection at many monasteries from around 950. After a career of robbing and slave-trading, Olaf Cuaran was heavily defeated at Tara by Maelsechnaill, high-king of Ireland. This moved Olaf to go on a pilgimage to Iona in 980, where he died the following year.

Gluniarvin, a son of Olaf Cuaran then became king in Dublin. When he was murdered in 989, a further son of Olaf Cuaran took over. He was Sitric Silkbeard. His long reign of forty-five years saw Dublin develop as a prosperous and stable trading centre.

7.4 Conversion to Christianity

Some hints have been given about the conversion to Christianity of the Norsemen in Ireland during the decade 940 t0 950, but such dates may have been derived from the date of baptism of Olaf Cuaran at the court of King Edmund in 943. It is difficult to discern any positive encouragement that Olaf Cuaran gave to churches in Dublin during his reign.

At a later date, an incident occurred during a raid on Dublin by the Irish king Maelsechnaill in 995. He carried off two items, the Ring of Tomar and the Sword of Carlus. Very likely, this ring was 'Thor's Ring', the armlet worn by the king-priest who presided over assemblies at the Thingmount. However, Curtis held the opinion that this sacred object would not have been yielded up unless it had already ceased to be used (4).

The citizens of Dublin were primarily of Norse extraction, but this seaport may have sheltered other elements, giving a social structure of a more open kind than one based on land ownership. Ryan believed that up to about 975, paganism was still widespread among the people of Norse descent in Ireland (5). On the other hand, it seems possible that soon after 940, there may have been minority groups of Christians in Dublin.

7.5 Churches in Dublin

When Sitric Silkbeard went on a pilgrimage to Rome in 1028, he was impressed by the organisation of the Roman Church. He retired from his position as king in 1036. His sucessor was his nephew Eachmarcach Reginaldson, who was king up to 1038 and for a second period later. Some writers have suggested that Christ Church Cathedral was established soon after 1028 while others believe that this occurred around 1038. The first bishop was Dunan or Donatus. He was born in Ireland but may have been of Norse descent.

After Dunan's death in 1074, the succession of bishops at Christ Church was: Patrick 1074 to 1084; Donatus O'Haingly 1084 to 1095; Samuel O'Haingly 1096 to 1121; Gregory 1121 to 1162; Laurence O'Toole 1162 to 1180. The first bishop at Waterford was Malcus, 1096 to 1135. Further details of these bishops need not be given, but it is noted that all were consecrated by the Archbishop of Canterbury. This shows that the Norse communities in Ireland set up a church organisation on an English model without paying any regard to the churches of the rest of Ireland. From 1175, a start was made to rebuild Christ Church in stone.

When Christ Church made its appearance in 1038, it might be thought that this was the first church to be established in Dublin. However, it is highly likely that other churches already existed, but no contemporary records are available. During the century following the establishment of Christ Church, many churches were built in Dublin, and at least some of these were built on older foundations.

The original church of St Andrew was at the west end of the present Dame Street. It was possibly a temple replacement, this saint being selected because his festival day of November 30 fell near the Yule festival. In recent times, a new church of St Andrew was built on the land vacated by removal of the Thingmount, where St Andrew's Street now runs.

The church of St Michael le Pole (that is, by the pool), stood just outside a gate in the south wall of the town at Ship Street. There is a tradition that it was originally the church of St Mac Tail, who was a monk of Kilcullen in County Kildare, and who died in 664. The church of St Michael le Pole had a round tower with a conical roof, the only round tower in Dublin. The church and tower were demolished in 1781.

St Brigit's Church, a little on the south side of the town wall, was pulled down around 1780, while the nearby church of St Kevin is now a ruin. The church of St Peter in this district stood until 1610 but nothing is now left of it.

The old church of St Mo Lua stood outside the west wall of the town. The most prominent Irish saint who was known by this name was Lugidus or Lugaid maccu Oche. He founded the monastery of Clonferta-Molua near Borris-in-Ossory in County Laois, sixty miles west of Dublin. The date of Molua's death has been variously given as 605, 609 or 622, his feast day being August 4. The church of St Mo Lua was in the district that later became the Cornmarket, in the parish of St Catherine. The church of St Catherine was first built in 1105, and it is possible that it was built on the site of Mo Lua's church.

The churches of St Martin and St Colum Cille within the town walls were still mentioned under these names in a charter of Archbishop Laurence in 1178, and they had evidently served the Norsae inhabitants. Soon after this date, St Martin's was rebuilt in stone and re-dedicated to St Werburgh, after a similar church in Bristol. The church of St Colum Cille was also rebuilt and named after St Audoen of Rouen, the patron saint of the Normans. The church of St Olave in Fishamble Street was locally called St Tulloch's, and belonged to the Augustinian monks who arrived with the Anglo-Normans. Churches built on new sites in the 12th century need not be mentioned here.

There were two prominent churches on the north side of the River Liffey. In the Oxmantown district, St Michan's Church, built in 1096, commemorates a Danish saint. In medieval times, St Mary's Abbey became the wealthiest of the religious houses in Dublin. This abbey was founded as a Benedictine house in 1139 (2). A church on the Howth was set up by the Norse in 1042, and was enlarged and dedicated to the Virgin Mary in 1235.

The general impression gained from the above notes is that when the Norse inhabitants of Dublin adopted Christianity, they built a series of churches, some of them being on the sites of older Celtic churches. To each of them they attached the name of an Irish saint. Prior to the appointment of a bishop, these churches would be owned by groups of townspeople. Following the establishment of the cathedral, these churches were rebuilt in a more substantial way. During a period of increasing English influence in church affairs, and particularly after the arrival of the Normans, churches were re-dedicated to non-Irish saints, excepting the churches of St Patrick and St Bridget.

St Patrick's Cathedral, to the south of the town wall, was built in 1192 by Cumin, the Norman archbishop. The site was not ideal as it was liable to flooding, but was used because this was the site of an earlier church of St Patrick, with its associated well. The churches of St Patrick and St Briget probably stood on the sites of Celtic churches. It seems likely that during the tenth century, these churches were taken over by the Norse townspeople and were given the names of St Patrick and St Bridget at that time. This is an interesting question, as it may reveal the place where the Norsemen made their acquaintance with St Patrick and St Bridget, whose

84

names they carried abroad during the second half of the tenth century.

A group of saints commemorated in Dublin such Andrew, Michael, Patrick and Bridget can also be found among the church dedications in the Isle of Man. It seems a little unlikely that church-building activities in Dublin were so far advanced as to set an example to other Norse colonists around the Irish Sea. However, the Norsemen possibly had some respect for the record of literacy possessed by the indigenous Irish people. They did not, at this time, have any saints of their own, so they were willing to adopt Irish saints when the need arose. Further, the Norsemen may have been encouraged to adopt Irish saints by the Irish priests whom they employed.

At this point, a wider view must be taken of events in other parts of the British Isles during the 10th century.

References for Chapter 7

(1) H.B.Clarke, 'The Topographical Development of Early Medieval Dublin', in, *Medieval Dublin,* (editor: H.Clarke), Irish Academic Press, Dublin, 1990, p.63

(2) A.Gwynn and R.N.Hadcock, *Medieval Religious Houses: Ireland,* Longman, London, 1970, pp.70, 130

(3) G.T.Stokes, *Ireland and the Anglo-Norman Churches,* Hodder & Stoughton, London, 1889, pp.59, 110

(4) Edmund Curtis, 'Norse Dublin', 1941, reprinted in *Medieval Dublin,* (editor: H.Clarke), Irish Academic Press, Dublin, 1990, p.98

(5) John Ryan, 'Pre-Norman Dublin', 1949, reprinted in *Medieval Dublin,* (editor: H.Clarke), Irish Academic Press, Dublin, 1990, p.110ok

Chapter 8
NORSEMEN AROUND THE IRISH SEA

A glance at the map of Cumbria shows that many of the place-names are of Scandinavian derivation. This is a result of an immigration of people of Norwegian descent following the Danish invasion of the eastern side of England. The purpose of this chapter is to illustrate the environment of the Irish Sea in the century 900 to 1000. In this arena, the untutored Norsemen came face to face with Anglo-Saxon civilization. Information will be gathered relevant to two questions, the way in which these intruders interfered with existing churches, and the way in which they eventually adopted Christianity and built churches of their own.

8.1 Danish Invaders and the House of Wessex

The Danish army under Ivar the Boneless assembled in East Anglia in 865. The following year they marched northwards and captured York. These men, during their advance, had no respect for any of the institutions they found. For example, the monastery of Streoneshalch at Whitby was desecrated and remained deserted for two centuries. Over large areas of Lincolnshire and Yorkshire the Anglian churches were destroyed. On the death of Ivar in 873 his brother Halfdan took charge of the army and in 875 he allotted farm lands to his followers in the eastern parts of England.

Wulfhere, the archbishop of York, saw that he had to collaborate with the newcomers. After Halfdan, the next king in York was Guthfrith. In 882 he permitted the monks of Lindisfarne to settle at Chester-le-Street. When Guthfrith died in 895, Wulfhere was able to arrange a Christian burial for him in York Minster.

Turning now to Wessex, Alfred became king there in 870 at the age of twenty- one. He rapidly gained experience in combat against the Danish army. One of these occasions is described in the Anglo-Saxon Chronicle under the year 877 (1):

"In this year the (Danish) army stole away to Wareham (in Dorset)... and after that the king (Alfred) made peace with the army, and they gave the king as hostages those who were most honourable in the army, and they swore oaths to him on the holy ring which they before would not do to any nation, that they would speedily depart from his kingdom."

It is seen that the Danes had a code of honour backed by a religious ritual. Later, Guthrum, the commander of the Danes drove Alfred back to the marshes of Somerset. After assembling an army, Alfred was able to make a successful attack at Edington in Wiltshire. By a treaty of 879, Guthrum agreed to be baptized, while Alfred recognised Danish rule in the Danelaw, that is, in the lands east of a line running roughly from London to Chester. Alfred built fortified towns in his territory and promoted cultural projects such as translation of books into the Anglo-Saxon language.

On his death in 899, Alfred was followed by his son Edward the Elder, a good military strategist. When Edward died in 924, his eldest son Athelstan came to the throne. He consolidated his position by military power, by new legislation and by making himself guardian of the Catholic Church. Athelstan took ill and died in 939 at the age of forty-four.

8.2 Mercia and the Growth of Chester

The Anglo-Saxon kingdom of Mercia stretched from Chester in a broad band through the East and West Midlands to London. When Penda, the last pagan king died in 655, Mercia was ruled for the next fifty years by his sons Peada, Wulfhere and Aethelred. The king 658 to 675 was Wulfhere, who brought priests from Lindisfarne. These included Chad, who established his bishop's seat at Lichfield in 669. According to tradition, Aethelred built the church of St John the Baptist at Chester in 689. After being rebuilt at various times, this church is still in use. Under Aethelbald, who ruled from 716, Mercia gained military strength. This strength reached a peak under Offa, who died at his chief residence at Tamworth in 796.

The boundary between Mercia and Northumbria became fixed at the River Mersey. Soon after the Scandinavians were expelled from Dublin in 902, a party of them under the leadership of Ingimund settled in Wirral. When they became unruly in 907, the fortifications of Chester had to be renewed. During the reigns of Edward and Athelstan, the town of Chester grew rapidly. Scandinavians who had settled outside the walls soon played a part in the rise of Chester as a commercial centre.

In 959, Edgar son of Edmund, at the age of sixteen, became king of the united kingdom of England. He delayed his coronation until 973. Soon afterwards, he called a number of sub-kings to Chester to swear allegiance. These included Kenneth, king of Scotland, Dufnal, king of Strathclyde and his son Malcolm, king of Cumbria, with Iago, king of Gwynedd and Macco (Magnus) son of Harald who was king of the Sudreys. As described by Simeon of Durham, these kings rowed Edgar in his ship from his palace to St John's Church and back again (2). Edgar was conscious of his position as high-king of all Britain and as protector of the Roman Church. Since 940, the Anglo-Saxon Church had collected tithe, and this arrangement was confirmed by Edgar's statute of 970.

Ecclesiastical developments in Chester are now followed. Wulfhere, king of Mercia had a daughter Werburgha. After a lifetime of superintending nunneries, she died in 690. Her remains were brought to Chester in 875 and housed in a chapel there. This chapel was granted land by King Edgar in 959 and was granted further endowments in 1057. At the time of the Domesday Book, Chester had churches of St John, St Werburgh, St Peter and St Mary.

Benedictine monks were installed at St Werburgh's in 1093. Within a few years, Chester possessed churches St Michael, St Martin, St Bridget, St Oswald and St Nicholas. The church of St Olaf, on record since 1110, shows that the Scandinavian inhabitants had not forgotten their origins. Through medieval times, the monastery of St Werburgh became wealthy and dominated the town of Chester, which, at that time, lay within the diocese of Lichfield. At the

Reformation, the abbey church at Chester became the cathedral of a new diocese.

8.3 The Dublin-York Axis

From their bases in Ireland, the Norsemen sailed unchallenged around the Irish Sea. Soon, York attracted the attention of the Dublin kings, who were descendants of Ivar the Boneless. From 910 onwards, Ragnald Ivarson was fighting in North Britain. In a battle at Corbridge in 918 he defeated the combined forces of Ealdred, the chieftain at Bamborough and of Constantine, king of Scotland. This campaign culminated in Ragnald's capture of York in 919. He died the following year.

Ragnald was succeeded by Sitric Ivarson, called Sitric Gale. In 926, Athelstan, who had just become king of England, called Sitric Gale to a meeting at Tamworth. Sitric promised to renounce his heathen religion and took Athelstan's sister Eadgyth as his wife. However, he died before a year had elapsed. His place was taken by his brother Godred Ivarson.

During the year 927, Athelstan expelled Godred from York. He then went to Dacre on the River Eamont near Penrith to receive pledges of peace from Ealdred lord of Bamborough, Constantine king of the Scots and Eugenius (Owain) lord of Cumbria. He extracted promises that they would not make any alliance with heathens. It appears that when the Norsemen captured York, the Britons of Strathclyde proceeded to occupy the former Northumbrian territory around the Solway, without meeting with opposition. So by the date of Athelstan's conference, the boundary of British territory extended as far south as Penrith (3).

Constantine did not adhere to his pledges, and in 934, Athelstan led his army northwards again. He stopped at the shrine of St Cuthbert at Chester-le-Street and also at Beverley where he left gifts. He then marched to Edinburgh to receive new oaths of allegiance. He had already appointed Wulfstan archbishop of York.
The most serious challenge to Athelstan's authority came very soon.

The rebel leader was Olaf Godredson who had succeeded his father Godred Ivarson as king of Dublin. He was supported by Constantine, king of the Scots. Groups from Cumbria and the Hebrides also arrived. This Norse confederation was met by Athelstan at the battle of Brunanburh in 937. There is not complete agreement about the exact location of this battlefield. It was a hard-fought battle with a large loss of life, but it left Athelstan in a clear position of superiority. When Athelstan died in 939, he was followed by his half-brother Edmund.

Olaf Godredson, after his defeat at Brunanburh, retired to Dublin, but when he heard of Athelstan's death, he went immediately to York. He then marched south with his army to Tamworth to confront the young King Edmund. Accompanying Olaf was Archbishop Wulfstan of York. Likewise, Edmund had in his camp Archbishop Odo of Canterbury. A treaty was arranged by which Olaf Godredson was confirmed king of York and also of the Danelaw, this being the area that included Lincoln, Nottingham, Derby, Stamford and Leicester. Also Olaf agreed to be baptized. Olaf celebrated his good fortune with an issue of coins from the mint at York displaying the Norse symbol of an eagle with outstreched wings. His triumph as senior king of the Dublin-York empire was short-lived, as he was killed in Scotland in 941.

He was replaced by Olaf Cuaran, son of Sitric Gale, then aged twenty-one. In 943, Olaf Cuaran agreed to be baptized at the court of King Edmund. However, Olaf failed to hold the trust of his supporters and was forced to withdraw. Ragnall (Reginald) was then selected by the Northumbrians as king at York. He was a brother of Olaf Godredson, formerly king in York. Although Ragnall complied with Edmund's request that he should be baptized, Edmund expelled him in 945 and personally took possession of York. When King Edmund died in 946 his place was taken by his brother Eadred.

King Eadred immediately came to receive the submission of the Northumbrians, whose spokesman was Archbishop Wulfstan. The Northumbrians very soon broke their promises by inviting Eric Bloodaxe to rule in York. Eric, son of Harald Fairhair, was a ruthless pagan who had been expelled as king of Norway. King Eadred was irritated to hear of Eric's arrival, and began ravaging the countryside around York. Threatened in this way, the Northumbrians were forced to expel Eric.

Olaf Cuaran had been waiting for this opportunity, and on his arrival in York, he was accepted as king there for a second time in 948. His stay did not last long as he was displaced in 952 by Eric Bloodaxe, who had returned after travelling abroad.

Although the English kings had tolerated these Norse rulers in York, King Eadred now acted decisively. Archbishop Wulfstan was removed and was replaced by Osketel. Eric Bloodaxe was assassinated at Stainmore in Cumbria in 954, and Oswulf, Earl of Bamborough was put in charge at York. As a kingdom, Northumbria ceased to exist.

The efforts of the English kings to pacify the Scandinavian chiefs by baptizing them may be summarized here. King Athelstan secured the baptism of Sitric Gale in 926 and of Olaf Godredson in 939. His sucessor King Edmund secured the baptism of Olaf Cuaran in 943, and of Ragnall Godredson a year or so later, while it is said that Eric Bloodaxe received baptism before his death in 954. To these people, baptism was a matter of expediency, and it had little effect on their personal behaviour.

8.4 Norse Immigration into Cumbria

Although Cumbria, as far north as Penrith, was nominally Northumbrian territory, no attempt was made to repel immigrants. Of the Scandinavians that were driven out of Dublin in 902, some went to the Isle of Man and quite a number went to Wirral, but only a few went further north. One of the early coastal settlements was at Aspatria in Cumbria.

A little later, hordes arrived on the coast of Cumbria from Dublin, the Isle of Man and the Hebrides, the numbers reaching a peak between 910 and 930. Although much of the fertile land was already occupied by Northumbrians, there was still plenty of land for immigrants. They settled along the western fringe of Cumbria, on land adjoining the River Kent and for some miles on either side of the River Derwent, also in the central Eden Valley, sheep-farming being a one of their principal activities.

One of the rare documents relating to settlement in north-west England shows that in 934, King Athelstan granted to the Bishop of York a piece of land in the Hundred of Amounderness. He had purchased this `from the pagans', as mentioned by Mills (4). This area, to the north of Preston, was settled by Norsemen who arrived under the leadership of Agmund. This document shows that they had arrived prior to the above date, and that they were not Christians at the time when they arrived. Further north, Norsemen settled at Heysham. There, they built their own chapel of St Patrick near to the existing Anglian church of St Peter, as mentioned by Collingwood (5).

8.5 Anglian Churches in Cumbria

Heversham is in Westmorland, on the Kent estuary. At this monastery there was a cross, nine feet high, with Anglian decoration, dated to around 800. An existing document describes how Tilred, abbot of Heversham, decided to leave at some date during King Edward's reign, which was 901 to 925. Apparently, he was alarmed by the arrival of Norse settlers on the coast (6). This monastery with its estates came to be surrounded by many villages bearing Norse names. Higham suggested that in such surroundings, paganism may have persisted for a while (7). No masonry of the existing church at Heversham is older than the twelfth century, and the dedication of the church to St Peter was not recorded until 1360.

Another Northumbrian monastery was situated at Dacre, four miles south-west of Penrith. It already existed in 728 when it was mentioned by Bede (7). Excavation has shown that the buildings of the monastery were of wood (8). A monument in the Anglian style called the `St Mark carving' dates from the ninth century. Norse influence is revealed in the `Adam and Eve' stone dated to the tenth century. These monuments show that control of the resources needed for commissioning sculptural work had passed to a Norse aristocracy. Parts of the Norman church date from the 12th century, but the dedication to St Andrew was not recorded until 1359. Possibly, the monastery at Dacre can be regarded as being analogous to that which existed at Maughold during the 8th century.

Typically, lands belonging to an Anglian monastery became the centre of an estate belonging to a Norse chieftain. As priests could not continue without income, churches would be abandoned. Up to a date around 930 it is expected that many of the immigrants were pagans or relapsed Christians. While these settlers did not destroy church buildings, they allowed them to fall down, but made use of the cemetery. In Cumbria, this phase was of short duration, perhaps less than thirty years. However, a fundamental change in church organisation occurred. Previously, the church was controlled by a monastic abbot but now the church came into the possession of the new landowner, who was responsible for appointing and supporting a priest. It is likely that church leaders in York encouraged missionary work among the colonists of Cumbria, as suggested by Higham (8).

One of the Norse settlements was on the peninsula west of Duddon Sands. The Scandinavian name, first recorded in 1065, was *Hougun*, but this was later changed to Millom, the present name. Adjacent to this village was *Chapel sucken*, a name signifying a district occupied by `sokemen', that is, by free-men retaining their Norse laws and customs. Within this district, the village of *Santacherche*, was noted in the Domesday Book of 1083. This village, now called Kirksanton, will be considered again a little later.

At a dozen churches in Cumberland and Westmorland, eighth-century Anglian crosses have been found. However, no documents become available until Norman times. This time interval is sometimes filled by Norse-Irish monuments that still remain on church sites. For example, at St Mary's Church, Gosforth, a wheel-headed cross fourteen feet high can be dated to around 1000. Gosforth is a village ten miles south-east of Whitehaven. At the same church, a portion of another cross has a panel illustrating the story of Thor's fishing expedition, taken from Norse mythology. This story is also illustrated on the Thor cross at Bride, Isle of Man, dated around 1030.

In recent years, efforts have been made to obtain more information about the period of Norse settlement through stylistic studies of stone monuments and through a study of place-names. By applying linguistic tests to place-names, it can be established that the early settlers in Cumbria used a fairly pure Scandinavian language. These settlements were secondary ones, in the sense that immigrants did not come directly from Norway but had already lived for some time at places around the Irish Sea. This is revealed by the occasional use of Irish loan-words. As Old Norse and Old English were languages of similar structure, transition to speaking English could proceed gradually. The Norse language was used in short runic inscriptions, but documents, when they appeared, were written in Anglo-Saxon.

Some parallels can be drawn between the settlement process in Cumbria and that in the Isle of Man, but there are also points of difference. In Cumbria, settlement occurred a century later than the land-taking in the Isle of Man. Existing churches were not destroyed, but some may have lain deserted for a while. Usually, small groups of settlers inserted themselves alongside the previous inhabitants, who were mostly Northumbrians. The newcomers in Cumbria had some respect for the Northumbrian culture that they found all around them. On the other hand, in the Isle of Man, the Norse colonists regarded the Celtic natives as inferior people whose culture was not worthy of their attention.

8.6 Churches of St Bridget

Bridget was widely known in England in the tenth century. So one can rarely be certain of the foundation date of a church dedicated to St Bridget, as written records come at a much later date. Five churches in Cumberland were dedicated to St Bridget. At Beckermet, six miles south of Whitehaven there is a church of St

John in the village and a further church of St Bridget half a mile away, as described by Collingwood (9). Possibly, St John's church belonged to an Anglian community. Norse settlers, when they arrived, may have built their own church of St Bridget. However, the name Beckermet is clearly Scandinavian, so this name must have replaced an earlier name of the village.

Tenth-century monuments have also been found at Bridekirk, two miles north of Cockermouth. The name was first recorded in 1210. This church has a twelfth-century font carrying an inscription in Norse runes, giving the name of Richard, the stone carver. Further churches of Bridget are found at Moresby and Kirkbride. At Kirkbride on the south bank of the Solway estuary, the present church is a restored 12th century building, the name being first recorded in 1163. As the three churches last mentioned have no monuments earlier than the tenth century, it is likely that at each place, the community was founded by Norse immigrants who adopted Bridget as their patron saint.

In the case of Brigham, the name is Anglian, meaning 'Bridge-town', and a piece of an Anglian cross has been found there. However, fragments of crosses in the Scandinavian style have also been found, dated to the 10th or early 11th century. We have two possibilities here. The Norse immigrants, on arrival, may have found an Anglian church of St Bridget, which is improbable. Alternatively, they attained a position of superiority and renamed the older Anglian church after St Bridget.

In the Wirral, immigrants arrived from Dublin in 902 or soon after. They built a church of St Bridget at their settlement at West Kirby. The date of this original church is not known, as the earliest masonry of the church is of Norman date. Twenty or more places called 'Kilbride' may be found scattered through Dumfriesshire, Galloway, Ayrshire and Lanarkshire. Possibly most of these names arise from a church dedication introduced by the Norsemen, as suggested by Graham and Collingwood (10).

Some elements of mythology concerning Bridget are found in the Isle of Man, such as the practice of leaving food out at nightfall in the hope that she would pay a visit. This mythology is the common property of all the Gaelic-speaking peoples from Ireland to the Hebrides. An example from Colonsay was given by Martin (11). This mythology appears to be associated with the pre-Christian Bride, daughter of Dagda and goddess of the hearthstone, some of whose attributes became transferred to the Christian Bridget. The persistence of such mythology in a particular district does not give any assurance that Bridget's name was attached to a church there in pre-Norse times.

8.7 The Norse in South-West Scotland

It is assumed that around 850, churches in the Isle of Man were rendered ineffective on account of their lands being appropriated by Norse colonists. Therefore, over the century 850 to 950, no interaction can be expected between churches in the Isle of Man, which did not exist, and the Anglian monasteries at Carlisle and Whithorn. Nevertheless, developments at these places will be briefly outlined.

A few Anglian monuments found in Carlisle tend to show that churches of some kind persisted there through most of the ninth century. In 875, Halfdan with his Danish army left York to ravage the kingdom of Strathclyde. At this time it is likely that the town of Carlisle with its Anglian monastery was plundered. It is likely that the town was again plundered in 915 by the army of Ragnald Iverson that arrived from Dublin. After this time, the town remained in a ruined state until it was revived by William Rufus in 1092.

According to the Royal Commission, the first Norse settlements in south-west Scotland can be dated to around 880 (12). However, substantial immigration of the Norse-Irish came later. By about 920, such numbers of these *Gall-Gaidhil* people had arrived that the country was given the name of `Galloway'. One of the places where a considerable number must have arrived was at Tinwald, four miles north-east of Dumfries. Here, as the name indicates, they established a Thing-mote. This can be identified as a gravel bank about ten feet high with a flat top. The parish church stands a hundred yards away. However, Radford suggested that Norse settlement did not quite extinguish the Anglian monastery at Hoddom (13).

At Whithorn, the succession of Anglian bishops came to an end around 830, possibly because conditions there became unsettled. Following the Norse occupation of York in 919, the territory of Galloway was taken into the kingdom of Strathclyde, until, in 1018, Strathclyde was absorbed into the kingdom of the Scots.

A recent discussion of post-Norse Whithorn has been given by Richard Oram (14). As he pointed out, place-name evidence suggests that Scandinavian settlement was chiefly confined to coastal districts of Galloway, such as the Machars peninsula and around the Dee estuary. The settlers came from the Western Isles of Scotland and also from Dublin, and intruded at a relatively late date into districts that were already occupied.

It seems that these settlers used the existing cemetery at Whithorn. Dr Radford has mentioned fragments of twenty headstones there of a type also found at other Scandinavian settlements, and dating from the later tenth century (15). Dr Radford believed that the monastery of some kind continued at Whithorn up to the time of Fergus, Lord of Galloway (13).

Some writers have suggested that the Norse element of the population in Galloway became dominant late in the tenth century. In support of this contention, it has been claimed that Galloway was one of the Scottish earldoms that belonged to Earl Thorfinn from 1034, which he held until his death in 1065. It appears that Magnus Barelegs, king of Norway had sufficient authority in Galloway to demand, in 1098, that timber should be shipped to the Isle of Man for building forts there.

King William of Scotland, at some time around 1175, granted four churches in Galloway to the abbey of Holyrood in Edinburgh. These churches were named as Kelton, Kirkcormack and Barnacrosh on the east of the River Dee, with Kirkandrews in the parish of Balmaghie. The point of interest here is that these churches previously belonged to Iona. These churches had very probably been founded in the Anglian period (15). Radford suggested that these churches must have been acquired by Iona during the period of Scandinavian supremacy in this region (16). However, it is most unlikely that ownership of these churches arose through any mission sent from Iona to the Scandinavian settlers in Galloway.

In 1125, Fergus, Lord of Galloway installed Gilla-Aldan as the first of a new series of bishops at Whithorn. Fergus, before he died in 1161, began building his cathedral church at Whithorn. Around this time, the Priory of Whithorn received a grant of land in the Isle of Man, restoring a relationship that had been in abeyance for three centuries.

8.8 Politics in the Isle of Man

During the time when the kings of Dublin were striving to keep a hold on York, that is, during the first half of the tenth century, it may be expected that the Isle of Man was under their control. Two of these kings were Sitric Gale, who died in 927 and Godred Ivarson who died in 934. At that time, the local ruler in the Isle of Man was MacRagnall. He was probably a son of Ragnall Ivarson, one-time king in York. MacRagnall was killed while fighting in Ireland in 941. After this, Olaf Cuaran may have been the overlord. At some point during this period, the people of Norse descent in the Isle of Man took steps towards accepting Christianity. David Wilson has written (17):

"In some fashion, the Viking community (in the Isle of Man) had taken to itself the faith of Christ. In what way they did this we cannot know. The circumstantial evidence of art-styles would certainly indicate that Christianity was introduced from the Christian Viking colonies of north-west Britain at some time after the Battle of Brunanburh in 937. We have no idea how this happened: there is no record of any priest until the end of the eleventh or the beginning of the twelfth century."

Evidence of art styles may only have the meaning that stone sculptors familiar with Anglian styles were ready to come when they were called. The north and west of Britain was at that time a cultural wilderness. The Anglian monastery at Carlisle was in ruins and quite likely, that at Whithorn was in a similar state. However, the date of the battle of Brunanburh may be a pivotal one, in that the Norse communities would then be under increasing pressure from England to make a positive declaration in favour of Christianity.

After King Eadred of England had expelled the Norsemen from York in 954, he considered that he had the right to make arrangements for the Sudreyan kingdom, which he granted to Magnus Olafson. He was a son of Olaf Godredson, one-time king of Dublin, and he continued in the Isle of Man until 962. At this time, King Edgar of England nominated or approved of Magnus Haraldson as king of the Sudreys. He was a son of Harald Sitricson, king of Limerick. Magnus Haraldson, or Macco remained in this position until 976. Over a period of more than twenty years, these two kings acknowledged the overlordship of the kings of England, who were Eadred, Edwig and Edgar. It will be remembered that Edgar called Macco to Chester to swear allegiance in 973.

The Isle of Man has a large number of cross-slabs carved in a distinctively Scandinavian style. It is widely accepted that they were first erected during the second quarter of the 10th century (18). They must have been erected in communal cemeteries after Christianity had become legally permitted. Very likely, a decision was taken by the king in the Isle of Man as a result of influence exerted on him from England, probably by King Athelstan, before he died in 939. Again, a similar influence would be exerted by King Eadred as part of his settlement of Northumbrian affairs in 954.

It seems that Irish people felt no strong urge to convert Norsemen to Christianity. Apparently, members of the Norse ruling class in the Isle of Man were persuaded to appoint priests. If Irishmen responded to this call, they did so as competent professionals who

99

happened to be available rather than as fervid missionaries. This point will be taken up again in the next chapter.

References for Chapter 8

(1) Benjamin Thorpe, *The Anglo-Saxon Chronicle*, Longmans Green, London, 1861, pp.63,64

(2) J.Stevenson *Simeon of Durham: A History of the Kings of England*, 1858, reprinted by Llanerch Publishers, Lampeter, 1987, p.93

(3) F.M.Stenton, *Anglo-Saxon England*, Clarendon Press, Oxford, 1971, p.332

(4) D.Mills, *The Place Names of Lancashire*, B.T.Batsford Ltd., London, 1976

(5) W.G.Collingwood, *Northumbrian Crosses of the Pre-Norman Age*, 1927, reprinted by Llanerch Publishers, Lampeter, 1989, p.15

(6) J.F.Curwen, *Heversham Church*, Trans.Cumb.& Westm.Arch.& Ant.Soc., Vol.25, 1925, p.28

(7) Leo Sherley-Price, *Bede: A History of the English Church and People*, Penguin Books, Harmondsworth, 1968, p.268

(8) Nick Higham. *The Northern Counties tp AD 1000*, Longman, London, 1986, pp.283-4, 331

(9) W.G.Collingwood, *The Lake Counties*, 1902, revised by William Rollason, J.M.Dent, London, 1988, p.67

(10) T.H.B.Graham and W.G.Collingwood, *Patron Saint of the Diocese of Carlisle*, Trans.Cumb.& Westm.Arch.& Ant.Soc., NS, Vol.XXV, 1925, p.1

(11) M.Martin, *A Description of the Western Isles of Scotland*, 1716, reprinted by James Thin, Mercat Press, Edinburgh, 1976, p.119

(12) Royal Commission on the Ancient and Historical Monuments of Scotland, *County of Dumfries*, HMSO, 1920, p.xx

(13) C.A.Ralegh Radford, *Hoddom*, Trans.Dumf.& Gall.Nat.Hist.& Ant.Soc., Ser.3, Vol.XXXI, 1954, p.174

(14) Richard D.Oram, `Scandinavian Settlement in South-West Scotland', in *Scandinavian Settlement in Northern Britain*, (editor: Barbara E.Crawford), Leicester Univ. Press, 1995, p.127

(15) Daphne Brooke, *The Northumbrian Settlement in Galloway and Carrick: An Historical Assessment*, Proc.Soc. Antiquaries of Scotland, Vol.121, 1991, p.295

(16) C.A.Ralegh Radford, *Excavations at Whithorn*, Trans.Dumfr.& Gall.Nat.Hist & Ant.Soc., Ser.3, Vol.XXVII, 1950, p.85

(17) D.M.Wilson, *The Vikings' Relationship with Christianity in Northern England*, Journ.British Archaeological Association, Ser.3, Vol.30, 1965, p.37

(18) A.M.Cubbon, `The Early Church in the Isle of Man', in *The Early Church in Western Britain and Ireland* (editor: Susan M.Pearce), British Archaeological Reports, British Series, No.102, 1982, p.257

Chapter 9

ST PATRICK'S CHURCH AND ROUND TOWER

Towards the middle of the tenth century, settlers of Norse extraction occupied a dominant social position in the Isle of Man. While they may have held diverse views about Christianity, they would tend to be influenced by the attitude of the reigning king. However, the position adopted by these kings has not been recorded, neither is their place of residence known with certainty, while the earliest churches may have been built of wood and have disappeared.

Some of the earliest masonry still surviving is to be found in buildings on Peel Island (St Patrick's Isle), notably St Patrick's Church with its Round Tower (Figure 4). Elsewhere in the British Isles, similar buildings were erected at about the same time, so some attention will be given to these analogous situations.

9.1 St.Patrick's Church

It is unknown whether a wooden church previously existed at the site of this church. Three phases of building in stone were distinguished by Robert Curphey (1). The first phase is represented by the foundations and portions of walls which now stand to a height of two feet along the western parts of the north and south sides. Internally, this part was 28 feet long and 18 feet wide. The building had *antae*, that is, the side walls projected beyond the outside of the gable.

This style was widely adopted when churches first came to be built of stone in Ireland during the tenth century. An example is the ruined cathedral at Clonmacnois, built in 908. The remains a similar church with antae can be found at Nendrum in Strangford Lough (2). It had internal measurements 26 by 16 feet and was built of rubble masonry with a door in the west gable. It was probably built before 974, when the monastery was burnt down.

So the stone church of St Patrick followed an Irish model, indicating a probable date of construction during the second half of the 10th century. This first stage of building may have occurred during the reign of Magnus Olafson (954 to 962) or Magnus Haraldson (962 to 976) or Godred Haraldson (976 to 989). Dr Ralegh Radford made an estimate of the date of construction based on both the historical record of these kings and on Irish parallels. His estimate was 960 to 985, that is, during the reign of the second or third of the above kings (3). This stone building lasted for over a century and was taken down around 1100, about the time when Magnus Barelegs erected fortifications on Peel Island.

In the next phase, the west gable was moved outwards by three feet and the foundation of the previous gable was taken up. The north and south walls were built with herring-bone courses, visible on both inside and outside of the walls. Decorative courses of this kind represent an English style of the early Norman period. Some slightly earlier examples of herringbone work occur in churches on the Welsh Border, discussed by J. and H. Taylor (4). It is reasonable to assign this phase of construction to the reign of Olaf Kleining, that is, from 1113 onwards.

Some centuries later, in a third phase of construction, the east gable was taken down and its foundation was removed. This gable was then rebuilt in grey slate to extend the church 18 feet to the east. The style of this work shows it to be of the 15th century. During this rebuilding, the door which had previously been in the west gable was moved to the north wall.

9.2 Later Connections with Dublin

Before the Round Tower at Peel can be considered, it will be necessary to gather a considerable amount of background information. The year 989 marks the time when Sigurd, Earl of Orkney was able to re-establish control over the Isle of Man, temporarily displacing the previous kings of the Dublin dynasty. Sigurd's deputy in the Sudreys was Earl Gilli, who was married to Sigurd's sister Nereide. Earl Gilli had his headquarters in the island of Colonsay. Following Sigurd's death at the battle of Clontarf in 1014, Earl Gilli continued to control the Sudreys until he died in 1025. During this period 989 to 1025, it appears that there was no resident king in the Isle of Man. So it is a little unlikely that any important buildings were erected there during this time.

Subsequently, Sitric Silkbeard, king of Dublin may have been the overlord in the Isle of Man. When he retired in 1036, control passed to Harald Godredson, otherwise Harald the Black of Islay. In 1040, Earl Thorfinn exerted his authority in the Isle of Man and put his nominee in charge. From 1050, his nominee was Sitric Reginaldson who was a nephew of Sitric Silkbeard and belonged to the dynasty of Dublin kings. Sitric Reginaldson continued as king of the Sudreys until he died around 1065. Meanwhile, his brother Eachmarcach Reginaldson was king in Dublin over the period 1046 to 1052. This illustrates the close political relationship between the Isle of Man and Dublin at this time.

Ties with Dublin are confirmed by coin hoards. From 997, the Dublin kings began to strike their own coins. Of the various coin hoards discovered in the Isle of Man, eleven contained Dublin coins, as described by Dolley and Graham-Campbell (6). From the dates when they were deposited, it can be deduced that the Isle of Man came within the sphere of influence of Dublin from 1025 to 1075, despite Thorfinn's intervention. It is likely that during this period, the Scandinavian communities in Dublin, the Isle of Man and the Hebrides kept in close contact with each other, not only through trade but also by intermarriage.

9.3 Round Towers in Ireland and Scotland

The Round Tower on Peel Island has often been compared with Irish towers, so a few words will be said about these. Over the period 900 to 1200, about 120 of these towers sprang up at monasteries in Ireland and about 80 still remain. Two categories can be distinguished, those that stand alone and those that form an integral part of a church. A tower of the first kind was often placed a little off the west gable of the principal church and off the axis of the church. The typical Irish tower tapered from ground level to a height of about 100 feet, the circumference at ground level varying from 40 to 60 feet. The wall thickness also tapered from bottom to top. The stone roof was conical.

Inside the tower, wooden floors were reached by means of ladders. The tower often had six storeys, each being lighted by a single window, but the top storey had four equally spaced windows. The door of the tower, which faced the west door of the church, was at some height above ground level, and was reached by a ladder, so that the tower could be used as a refuge. The jambs of the doorway sloped inwards and were covered by a single lintel stone. The date of erection of the tower can be estimated from the quality of the masonry. Earlier towers were built of flat stones, but later ones were built of ashlar, that is, squared blocks of stone. Round towers at the notable monastic sites of Clonmacnois and Glendalough are late examples belonging to the 12th century.

Two round towers in Scotland are now examined to see whether they have any features in common with the Irish towers. At the sites to be considered, the church has been rebuilt while the tower continued to stand, so the relationship of the tower to the original church is not now obvious.

At Brechin in Angus, an older Pictish church already existed when the Scots king Kenneth mac Malcolm selected this place for a new monastery. Around 977 he granted land and built a church dedicated to the Holy Trinity, and installed a college of Culdees. The tower has a height of 86 feet up to the base of the octagonal spire, which was built later. Externally, the tower is tapered, but the inside diameter is eight feet throughout, the wall thickness at ground level being three and a half feet. The tower is built of large blocks of sandstone, each dressed to the curvature of the wall, with thin mortared joints. The doorway is six feet above ground level. The door jambs are single stones with pelleted borders, inclined inwards. On each, a figure of a bishop carved at mid-height. The lintel carries a Crucifixion carving. The carvings are distinctly Irish in style.

Simpson bracketed the date of construction of this tower between 990 and 1012 (7). However, others have suggested a date as late as 1100. A recent review has been given by Cameron (8). Culdees continued at Brechin until after 1200.

Abernethy near Perth was an old Pictish centre. The tower there now stands to a height of 76 feet with an inside diameter of eight feet. The walls are three and a half feet thick at ground level, reducing to two and a half feet at the top, so that externally, the tower has a slight taper. The building blocks were all dressed to the curvature of the wall. The lower courses up to the doorway are of a reddish-grey stone, as described by Dr Simpson (7). The upper part of the tower, including the doorway and the belfry windows, is of yellow freestone. The doorway is two and a half feet above ground level. Each of the inclined door jambs consists of a single stone without decoration.

Dr Ralegh Radford estimated the date of the first phase of construction as 1050 or a little later (9). The upper part of the tower, including the belfry windows, represents a subsequent rebuilding. Resident Culdees were first mentioned at Abernethy in 1093, but were probably there much earlier (7). They remained there up to 1272.

At Egilsay in the Orkney Isles the ruined cathedral has a round tower dated about 1130, but this tower bears no architectural relationship to the Irish towers.

Some historical points are now mentioned. The policy of the Pictish kings was to adopt Roman practice in their churches. Resistance offered by Columban monks led King Nechtan to expel these monks from his kingdom in 717. Later, Constantine, who was king of the Picts 789 to 820, set up a church at Dunkeld in Strath Tay.

A turning point was reached when Kenneth MacAlpin of the Dalriadic Scots gained control of the combined kingdoms of the Scots and Picts in 843. Kenneth made Dunkeld his ecclesiastical centre and brought relics of St Columba from Iona. However, there

106

Fig. 1 Irish Sea region - AD 600.

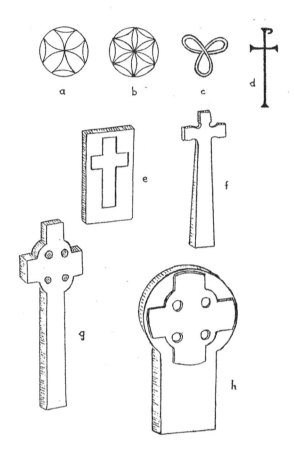

Fig. 2 Features of cross slabs.

(a) Maltese Cross enclosed in a circle, (b) Marigold figure of compass-drawn arcs, (c) Triqueta or knot, (d) Latin Cross with expanded terminals and Rho sign, (e) Incised double-line Cross, (f) Free-standing Cross with rounded armpits, (g) Celtic or Irish Cross with ring head, (h) Wheel-head Cross with Celtic Cross ornamentation.

Fig. 3 Regions of Norse Penetration.

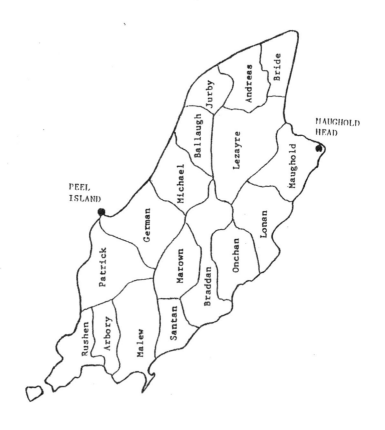

Fig. 4 Isle of Man - Parishes.

Fig. 5 Tracing of the Thorwald Cross from Andreas.

This tenth-century carving illustrates the conversion of the Norsemen and shows a priest carrying a book and a staff.

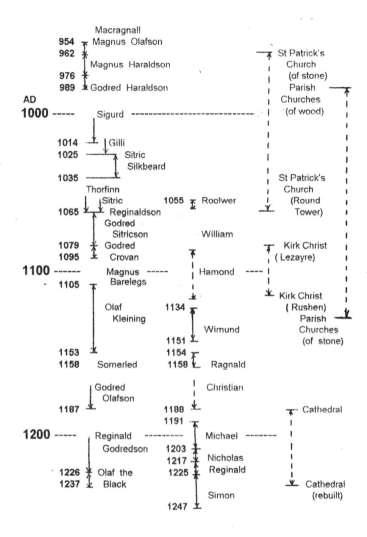

Fig. 6 Time-Scale for Kings, Bishops and Buildings.

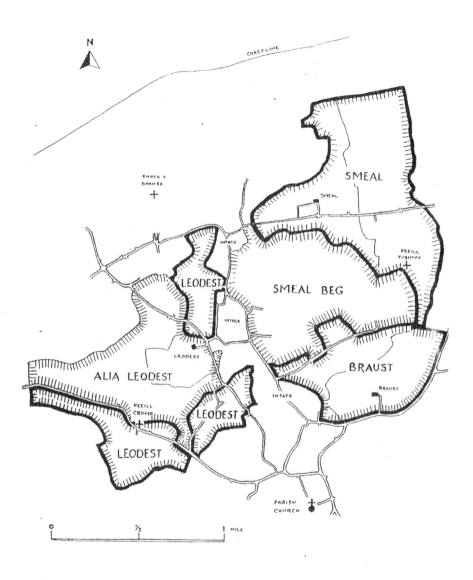

Fig. 7 Five Treens in the Parish of Andreas.

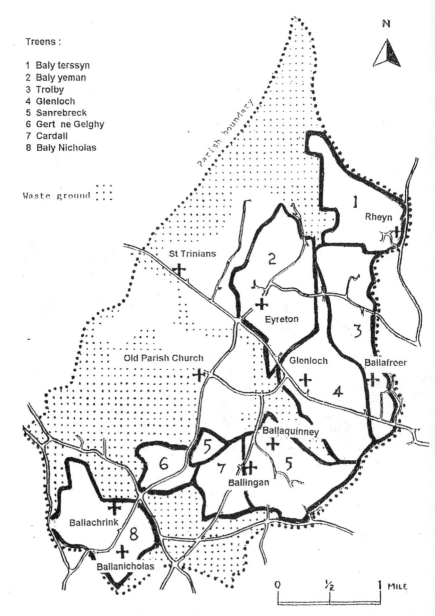

Treens:

1. Baly terssyn
2. Baly yeman
3. Trolby
4. Glenloch
5. Sanrebreck
6. Gert ne Gelghy
7. Cardall
8. Baly Nicholas

Waste ground

N

Rheyn

St Trinians

Eyreton

Glenloch

Ballafreer

Old Parish Church

Ballaquinney

Ballingan

Ballachrink

Ballanicholas

0   ½   1 MILE

Fig. 8 Treen boundaries and Keeill sites in the Parish of Marown.

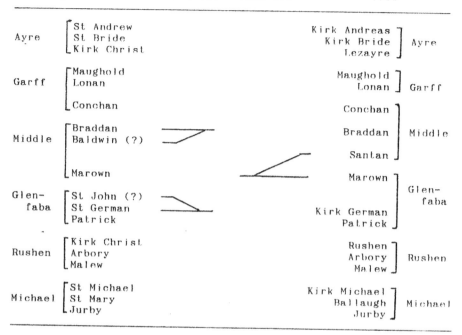

Sheading	Parish	1079 (?)	1266 (?)	1796	
Ayre	St Andrew St Bride Kirk Christ			Kirk Andreas Kirk Bride Lezayre	Ayre
Garff	Maughold Lonan Conchan			Maughold Lonan Conchan	Garff
Middle	Braddan Baldwin (?) Marown			Braddan Santan Marown	Middle
Glen- faba	St John (?) St German Patrick			Kirk German Patrick	Glen- faba
Rushen	Kirk Christ Arbory Malew			Rushen Arbory Malew	Rushen
Michael	St Michael St Mary Jurby			Kirk Michael Ballaugh Jurby	Michael

Fig. 9 Sheadings and Parishes.

This shows the conjectured subdivision of the original sheadings
into parish districts, the names of which are not known.
Subsequently, parishes were combined,
and in 1796, the sheadings were rearranged.

is no indication that Columban monks were brought. It is known that later, the church at Dunkeld was served by Culdees, and they remained until 1127 when a move was made to displace them.

Malcolm Canmore ruled in Scotland 1057 to 1093. During the time of Malcolm's sons, particularly of David who ruled 1124 to 1153, new dioceses were set up under the direction of bishops of the Roman Church. When these bishops arrived, they found that churches in Scotland were being served by Culdee priests. Buildings previously erected over the century 1000 to 1100 at Brechin, Abernethy and other places had been the work of these Culdee priests. Irish features of the churches of this time are sufficiently accounted for by the presence of these Culdees and need not have been inspired by any political ideology. It is now necessary to inquire where these Culdees came from.

9.4 Culdees

The Irish name *Céle Dé*, 'servant of God' was adopted by the monks at Tallaght on the south side of Dublin when their monastery was founded by Maelruain in 769. This sect set themselves a high standard of conduct and literacy, perhaps as a reaction to the laxity prevailing elsewhere. The monastery at Tallaght continued through the time of the Norse occupation of Dublin. All the Culdees did not necessarily come from Tallaght, but they formed a confederation or independent order of monks who followed the rule of their founder.

A few words may be said about the reasons why the Culdees came into prominence. In Celtic lands, monastic property was vested in the founder and was inherited by members of his family. The hereditary abbot collected the revenues, but he was sometimes a layman who paid out only as much as he wished for the support of the monks. Under these circumstances, Culdee monks were prepared to join an established monastery and to undertake duties there, sometimes acting as choristers or repairers of buildings.

Some Culdees may have been hermits but most lived in a community which typically consisted of a prior and twelve monks.

107

For example, it is recorded in the Annals of Ulster that Culdees were working at Armagh when the monastery was raided in 921 by Godred Ivarson. It has also been recorded that Culdees were present at Iona at the late date of 1164, but may have been there much earlier. However, writers of repute emphasize that the Culdees had no essential connection with the Columban Church (10). Initially, they adhered to the strict rule of their founder, and candidates were received into the order after a novitiate of seven years. When Culdees joined an existing monastery, they kept themselves apart and conducted their own mass.

Although the Culdees had no bishops, their religious observances were not significantly different from those of the Roman Church. A litany used by the Culdee community at Dunkeld has been reproduced by Forbes, but it is of uncertain date (11). This litany, after listing the biblical saints and the leading Irish saints, included Scottish saints such as Ninian, Kentigern, Blane and Adamnan and also the martyr Constantine Rex, who was presumably the missionary who was murdered in Kintyre. The Culdees held St Patrick in high esteem, but did not acknowledge the jurisdiction of the Pope, except when it was expedient for them to do so.

Activities of the Culdees in Scotland are now outlined. A community may have lived on St Serf's Island in Loch Leven from the 9th century, and a document of 955 confirms that the *Keledei* were living there. Subsequently, the monks of Loch Leven were generously treated by the kings of Scotland until they were ordered by King David in 1150 to become regular canons under the supervision of the bishop of St Andrews (12). During this long period, groups of Culdees came to occupy dominant positions in the principal churches of Scotland. During the 12th century, Culdees relaxed the strictness of their conduct and many of them took wives and acquired property (10).

At this point, it may be asked whether there is any evidence for the presence of Culdees in the Isle of Man. The collection of monuments at Kirk Andreas Church includes the tenth-century Thorwald's Cross (No.128). One side shows a scene from Norse mythology while the other side shows the arrival of a Christian missionary. Mr Cubbon and others believe that this scene represents the conversion of the Norsemen (13). The missionary is shown as a bare-headed figure carrying a book in one hand and a staff in the other (Figure 5). The top of the staff is of cruciform shape. If the sculptor had wished to portray a bishop, he would have given him appropriate insignia, including a crozier. It is suggested that this figure represents not a bishop but a Culdee prior. The implication is that Culdees had been brought by a Norse king to supervise the new temple-replacement churches.

9.5 The Round Tower at Peel

This tower is cylindrical, not tapered, and has a uniform wall thickness. It has an outside circumference of 45 feet and an inside diameter of 6 feet. The presence of four windows at a height of 35 feet, just below the parapet, reveals the original height of the uppermost storey. The overhanging parapet, which now brings the overall height to 50 feet, was added at the time when battlements were added to the cathedral towers in 1392. Daniel King's drawing of 1644 showed a conical roof, probably of wood, which has now disappeared. It is not known whether the tower originally had a conical stone roof.

The tower is built of rubble consisting of local red sandstone with a few pieces of limestone. Although a hard mortar was used, the quality of the masonry is poor and will not bear comparison with the ashlar masonry of the Scottish towers. There is not much about this tower that relates to the Irish towers except the doorway. This faces the west gable of the church and is seven feet above ground level. The jambs of the doorway slope inwards and are built of squared blocks. The doorway has a rounded top consisting of two blocks with a central joint.

This round tower has nothing to do with a Celtic monastery. It stands on the centre-line of St Patrick's Church at a distance of 40 feet from the west gable. This indicates that the tower was built as an ornamental addition to the original stone church. The time of construction of St Patrick's Church and the Round Tower is often

109

bracketed between 950 and 1050, and indeed, this is quite likely, but these buildings were not necessarily erected at the same time.

Building the tower would require resources that were available only to the kings of the Sudreys. It is noted that during the period 1050 to 1075, the Sudreys were ruled by Sitric Reginaldson and his son Godred. Sitric minted his own coins in the Isle of Man, as remarked by Young (5). It seems possible that the Round Tower was built as a further statement of his independence. Sitric lived in the Isle of Man, and if the tower was built during his reign, there is a presumption that he lived at Peel, even though Mr Young thought that his residence may have been near Ramsey (5).

It has already been mentioned that there was a political relationship between the Isle of Man and Dublin during the reign of Sitric Reginaldson. However, Irish features of the Round Tower at Peel need not have any ideological significance. It is suggested that St Patrick's Church had been administered since its inception by a community of Culdees. When these priests were asked, around 1050, to build the Round Tower, they would be likely to incorporate Irish features. This would be in keeping with the response of the Culdees in Scotland who set about building church towers at a similar time.

9.6 St Patrick's Isle

In the Annals of Ulster, an entry relating to the year 798 gave (14):

"Burning of Inis Patraicc by the gentiles; and they took away tribute from the provinces and Dochonna's shrine was broken by them, and other great incursions were made by them, both in Ireland and in Scotland."

For a long time this was taken to refer to Peel Island. However, it is now recognised by Megaw and others that the island mentioned in this passage was St Patrick's Island off Skerries in County Dublin (15). Dochonna was a saint otherwise known as Mochonna or Conna Cuairne.

A story from the Icelandic Sagas can now be considered, concerning the family of Ketil Flatnose. Mr Young estimated that Ketil was born around 815 (5). By 850 he had attained a position of leadership in the Western Isles of Scotland. Ketil's nephew Orlyg was educated by a certain Patrick, bishop of the Hebrides. When Orlyg wished to emigrate to Iceland, the bishop supplied various items, including consecrated earth to be put under the church that was to be built and dedicated to St Columba. The *Landnamabok*, from which this information comes, was written in the early 12th century, after the information had been transmitted orally for a couple of centuries.

Mr Young considered that prior to his departure, Orlyg may have lived in the Isle of Man and that Bishop Patrick may have lived on St Patrick's Isle (5). Dr Ralegh Radford considered that Bishop Patrick was probably the refounder of the Chistian community on St Patrick's Isle (3). These deductions do not appear to be justified by the information available. There seems to be no good reason for thinking that this Bishop Patrick had any connection with the Isle of Man, and other writers who have discussed this incident have not mentioned the Isle of Man. It seems fairly safe to assume that St Patrick's Isle took its name from the church of St Patrick that stands there, a proposition supported by Megaw (16).

References for Chapter 9

(1) R.A.Curphey, `Peel Castle', from *Ancient Centres of Government of the Isle of Man*, Manx National Heritage, Douglas
(2) *An Archaeological Survey of County Down*, HMSO, Belfast, 1966, pp.128-9, 292-6
(3) C.A.Ralegh Radford, `St Magnus Cathedral, Kirkwall and the Development of the Cathedral in Northwestern Europe', in *St Magnus Cathedral and Orkney's Twelfth Century Renaissance*, (editor: Barbara E.Crawford), Aberdeen Univ.Press, 1988, pp.14-16
(4) Joan and Harold Taylor, `Pre-Norman Churches of the Border', in *Celt and Saxon: Studies in the Early British Border*, (authors: K.Jackson *et al*), Cambridge Univ.Press, 1963, p.210

(5) G.V.C.Young, *The History of the Isle of Man under the Norse*, Mansk Svenska Publishing, Peel, 1981, pp.196, 52, 59, 13, 21

(6) J.Graham-Campbell, 'The Viking-Age Silver Hoards of the Isle of Man', in *The Viking Age in the Isle of Man*, (editors: C.Fell *et al*), Viking Society for Northern Research, Univ. College, London, 1983, p.53 (see pp.61-2)

(7) W.D.Simpson, *The Ancient Stones of Scotland*, Robt. Hale, London, 1965, p.115

(8) Neil Cameron, *St Rule's Church, St Andrews and Early Stone-built Churches in Scotland*, Proc.Soc.Antiquaries of Scotland, Vol.124, 1994, p.367

(9) C.A.Ralegh Radford, *The Early Christian Monuments of Scotland*, Antiquity, Vol.XVI, 1942.

(10) William Reeves, *The Culdees of the British Isles*, 1864, reprinted by Llanerch Publications, 1994, pp.31, 59

(11) A.P.Forbes, *Kalendars of Scottish Saints*, Edmonston & Douglas, Edinburgh, 1872, p.lvi

(12) A.C.Lawrie, *Early Scottish Charters*, James MacLehose, Glasgow, 1905, p.187

(13) A.M.Cubbon, *The Art of the Manx Crosses*, Manx Museum, 1977, p.32

(14) A.O.Anderson, *Early Sources of Scottish History*, Vol.1, Oliver & Boyde, Edinburgh, 1922, p.256

(15) Basil and Eleanor Megaw, 'The Norse Heritage in the Isle of Man', in *The Early Cultures of North-West Europe*, (editors: C.Fox & B.Dickins), Cambridge Univ.Press, 1950, p.143

(16) Basil Megaw, 'Norseman and Native in the Kingdom of the Isles', in *Man and the Environmenmt in the Isle of Man*, (editor: Peter Davey), British Archaeological Reports, British Series No.54(i), 1978, p.265 (see p.268)

The name `Maughold' appears to be a name of two parts. In the Germanic languages such as English and Norse, the adjectival part comes first and carries emphasis. An example is `Castletown'. In Gaelic, the adjectival or descriptive part still carries emphasis but comes after the substantive part, for example, `Ballachastal'. The name `Maughold' has stress on the first syllable, so it is suspected as being a Germanic word rather than a Gaelic *magh-* formation. The name in its earliest written form had already been latinized to *Maghaldus*. It is unlikely that the final `d' arose through latinizing. For example, the Irish name Mac Caille latinized to Machalus without an intrusive `d'. Terminations in *-ld, -lm* and *-ln* are common in Norse words but rare in Gaelic words. So it is not surprising that the final `d' was dropped in the Manx form *Maghal*, which is still followed in local speech. It seems that the written form preserved a significant final `d', which again points to a non-Gaelic origin.

By 795, the Vikings had started robbing exposed places on the coast and it is unlikely that they omitted to rob the monastery at Maughold. Soon afterwards, possibly around 830, colonists arrived in the neighbourhood, and took possession of all the arable land. Deprived of resources, the monastery could not continue. The sequence of monuments in the churchyard appears to break off at this time. Buildings may have been of timber, as in contemporary Northumbrian monasteries. Over the next century the Norsemen made use of the cemetery, as shown by graves containing weapons. Dr Shetelig dated one of the swords to the year 900.

10.1 Mythical Saints and St Maughold's Well

On a number of occasions, it has been assumed that the name possessed by a church is that of a saint, when in truth, it was a name associated with the locality before the church was built. An example occurs at St Bees in Cumbria. A bracelet (Old Norse: *baugr*) was kept there and was used by Norse settlers as a sacred object on which oaths were sworn. When a church was built, the bracelet remained there, and gave the church the name of `Bega-church' (1). A story was then devised to account for the name. One version claimed that the church was founded by Begu, a nun from Hackness in North Yorkshire, while another version gave details of how Bega, an Irish princess, founded a nunnery there.

Again, St Alkelda is patroness of the Yorkshire churches at Giggleswick near Settle and at Middleham in Wensleydale. At each of these places a bubbling spring is found, to which the Scandinavians gave the name *ölkelda*, that is, `ale-well' (1). Eventually, the story was told that the well was named after Saint Alkelda, and it was explained that she was an Anglo-Saxon princess who had been murdered by the Danes.

Place-names embodying the word *kelda* are quite numerous over areas of Norse settlement in the north of England, but in the spelling now used, this syllable is often found to have become distorted on account of its meaning becoming forgotten. An example is a spring near Greystoke Castle, west of Penrith which was named Mary Keld, that is, St Mary's Well, but by 1705 it was called Marigold Spring (2). A number of examples of the name `Halikeld' can be found, meaning Holy Well. As Norsemen used the church-yard at Maughold, they would have been familiar with Branhui's well. It is suggested that they gave this place a *kelda* name.

The significance of the first syllable of `Maughold' is not obvious, but one suggestion is that it represents the Old Norse *makt*, meaning `power'. This epithet may have been inspired by the physical vigour of the spring, which was given the name *Makt-kelda*. It is not possible to retrieve this form of the name, as by the time that the first written records appeared in the twelfth century, the name of the spring had already been turned into the saint's name of `Maghaldus'. This became de-latinized to `Maghald', losing the last syllable of the original name.

The earliest record of this name appears to be in Jocelin's `Life of St Patrick', written around 1186. A passage is reproduced here from the translation by Swift (3):

'And in the Caemetery of its church is a Sarcophagus of hollowed stone, whereout a spring continually exsudeth, nay, sufficiently floweth forth, the which is sweet to the draught, wholesome to the taste and healeth divers infirmities... And in that stone are the bones of Saint Machaldus said to rest, yet therein is nothing found save only clear water. And though many have often times endeavoured to remove the stone, and especially the King of the Norici, who subdued the island... yet have they all failed in their attempt ...'

From this passage it may be noted that spring was a vigorous one, for which the Old Norse term *kelda* is appropriate. It appears that the well had been consecrated in the name of St Maughold. The king who attempted to dig up the stone reservoir was Magnus Barelegs, who came in 1098. He had an interest in antiquities. Before leaving Norway he had opened the tomb of St Olaf, and on his journey to the Isle of Man he entered the chapel where the shrine of St Columba was kept at Iona.

Mr Gill agreed that this was the original St Maughold's Well (4). At a later date, possibly at the Reformation, the spring or water conduit became stopped up, as there is no sign of it at present. Attention was diverted to a rock basin on the cliff top at Maughold Head, which then acquired the name of St Maughold's Well. A new resting place then had to be found for St Maughold's bones. The story given in the 16th century `Traditionary Ballad' is (5): "Maughold died and he lies also in his own church too at the Head".

It will be recalled that according to Muirchu's "Life", St Patrick sent Mac Cuill to the Isle of Man. When Jocelin wrote his `Life of St Patrick' he used this story, and took St Maughold to be the same man as Mc Cuill. His actual words were (4): "And in Ulydia was Magiul, a Heathen, who was also called Machaldus". Jocelin's background will be considered later. For the moment, it is noted that none of the Irish annalists equated Mac Cuill with St Maughold, and there is no good reason for doing so, as the resemblance between the names is only superficial.

Mac Caille was the bishop who placed a veil on the head of St Bridget at his church at Croghan, Co. Roscommon, and the ancient martyrologies gave his festival day as April 25. An entry in the Annals of Ulster recorded his death in 489. Hennessy pointed out that in two copies of the Annals, this entry had the added word "Mannensis" (6). He called this "an idle gloss", but did not indicate its date.

However, Scottish historians, searching for bishops of 'The Isles', made a determined attempt to identify Mac Caille or Machalus with St Maughold. Hector Boece, in his *Scotorum Historiae* of 1575 claimed that Bridget was confirmed by the bishop of the Isles in the Isle of Man, as quoted by Forbes (7). In Keith's 'Calendar of the Scottish Bishops' of 1755 it was claimed that Machalus, 'also called Mauchold', was bishop of Sodor, again quoted by Forbes (7). The real Mac Caille did not leave Ireland, and Machalus, his partner in the Isle of Man is fictitious.

A further saint was Machan or Machanus, who was commemorated on Sept.28, particularly in the region of Glasgow, but he had no connection with either Machalus or Maughold. Kneen mentioned a saint celebrated on Aug.9 at Fortingall and Logierait in the district of Atholl (8). He was Machead, Mochoat or Macoit, but likewise, he would not seem to be relevant.

10.2 The Miracle of St.Maughold.

A new church was eventually built at Maughold, as shown by cross slabs carved in a distinctively Norse style. Cubbon has dated the Boar Fragment (No.133) to the late tenth century (9). In passing, the interment of Bishop Roolwer at Maughold around 1060 is noted.

A story relating to Maughold Church has come to be called 'The Miracle of St Maughold'. It was written down in the *Chronicon Manniae* around 1250, but relates to an earlier historical incident. In 1158, Somerled of Argyll landed at Ramsey with the intention of

116

taking control of the Isle of Man. Extracts from Young's translation are given here (10):

'One of the principal chiefs called Gilcolum maintained that it would be no violation of the asylum of St Maughold to drive off, for the supply of the army, the cattle that were grazing outside the precincts of the cemetery. A rumour in the meantime reached the church... The weaker sex, with dishevelled hair and mournful accents wandered around the walls of the church, loudly crying "Where art thou now, oh Maughold ? Where are thy miracles which till now thou hast worked in this place ?". Moved, as we believe, by these and similar supplications... St Maughold delivered them from imminent danger.

For when the aforesaid Gilcolum had fallen asleep in his tent, St Maughold appeared to him clothed in a white garment and carrying his pastoral staff... he raised on high the staff that was in his hand and drove the point through Gilcolum's heart. His sons and followers... hastened to him, inquiring what had happened... he answered... "Go quickly to the church and bring the staff with the priests and clerks that they may intercede for me with St Maughold"... Thus he did expire in great torture '.

In this account, no monastery is mentioned. The church was a collegiate church staffed by priests, some of them being married. Emphasis was placed on the power of the saint's crozier. A similar story can be found in the `Annals of Clonmacnois' under the years 843 and 844 (11):

'All the Termynlands belonging to St Queran were preyed and spoyled by Felym mcCriowhainn without respect of place, saint or shrine... As king felym (soone after his return into Mounster) was takeing his rest in his bed, St Queran appeared to him with his habit and bachall, or pastoral stafe, & there gave him a push of his Bachall in his belly whereof he tooke his disease and occation of Death...'

Feidlimid mac Crimthainn was the king at Cashel and the saint was Ciaran of Clonmacnois, who had been dead for three centuries. The

117

monks were giving warning that if anyone violated their precincts, their saint had the power to arrange a divine retribution.

It can be taken that the details of the Miracle of St Maughold were devised by the priests at Maughold shortly after Gilcolm's raid. In Scotland at this time, churches depended to a large extent on the services of Culdee priests. So it would not be unreasonable to assume that Culdees continued to serve churches in the Isle of Man until late in the twelfth century, under the supervision of the regularly appointed bishops. If they were present at Maughold, this would account for Irish details of the Miracle. However, they were serving in a Norse church that had already stood on this site for two centuries.

Veneration of shrines containing relics of saints goes back to early times. The Second Nicene Council of 787 decreed that no church should be consecrated without relics. These gave a church an indentity and a degree of prestige and also a source of income. The practice of keeping shrines in churches gained strength through Norman times until it was suppressed at the Reformation. The Miracle of St Maughold was filled out with details designed to promote St Maughold as a founder-saint and miracle-worker. As his bones were not available, his relic took the form of a staff.

10.3 Saint Malachy

At this point, the church at Maughold was about to be affected by developments at places farther afield, to which attention must now be given. In the eleventh century, the Irish monastic churches were in an unsatisfactory state as their endowments were held by hereditary abbots. An early leader of the reform movement was Gilbert, appointed in 1107 as the first bishop of the Norse settlement at Limerick. He was supported by Cellagh, who had been the lay abbot of Armagh but took orders as a bishop in 1105. Gilbert, as papal legate, took the chair at the synod that was held in the year 1111 at Rathbreasail near Limerick. This synod divided Ireland into dioceses.

The next outstanding figure to emerge in the reform movement was Malachy O'Morgair. He was born in 1095, son of the chief professor at Armagh. At the age of twenty-five he was appointed chief assistant to the abbot of Armagh. A period of study under Bishop Malchus in Waterford gave him an appreciation of church organisation in England. His appointment as bishop of Connor (Antrim) in 1125 allowed him to put his ideas into practice.

Looking back to Viking times, Comgall's ancient monastery at Bangor on Belfast Lough was repeatedly raided and by 930 it was in ruins. In the intervening two centuries the lands of the monastery had remained in the possession of Comgall's relatives. According to James Kenney, Malachy's mother happened to be related to the Coarb of Bangor (12). When this man died, Malachy took the opportunity to procure the site of the ruined church. On this site Malachy built a wooden church in 1124 and installed Augustinian canons. After Malachy had waited for some years, he was invited, in 1134 to accept the position of abbot of Armagh, thus terminating the hereditary succession at that place.

In 1140, Malachy built a new stone oratory at Bangor and a new church on the ruins of Patrick's ancient church at Sabhal. There had been about two hundred monasteries in Ireland, but Malachy succeeded in replacing many of these by over forty reformed houses under the control of regular bishops. With his support, the first Cistercian monastery was set up in 1142 at Mellifont near Drogheda. While on a visit to Rome, Malachy died in 1148 at St Bernard's monastery at Clairvaux in France. His hopes were fulfilled in 1152 when the Synod of Kells set up provinces for four archbishops at Armagh, Tuam, Cashel and Dublin. Malachy was canonised as St Malachias by Pope Clement in 1190. After this sketch of affairs in Ireland, further attention can now be given to the church at Maughold.

10.4 The Church of Juan the Priest

Jocelin said, when he wrote about St Maughold in 1186: "And in that island was a city after him named of no small extent, the

119

remains of whose walls may yet be seen". The present boundary wall encloses a plot of five acres. Jocelin did not mention the Romanesque church which had already been built, nor the keeills in the churchyard. These may have been chapels of Norse land-owners. The North Keeill is known to have been built on top of slab-lined graves, confirming that was built at a relatively late date. A runic cross, the Hedin Cross, found just outside this chapel may indicate that a burial plot was reserved for the chapel, as suggested by Kermode (13). The claim has been made that one of the four keeills was named after St Michael. This is now thought to be a mistake, as such references properly relate to the parish church at Kirk Michael (14).

Keeill Woirrey is situated quarter of a mile west of the farmhouse of Upper Cornaa in the parish of Maughold. This keeill was quite an important one, as Cornaa Fair was held there. At this place, a slab has been found (Manx Museum No.144) having a runic inscription in the Norse language, which has been transcribed by Page (15). This may be translated: "Christ, Malachy and Patrick, Adamnan: but of all the sheep is Juan priest in *Kurnadal*". A further stone (No.145) has been found at Maughold Church, inscribed in runes with additional ogham characters, which reads: "Juan the Priest cut these runes". From the canonized saints cited, it can be deduced that Juan was a regular priest of the Roman Church who officiated at both the parish church and the chapel at Cornaa-dale, and the date can be set at around 1200.

The church at Maughold may have belonged to local landowners in earlier times, but after Godred Crovan's time, it probably belonged to the king. According to Mr Young, King Godred Olafson granted lands adjacent to the church to the Priory of St Bees in 1175, but apparently he retained the church itself (6). So it seems that when Juan the Priest was there, around 1200, his church belonged to King Reginald Godredson and formed part of the diocese of the Sudreys.

Juan's notice erected at Cornaa conveyed that he was acting by the authority of the saints he cited. Why Malachy was included is an interesting question. Maybe it is relevant to note that Bishop

120

Christian of the Sudreys who died around 1190 and Bishop Nicholas who died in 1217 were both buried at Bangor Abbey. Possibly, Juan the Priest had been trained at Bangor Abbey, which had received a grant of land in the Isle of Man, the probable date of the grant being around 1180.

10.5 Staff Lands

In Maughold, certain pieces of land in the vicinity of the parish church have been called Staff Lands. The origin of this and similar terms will now be investigated. Mr A.W.Moore maintained that holders of these lands had certain obligations (15):

"Probably formerly subject to the customary service of caring for the pastoral staff of the Saint Maughold to whom the parish church was dedicated and of producing it for processions when required."
koko
First, attention can be given to the Manx name `Ballaterson'. Mr Kneen explained that this name is derived from the Gaelic *trosdan*, a crozier or staff. He cited the parish of Ballytrustan near Portaferry, County Down, which belonged to the Knight Hospitallers (8). So the name Ballaterson can be taken to mean a farm belonging to a staff.

The concept of property belonging to a relic was quite foreign to the Celtic Church and did not come from Ireland, but from medieval England. As an example, the successors of the abbots of Lindisfarne acquired large grants of land which were said to belong to St Cuthbert. The person who collected the income from this property was the bishop of Durham, who kept Cuthbert's bones securely in his cathedral (16). Thus, property was vested in the relic and possession of the relic conferred rights to the property, before the days when written deeds were much used. Through the twelfth century, which is the setting of the Miracle of St Maughold, it would be accepted that the glebe lands of Maughold Church were the property of the sacred relic, which was the Staff of St Maughold.

121

As pointed out by Mr Kneen, there were treens called Ballaterson in each of the parishes of Maughold, Ballaugh, Marown and German, and in each place, this treen was adjacent to ecclesiastical lands. The Bull of Pope Gregory of 1231 listed lands in each of the above parishes which were named as lands of *St Maughaldus*, of *St Mary of Ballalaughe*, of *Kirkemarona* and lands of the *Staff of St Patricius*. While this document was probably written at a date later than the date attached to it, the writer apparently wished to claim that the lands listed had been properly surrendered to the bishop. It might be supposed that at an earlier date, these lands had belonged to particular churches.

We may now turn to the Manorial Roll of 1515, which clearly lists the four estates called `Ballaterson' as treens, that is, as lands subject to Lord's Rent. A possible interpretation of this situation is that the estates called Ballaterson were once ecclesiastical lands, at which time they gained their name. They were later taken back into the possession of the Lord of Man to form newly created treens, which retained their older name.

In Maughold, the name of Staff Lands continued to be applied to scattered plots totalling about a hundred acres. At some time in the remote past, this land probably belonged to Maughold Church, but was eventually taken from this church and granted to the Barony of St Bees. When the monasteries were disbanded, most of their property in the Isle of Man was taken by the English government but the Barony of St Bees was acquired by private owners (15). At this stage, tenants may have continued to claim preferential conditions of tenure, putting forward fanciful arguments about their rights as guardians of the Staff of St Maughold. As late as the time of Woods' Atlas of 1867, the Staff Lands were still listed as being part of the Barony of St Bees, even though this Barony no longer existed.

Mystery surrounds what happened to actual staff of St Maughold, which may have been one of the "Three Relics of Man", but it was probably destroyed at the Reformation.

References for Chapter 10

(1) T.H.B.Graham and W.G.Collingwood, *Patron Saints of the Diocese of Carlisle*, Trans.Cumb.& Westm.Ant.& Arch.Soc., Vol.XXV, 1925, p.1 (see p.15).

(2) A.M.Armstrong, A.Mawer, F.M.Stenton and Bruce Dickins, *The Place-names of Cumberland*, Part I, Cambridge Univ. Press, 1950, p.197

(3) Edmund L.Swift, *Jocelin's "Life of Patrick"*, Hibernia Press, Dublin, 1809, pp.202-205

(4) W.W.Gill, *A Manx Scrapbook*, Vol.1, Arrowsmith, London, 1929, p.29

(5) A.W.Moore, *Manx Ballads and Music*, G. and R.Johnson, Douglas, 1986, p.9

(6) Wm.M.Hennessy, *Annals of Ulster*, HMSO, Dublin, 1887, Vol.1, pp.29, 279

(7) A.P.Forbes, *Kalendars of Scottish Saints*, Edmonston & Douglas, Edinburgh, 1872, p.288

(8) J.J.Kneen, *The Place-names of the Isle of Man*, Manx Society, Douglas, 1925, pp.273, 156

(9) A.M.Cubbon, *The Art of the Manx Crosses*, Manx Museum, 1977, p.25

(10) G.V.C.Young, *The History of the Isle of Man under the Norse*, Mansk Svenska Publications, Peel, pp.142, 143, 209

(11) Francis J.Byrne, *Irish Kings and High-Kings*, B.T.Batsford, London, 1973, p.226

(12) J.F.Kenney, *The Early History of Ireland - Ecclesiastical*, Irish Univ.Press, Dublin, 1929, p.766

(13) P.M.C.Kermode, *List of Manx Antiquities*, Louis G.Meyer, Douglas, 1930, p.48

(14) William and Constance Radcliffe, *A History of Kirk Maughold*, Manx Museum, 1979, p.165

(15) A.W.Moore, *A History of the Isle of Man*, T.Fisher Unwin, London, 1900, p.872

(16) David Rollason, *Saints and Relics in Anglo-Saxon England*, Basil Blackwell, 1989, p.197

Chapter 11
NORSE PARISH CHURCHES

Early in the period of Norse rule, a scheme of civil administration was set up. Later, a distribution of churches appeared. It will be argued here that these churches fitted into the previously existing administrative structure. Attention will therefore be given to the system of government introduced by the Norse colonists. Guidance can be obtained from practices followed in Scandinavian countries, as the Norse colonists arriving in the Isle of Man continued in the way of life to which they had been accustomed.

A century or so later, most of the settlers had intermarried with the original inhabitants. At this stage, a decision was reached to legalize Christianity. Circumstances surrounding this step will be discussed. Also, the particular churches at Braddan, Santan and Malew will be examined.

11.1 Sheadings

In the Scandinavian countries, each `herred' district provided the ruler with a warship and crew. This may have been so in the Isle of Man. However, the word `sheading' itself has a simpler meaning. In the Manx Statutes of the period 1408 to 1430 the word is found to be spelt a couple of times as `shedding'. In Middle English and present-day North of England dialect, the word `shedding' means a process of dividing or a division. This term may have been introduced in the Isle of Man around 1400, and if so, the land division must have had an earlier name which has become lost.

Each sheading had a court which met at a Thing-field, a view supported by Canon Kermode (1). The Icelandic Sagas make two important points about Thing-fields. It was necessary that each should have a temple where an opening ceremony could be performed, as this gave validity to the proceedings and permitted witnesses to swear oaths on a sacred ring. Further, those taking part had to be of one mind in accepting to the pagan deities. It has been seen that this led to a crisis in Iceland when a significant number of freemen dissented. Sheadings must have been set up for taxation purposes at a very early stage of the land-taking. Taxation methods in the Isle of Man have been compared with those in the Orkney Isles by Loyn (2).

It is noted that each of the `herreds' in Iceland possessed not one temple, but three. When ecclesiastical parishes emerged in the Isle of Man in later Norse times, most of the sheadings contained three parishes. A chief cemetery can still be recognised in at least some of the sheadings.

The earliest written records date from the period of Stanley rule. A scheme for the goverment of the Isle of Man was approved by Michael Blundell, the governor who arrived in 1405. This scheme consisted of an assembly of twenty-four Keys (representatives) and two Deemsters (judges). These arrangements were confirmed at a court held at Castle Rushen in 1422, when one of the pronouncements was:

'Alsoe we (the Deemsters) give for law that there was never xxiiij Keys in Certainty, since they were first that were called Taxiaxi, those were xxiiij free Houlders, viz. viij in the Out Isles, and xvj in your Land of Man, and that was in King Orryes Days; but since they have not been in Certainty'.

King Orry, otherwise Godred Crovan, apparently wished to have a representative body for his kingdom of the Sudreys which had sixteen members for the Isle of Man. In order to have one representative per parish he may have found it convenient to adjust the number of parishes to sixteen from an unknown previous number.

One might start with the sheading of Glanfaba which still contains Tynwald Hill and the adjacent St John's Chapel. Mr Kneen proposed that the name Glanfaba was related to the name of the River Neb which flows out to Peel (3). It seems that an existing topographical name was used when the sheading was defined.

Thwaites wrote (4): "According to tradition, the chapel of St John is built on the site where once stood a temple of Thor". Although little weight can be attached to such traditions, further evidence supports this idea. Kermode mentioned that grave goods were recovered from an excavated burial mound near Tynwald Hill (5). When the old chapel of St John the Baptist was demolished in 1847 a cross-slab with a runic inscription was found (6). This monument could be taken to mean that a chapel had replaced a heathen temple during the 10th century.

Much later, when a written record appeared in 1408, the officer who kept order at the Tynwald ceremony was the Coroner of Glanfaba. The "Shedding of Glanfaba" was mentioned at a court held at Castle Rushen in 1430. St John's Chapel was named as the place where a Tynwald Court was held in 1577. It is reasonable to suppose that a sheading centre was set up at Tynwald Hill very early in the period of settlement. It is just possible that the district of St John's was a separate sheading subdivision before it was absorbed into the parish of German.

A few late records may give some rather uncertain glimpses of the possible locations of sheading centres. The sheading of Ayre has a Norse name which refers to the northern plain and includes parishes of Andreas, Bride and Lezayre. A court was held in Andreas Church in 1417 by John Litherland, governor for John Stanley. This event may only signify that a parish church was a convenient building in which to hold a court. However it is possible that the old sheading centre had been here, as will be mentioned later.

In 1422, a Tynwald Court was held at Kirk Michael on the 'Hill of Reneurling', the purpose being to indict leaders of a rebellion. The location of this hill is not known with certainty, but some possibilities have been mentioned by Cubbon (6). The sheading of Michael embraces the parishes of Michael, Ballaugh and Jurby. As the sheading is now named after the church at Kirk Michael, it must have had some other name prior to the time when the church was founded.

In 1428 another Tynwald Court was held at *Killabane*, that is, at the chapel of Keeill Abban in Baldwin. The Thing-mote at this site has been removed but its position is marked by a circular stone wall of recent construction (6). According to Mr Gill, the owner of Awallan, the farm standing to the west of the chapel was traditionally responsible for the upkeep of Keeill Abban (7). Perhaps we can see here the successor of the `Godi' who looked after the Thing-field temple. Whether this rather remote place was the main centre for the sheading of Middle is uncertain. So while it might be supposed that there were originally six sheading centres, it is now difficult to point to their locations on account of the many changes that have taken place during times when no records were kept.

It will be recalled that a national Althing was set up in Iceland in 930. However, it would be speculative to suppose that a similar Tynwald Court existed in the Isle of Man. The king probably made his wishes known to the sheading courts. At some time around 940, the king must have requested that temples should cease to be used. It is likely that a temple toll continued to be collected, as in Iceland, to provide for the building of churches and payment of priests. No bishop exercised central control, and priests were appointed by the leading landowner of each district. In these circumstances, the name given to a church would be selected by the local head-man, in consultation with his priest. For example, the people of Jurby wished to name their church after St Patrick, even though there was already a church of this name at Peel.

11.2 Circumstances of the Conversion

After the original Norse colonists had been interred in private burial mounds, the next generation used communal cemeteries. The earliest of these burials continued to be accompanied by weapons, in pagan style. A little later, Christian monuments appeared. The present-day distribution may be affected by destruction of these monuments through the ages. Concerning the church at Kirk Bride, Kermode remarked (8):

'Many pieces of "Picture stones" I am informed by one of the masons concerned, were broken deliberately and built into the present Church '.

Major cemeteries on the north-side include Maughold, Kirk Andreas and Kirk Michael, and on the south-side, Kirk Braddan and Malew. Concerning these cemeteries, Basil and Eleanor Megaw have stated (9):

'Only in the case of Maughold, however, can we as yet feel sure that there really was a Christian graveyard already in existence at the place before the Vikings were interred there... there are certainly no monuments older than the Viking age at the parish churches of Michael, Jurby and Andreas '.

Some considerations about the dating of the first Norse churches are now mentioned. A warning was given by W.G.Collingwood that dated gravestones do not necessarily imply that a contemporary church existed. He cited the churchyard at Hexham, which was used for two centuries after 875 while the church was in a ruined state. However, it has been seen that at least some of the Manx burial grounds did not exist as such before Scandinavian times. Here, a transition from heathen to Christian burials implies that a new church had been built.

Some Christian grave markers may have been made of wood and have disappeared. However, it is assumed that these, if any, were not of earlier date than the stone crosses which have survived. Furthermore, particular families may have adopted Christianity some time before this was accepted as a legally permitted practice. This may have been so, but such families would have been constrained to erect their monuments in private graveyards.

It has sometimes been claimed that memorial slabs depicting scenes from Norse mythology reveal an incomplete acceptance of the Christian faith. The suggestion has been made that Christ was merely added to the list of Norse gods. However, all existing monuments are seen to be in the form of a Christian cross, with added ornamentation. It is reasonable to view this ornamentation as an expression of pride in Scandinavian ancestry. Inscriptions, which were always in Norse runes, further emphasised class distinction. The Norse language was, of course, the language of the king's court.

The part played by the indigenous Celtic Church in the conversion of the Norsemen has often been discussed. Perhaps it did not play any effective part. At the relevant time in the mid-tenth century, pre-Norse churches had already lain in ruins for a whole century after they had been plundered by the first Norse colonists. While the priests of these churches were not necessarily murdered, they had no relevance to the social order initially set up by the settlers. An examination of place-names suggests that this social order penetrated to all districts of the Isle of Man without leaving Celtic enclaves of any appreciable size. When members of the lower social strata had to bury their dead, one must assume that they continued to use old keeill sites, but without the assistance of an organized clergy.

In the past, the opinion has been expressed that the foremost Celtic keeill in each parish developed into a parish church. This opinion is not well founded. In general, sites now occupied by parish churches had not been previously occupied by Celtic keeills, as already mentioned. In the Orkney Isles, the typical parish church developed from the chapel of the largest estate in the locality. Generally, in the Isle of Man, this was not so, but there may have been one or two exceptions.

District churches remained under the control of local landowners. Roolwer, who was Earl Thorfinn's bishop, visited the Isle of Man around 1060. Monuments having lavish decoration in Norse styles ceased to be erected at this time. Possibly, these monuments were disallowed by Roolwer. When Godred Crovan imposed his rule in 1079, it is likely that he made a more positive attempt to put the district churches under the control of Hamond, his bishop.

Three parish churches are now examined. Questions to be investigated include the identity of the patron saint and the reason why he was chosen.

11.3 Braddan Church

Of the monuments found at Braddan churchyard, none can confidently be given a pre-Scandiavian date. However, the cemetery has been in use from an early time as shown by Viking graves containing weapons (9). One of the earliest of the monuments is a large wheel-headed cross (No.72) having a carving popularly believed to represent "Daniel in the Lion's Den". Wheel-headed crosses have been found at the parish churchyards of Braddan, Onchan and Lonan. This type of monument consists of a heavy disc on a short shaft with a ringed cross carved on one face, a design inspired by the Irish high crosses (see Figure 2). Although there are no distinctively Norse details, it is now considered that these monuments were carved under the sponsorship of Norse proprietors during the first half of the 10th century. Braddan Church is not obviously associated with a sheading centre, and possibly it was first built as a private estate chapel.

A later Norse monument (No.135) has a runic inscription: "Thorleif Hnakki erected this cross to the memory of Fiac his son, brother's son to Hafr". Mr Cubbon pointed out that although the father and uncle had Norse names, the Gaelic name of the boy might indicate that his mother was a Celt (10). This cross is carved in the elaborate Mammen style and is attributed to the sculptor Thorbjorn who worked around the year 1000. This art-work has been taken to mean that members of the Norse community kept up communication with Norway.

It has been seen that many saints emerged from the northern part of Ireland in the sixth century to work along the western coast of Scotland, Brendan being one of the first of them. Brendan would appeal to a Norseman by reason of his reputation for seamanship and his power to calm stormy seas. The men of Bute came to hold Brendan in such high respect that they called themselves Brandanes. Brendan's name never gained a place in English church calendars, but was well known in Scotland and was transmitted northwards where it was found by 1200 in the calendar of the cathedral at Nidaros (11). His name also travelled southwards with the Dublin traders who had a settlement in Bristol. There, they had a chapel on

Brandon Hill, a name first recorded in 1192 (12). These records appear too late to be very useful, but may give an indication of earlier trends.

The earliest authentic record of the church at Braddan seems to be the report of a synod held by Bishop Mark at the *Ecclesia Sancti Bradani* in 1291. Documents of the period 1500 to 1700 mentioned the saint's name as Brandanus or Brendinus, showing that the saint was understood to be the Irish Brendan. However, by the nineteenth century, there were some odd ideas in circulation, and William Thwaites, writing in 1863 expressed the view (4):

'This church is dedicated to St Brandan or Brandon, bishop of the Island in the eleventh century. He is said to have been much respected and had churches in Britain dedicated to him. He died in the Isle of Arran in 1066 '.

There was an abbot called Brandan associated with Culross in Fife. The date of his death, as given in this passage, can be traced back to a calendar compiled by the Scotsman Adam King in 1588. The above reference to Arran seems to be the result of confusing this Brandan with the Irish Brendan who left his name in the Western Isles of Scotland five centuries earlier. It is fairly certain that the saint whose name was transmitted to the Isle of Man was the Irish Brendon, and that his name arrived by way of the Scottish Isles in the form of Brandon. This opinion was endorsed by Moore (13).

11.4 Churches of St Sanctan

First, the earliest manuscripts relating to St Sanctan may be examined. The Martyrology of Tallaght consists of a list of saints compiled around 790, but additions were made to it up to about 900. This lists Sanctan under his festival day of May 9. An added note says that he belonged to *Cell da Les*, but the location of this place has never been determined. Additionally, a further Bishop Sanctan is listed under June 10. The Martyrology of Oengus is a versified list made up of names selected from the Tallaght list and was finalized around 800. Oengus mentioned only one Sanctan, and he

131

was 'Bishop Sanctan the Famous', under May 9.

Sanctan's name occurred again in the Hymn of St Sanctan. This was included in the *Liber Hymnorum*, a book of the early 11th century now in Trinity College, Dublin (14). The preface to this hymn reads:

'Bishop Sanctan made this hymn, and it was on his going from Clonard westward to Inis Matoc that he composed it. He was a brother to Matoc, both of them being of the British race, but Matoc came into Ireland earlier than Bishop Sanctain... The true Irish tongue he (Sanctan) did not have until that time, but God promptly gave it to him '.

It is likely, but not certain, that Sanctan the Hymn-writer was the same person as Bishop Sanctan the Famous.

The village in Cumbria called Kirksanton is situated a couple of miles west of Millom. The first reference is that in the Domesday Book of 1086, which gives the name *Santacherche*. By 1185, the manor of *Kirkesantan* had passed to the De Boyvill family. By 1338, this land belonged to Furness Abbey, but the church continued as a chapel of the parish church of Millom. Soon after this time, the chapel must have become disused, as there is no later record of it. No reports are available on the site of this chapel.

The period of Norse-Irish settlement on the coast of Lancashire and Cumbria may have extended from 902 onwards to about 930. It does not seem possible that a British or Anglian church previously existed at Kirksanton. Sanctan had spent his life in Ireland and had established his reputation there, so his name must have been brought to Cumbria from Dublin. Historians in Cumbria, including Canon James Wilson and W.G.Collingwood, are agreed that Kirksanton was a name imported by a Norseman (15).

A Cumbrian genealogy is now followed up. According to *Harleian Manuscript No.19*, Pabo Post Prydyn was descended from the Ayrshire king Coel Hen. He lived somewhere around Cockermouth and had a son Dunod and another called Sawyl or Samuel Cendisel.

132

Sanctan and Matoc were sons of Sawyl. Dr Molly Miller suggested that this family tree may have been devised at Furness Abbey in the 12th century and transmitted to Ireland by way of the Cistercian abbeys in County Down (16). It is noted that the abbey of Mellifont was established in 1142. In this way, dubious speculations may have been incorporated into the Book of Leinster, which was compiled in Ireland from 1152 onwards. While personal details of Sanctan are uncertain, there seems to be sufficient evidence to show that he was born in Cumbria. He probably left at some time during the 7th century when conditions there became unsettled.

Attention is now given to the site of Cell Espuig Sanctain, located at St Anne's Wells, a village eight miles south-west of Dublin in the valley of Glennasmole. A graveyard there contains a ruin called Kill-Saint-Anne, or St Anne's Chapel. This Romanised form of the name implies that the chapel persisted into medieval times, for the reason that St Anne the mother of the Virgin Mary was hardly known in the British Isles before 1300. Gwynn and Hadcock, in their authoritative listing of early ecclesiastical sites in Ireland, suggested that Cell Espuig Sanctain might have been associated with a certain Bishop Sanctan who was a disciple of St Finbar of Cork (17). Hence it is doubtful whether this particular Sanctan is relevant to the present discussion.

References to the church at Santan in the Isle of Man are now traced. The AVITUS monument at Santan dates from the sixth century, but if a church existed there at that time, there is no good reason for believing that it was named after Sanctan. No record is available until 1291, in the time of Scottish rule, when the church was mentioned as *Ecclesia Sancti Santani*. The parish name in the Manorial Roll of 1511 was *Parochia St Santan* and the Diocesan Register of 1634 gave `Kirk Sanctan'.

Like other parishes in the Isle of Man, Santan was intensively colonised by Norsemen, but they left no distinctive monuments to show that there was a cemetery at the site of this church. For this reason, the first church may have been a private chapel that was set up and named during the 11th century. The district of Santan was not made into a parish until later.

133

Mr J.J.Kneen has mentioned a report made by a vicar of Santan (3). This report was of a fair held at Santan on May 21 in the year 1755. At this time the calendar had already been changed, so it might be expected that the fair day Bishop Sanctan the Famous on May 9 would then be held eleven days later on May 20. This approximate agreement of dates may show the survival of a genuine tradition concerning the saint.

Historians in Cumbria are agreed that the Sanctans commemorated in Cumbria and in the Isle of Man are the same person. In the above discussion it has been suggested that Sanctan should be primarily identified with Sanctan the Hymn-writer, and he was probably the same person as Bishop Sanctan the Famous mentioned by Oengus the Culdee.

11.5 Parish of Malew

There is no archaeological confirmation that a Celtic foundation existed at the site of the parish church at Malew. A couple of burials with weapons are understood to mean that the graveyard was used by Norsemen at an early date. The Sigurd Cross here has been dated by Shetelig to around 950. It is one of four such crosses, others being from Maughold, Andreas and Jurby East, all of which depict scenes from the Sigurd Saga of Norse mythology (6).

The literary record starts with the grant of lands by King Olaf Kleining on the occasion of the founding of Rushen Abbey in 1134. These lands were listed in the Bull of Pope Eugene in 1153. The translation give by A.W.Moore is (13):

The lands of Carnaclet as far as the monastery of St Leoc with their appurtenances; the village of Thore, son of Asser; the village of Great Melan, the village of St Melius; the village of Narwe, Stainredale with their appurtenances, the lands of St.Corebric and Fragerwl '.

This is the only occasion on which the names Leoc and Melius have been recorded. Various writers have associated the village of St

134

Melius with some part of the parish of Malew, and the monastery of St Leoc with the site of Rushen Abbey, but these locations are uncertain. Whether these names can be usefully discussed in relation to the parish name of Malew is a little doubtful.

A few saints are now reviewed. Moluag of Lismore in Argyll was mentioned in an earlier chapter. The saint Molua of Clonferta-Molua has already been mentioned in connection with churches in Dublin.

A further saint gave his name to the parish church of Kilmalieu at the medieval town of Inveraray in Argyll, this site being a mile north of the present town. The church was mentioned in records of 1442, but nothing is now left of it (18). Watson mentioned a further church at Kilmalieu, formerly Kilmalew, on Loch Linnhe in Morvern (19). The names of these two churches suggest that a saint called Liba or Moliubha worked on the west coast of Scotland. Further saints of a similar name need not be mentioned here.

Records for the Isle of Man are now examined. The following two documents belonged to the episcopates of William Russell (1348 to 1374) and John Donegan (1374 to 1380). Mr Kneen quoted a letter sent in 1368 by Pope Urban V to the Archdeacon of Man concerning the *Ecclesia Scti.Lupi in Mannia Sodorensis diocesis* (3). Further, Canon Kermode gave the text of a declaration made in 1376 by Bishop Donegan at a general chapter held in the *Ecclesia sancti Lupi in Mannia nostre Sodorensis diocesis* (1). These two reliable references indicate that the patron saint was already taken to be Lupus of Troyes, a regular saint of the Roman Church. There is no record that his festival day of July 29 was observed at Malew.

Pope Urban died in 1370. A Bull of his successor Pope Gregory XI dated 1377 confirmed the appointment of Malcolm Ysaye as priest of the *Ecclesia Sti.Maliwe*. This appointment had been made by "John Lord of the territory of Islay", as mentioned by Moore (13). John Macdonald of Islay assumed the title 'Lord of the Isles' in 1354. Some writers have taken this church to be in the Isle of Man, but the above information suggests that this was not so.

135

A reference to the parish name occurs in a Statute of Tynwald of 1598, where the name `Kirk Malew' is given. This is the present-day spelling, the pronounciation being `Mall-loo', with the accent on the second syllable. This seems to be the earliest reliable record of the parish name.

A theory that has enjoyed some popularity is the the parish name is derived from the name of St Lupus through the use of the Irish prefix *Ma*, which was commonly attached to a saint's name. This gave the formation *Ma-Lupus*, as explained by Thwaites (4). It seems impossible that such a word-formation could arise in post-Norse times, Also, although Lupus was known from the writings of Bede, there was no good reason to commemorate him in the Isle of Man. The converse process is more likely. It might be supposed that during the 13th century, a need was felt to have a regular Roman saint as patron saint of the church at Malew. An imagined derivation of the parish name from *Ma-Lupus* then justified the selection of St Lupus.

It has been seen that as early as 1368, the accepted patron saint was St Lupus. Although it may be suspected that this saint supplanted an earlier one, it is difficult to find any authentic reference to the name of this earlier saint. It is concluded that the parish name may be derived from a saint's name, but derivation from a place-name cannot be ruled out.

References for Chapter 11

(1) R.D.Kermode, *The Annals of Kirk Christ Lezayre*, Norris Modern Press, Douglas, 1954, pp.13, 207
(2) Henry Loyn, *The Vikings in Britain*, Blackwell, Oxford, 1994, p.108
(3) J.J.Kneen, *The Place-Names of the Isle of Man*, 1925, reprinted by Manx Gaelic Soc., Douglas, 1973, pp.319, 133, 613
(4) Wm. Thwaites, *Isle of Man*, Sheffield Publ. Co., 1863, pp.343, 384, 410
(5) P.M.C.Kermode, *List of Manx Antiquities*, L.G.Mayer, Douglas, 1930, pp.13, 62, 29

(6) W.Cubbon, *Island Heritage*, Geo.Faulkner, Manchester, 1952, pp.105, 107-8, 57-65

(7) W.W.Gill, *A Manx Scrapbook, Vol.1*, Arrowsmith, London, 1929, p.70

(8) P.M.C.Kermode, *Catalogue of the Manks Crosses with the Runic Inscriptions*, 2nd. ed., C.B.Hayes, Ramsey, 1892, p.13

(9) B.R.S. and E.M.Megaw, `The Norse Heritage in the Isle of Man', in *The Early Cultures of North-West Europe*, (editors: C.Fox & B.Dickens), Cambridge Univ. Press, 1950, p,143, See pp.146, 144

(10) A.M.Cubbon, *The Art of the Manx Crosses*, Manx Museum, 1977, p.38

(11) A.A.King, *Liturgies of the Past*, Longmans, London, 1957, p.402

(12) A.H.Smith, *The Place-names of Gloucestershire*, Vol.III, English Place-Name Society, 1965, p.95,

(13) A.W.Moore, *A History of the Isle of Man*, T.Fisher Unwin, London, 1900, reprinted by Manx Museum, 1977, pp.75, 165, 202

(14) J.H.Bernard and R.Atkinson, *The Irish Liber Hymnorum*, Book 1, Henry Bradshaw Soc., Vol.XIII, 1898

(15) T.B.H.Graham and W.G.Collingwood, *Patron Saints of the Diocese of Carlisle*, Trans.Cumb.& Westm.Ant.& Arch.Soc., Vol.XXV, 1925, p.1

(16) Molly Miller, *The Commanders at Arthuret* Trans.Cumb.& Westm.Ant.& Arch.Soc., Vol.LXXV, 1975, p.96

(17) A.Gwynn and R.N.Hadcock, *Medieval Religious Houses: Ireland*, Longman, London, 1970, p.403

(18) Royal Commission on the Ancient and Historical Monuments of Scotland, *Argyll, Vol.7*, HMSO, 1992, pp.114, 85, 69, 74

(19) W.J.Watson, *History of the Celtic Place-names of Scotland*, Wm.Blackwood, Edinburgh, 1926, pp.304-5

Chapter 12

FURTHER MANX CHURCHES

As many Manx churches appear to be dedicated to Irish saints, it might be argued that the churches must have had continuity from Celtic times, but this argument is unsound. The practice of dedicating a church to a guardian saint belongs to the Roman Church. It was followed by Anglian churches and was adopted by Scandinavian settlers in the British Isles.

When names of Manx churches first become available in the 13th century, they had already been forced into the formula *'Ecclesia Sancti* (Saint)'. The name was sometimes that of a real saint and was sometimes the personification of a district. As soon as a parish church had received a name, the name of the parish was normally taken to be the same as that of the church. Again, it was found convenient, from the 13th century, to express the official names of Manx parishes by the formula `Kirk (Saint)'. Here, the parish churches at Arbory, Marown, Onchan and Lonan will be examined.

12.1 Saints or Fields ?

Often, a Celtic saint received, as well as his baptismal name, a further name expressing respect or endearment. This name was formed by adding a prefix *Ma-, Mo-*, meaning `my', with a diminutive suffix *-ac, -oc, -ag, -og*. For example, the name Lugaidh of Lismore in Scotland became Moluag when applied to his churches. Sometimes, this piece of information has been too readily seized upon for generating saints from church names beginning with the syllable *Ma*. Mackenzie recognised this when he said (1): "And here I would remark that some of the attributions to Celtic saints that I have seen are so plainly speculative as to arouse suspicion that the names are more topographical than saintly".

Two of Mackenzie's examples may be reproduced here. Kirkmabreck is a present-day parish in Kirkcudbrightshire. The

138

church from which the name came was located two miles south-east of Creetown as marked on old maps, though no trace is now left of it. The name may have arisen from the Gaelic *Magh breac*, 'speckled field', the conjectured name of the field in which the church was originally built. Forbes gave the opinion that the church was named after an unknown saint called Mabreck (2). A fifteenth-century form of the name was *Kirkmakbrik*, which has suggested to some writers a commemoration of the Irish saint Aed mac Bricc. This idea is not confirmed by the earlier fourteenth century form of the name *Kyrkemaberc* (3). The question remains controversial.

Kirkmadrine is another example, this being the site of a church in the Rinns of Galloway, where the well-known ancient monuments were found. Watson put forward an improbable argument that the church commemorated a person called Draigne (4). A simpler derivation is from the Scottish Gaelic *Magh an droighinn*, 'blackthorn field'. Other places in Scotland have names such as Auchendryne, which have the same meaning (4). There are parallels in Ireland.

The church at Ecclefechan in Dumfriesshire was named in medieval charters as *Ecclesia Sancti Fechani*. Forbes explained that this connoted the Irish saint Fechin of Fore (2). However, Daphne Brooke proposed the simpler interpretation that the British name Ecclefechan means 'little church'(5). In the north of England, the prefix 'kirk' has been occasionally attached to a place-name, for example at Kirkburton in West Yorkshire and Kirkbampton in Cumbria. At these places, the church, when it was built, took the name of the village, and then the village was renamed after the church. Here, no one would suggest that a saint was involved. Referring to place-names in Wales, Owen Chadwick has remarked (6):

'For the bulk of Celtic dedications, no early evidence exists. For very few churches indeed is there any extant evidence before the 11th and 12th centuries... But it appears that the 11th and 12th centuries, when the Welsh ecclesiastical system was being progressively assimilated to the English, was a time of movement from the common custom of calling a church by its place-name to calling it after a saint.'

If a saint eventually gave rise to a place-name of the `Llan (Saint)' type, the saint's name must have been transmitted orally for several centuries. Of course, this gives plenty of time for distortion of the name and accretion of folklore.

12.2 Parish of Arbory

The earliest relevant document is the Bull of Pope Eugenius III dated 1153, relating to a grant made by King Olaf Kleining to Rushen Abbey. These lands included `the lands of St Corebric', as cited by A.W.Moore (7). This writer gave his source as being the translation by J.W.Oliver of the Cartulary of Furness, printed by the Manx Society in 1861. Mr J.J.Kneen has also given this saint's name with slightly different spellings.

It is believed that `Kirk' prefixes came into use in the late 12th century. No examples from the Isle of Man were recorded at such an early date, but examples from Galloway have been given by Daphne Brooke (3). So around the year 1200, it is supposed that the church at Arbory had the hypothetical name of *Kirk Corebric*, and the parish would also take this name.

Use now has to be made of an important document, which will be introduced here. This is the Bull of Pope Gregory IX addressed to Bishop Simon and dated 1231. It purports to list lands on which the bishop had a claim. Extracts here are taken from the translation by A.W.Moore (7):

'Amongst these (possessions) we have thought fit to specify the following by their proper titles:- the place called Holme, Sodor or Pile, in which the aforesaid Cathedral is situate, and the church of S. Patrick of the Isle... and also the lands in the aforesaid island, to wit both the Holmetowen, from Glenfaba, from Fotysdeyn, from Ballymore, from Brottby, from the staff of S. Patricius, from Knockcroker, from Ballicure, from Ballibrushe, from Jourbye, from Ballicaime, from Ramsey, also the lands adjacent to the Church of

140

Holy Trinity in Leayre, of S. Mary of Ballalaughe, of S. Maughaldus and of S. Michael; and the lands of S. Bradarnus and of Kyrkbye, of Kyrkemarona, of Colusshill and the land of St.Columba called Herbery.'

This text exists only as a copy discovered at Bishopscourt in 1888, and the Vatican copy has never been found (7). The existing copy, made around 1600, has been closely examined by Megaw (8). He suggested that the document was a fabrication that could be dated to the episcopate of John Donegan, 1374 to 1392. Locations of the places listed have been examined by Kneen.

At the date when this document was written, it might be supposed that the earlier name of `Kirk Corebric' had developed into alternative written versions of `Kirk Herbery' and `Kirk kerbrey'. Herbery was taken to be a place, as in the Papal Bull. The name `Kirk Kerbrey' is as given on Speed's map of 1605 (9). Kerbrey or Carberry was taken to be the name of a saint, and enquiries were made about his identity.

Around 540, an old church at Coleraine in Antrim was refounded by Bishop Cairbre, whose festival day was November 11. He did not gain recognition as one of the premier saints of Ireland and it is not clear why he should be commemorated in the Isle of Man.

It might be remarked that papal bulls and early charters show a disposition to describe ecclesiastical lands in terms of saints' names, possibly because this tended to legitimize the proposed arrangements. So when the name of a district was already established, it rather easily came to be accepted as a saint's name. The name `Corebric' may be a place-name of Norse origin. One possibility is that it came from the Norse *Kjarr-brekka*, `wooded slope'. Mr Kneen has mentioned analogous names, one being Ingebreck in Braddan, interpreted as `Ingi's slope'. A Norse place-name is therefore put forward as being the most satisfactory source of the parish name of Arbory.

141

12.3 Parish of Marown

It so happened that Olaf Kleining, king of the Isle of Man married Affreca, the daughter of Fergus, Lord of Galloway. This may explain why, at some point during his reign from 1113 to 1153, Olaf granted land in the parish of Marown to Whithorn Priory. However, no charter seems to be available until his grandson Olaf the Black confirmed this grant in 1193, when he additionally granted the parish church of Marown to Whithorn Priory. In this document the church was referred to as *Ecclesia Sancti Runani*. A little later, Bishop Nicholas confirmed that the church of *St Runa* had been granted to Whithorn, as mentioned by Megaw (10).

Later documents of the 16th century gave names such as *Kirk Marowney* (11). A Statute of 1594 gave the modern spelling of `Kirk Marown'. The local pronounciation has the second vowel as in `house', rather than as in `round', stress being on the second syllable. The possible explanation of these names may be that the place-name `Marown' was taken to be a saint's name. As this name was believed to be a *Ma-* formation, the first syllable was removed when the name was latinized during the 12th century, producing a saint's name of Runus, Runa or Runan. Subsequently, suggestions have been brought forward about to who this saint might be.

Out of the many saints called Ronan, a few may be mentioned here with their festival dates : Ronan the Kingly, son of Fergus (August 8); Ronan bishop of Lismore in Waterford (February 9); also Ronan, abbot of Kingarth in Bute. All these saints can be passed over, for the reason that the name `Ronan' does not bear any close resemblance to the name `Runa' recorded in the Manx documents.

The `Traditionary Ballad' mentioned the bishops Germain and Maughold and then went on to say (12):

The next bishop that came after, as far as we know was Lonnan. Connaghan the next then came in, and then arrived Marown the third. These three are laid in Kirk Marown, and there they always will remain '.

142

This folk-lore gives a special status to the site that is hardly warranted. An area of around a thousand acres in the parish was granted to ecclesiastical bodies by various Norse kings, but it cannot be inferred that any large area of land belonged to a church there in Celtic times. Indeed, there is no good evidence that Marown Church was built on the site of a Celtic keeill, as the only pre-Norse monument kept there was brought from the keeill at Ballaquinney, some distance away. Lintel graves found in the vicinity of the church may show that Norse settlers used the graveyard, but they did not do so to any large extent. A Norse cross-slab kept at the church was brought from a keeill at the Rheyn in the north-east of the parish.

Further attention is now given to the name 'Marown'. It is suggested that this is a topographical name consisting of a *magh*-formation. An analogue for the second syllable may exist in the name *Munenyrzana* recorded in the *Chronicon Manniae* as being the forerunner of the treen name of 'Mullenlowne' in Kirk Andreas. The first syllable of this word is the Common Gaelic *muine*, a shrubbery. The second syllable, according to Kneen, may be derived from the Scottish Gaelic *rabhan*, meaning a kind of grass that grows in pools (11). Hence a name *magh-rabhan* or *magh-raun* can be constructed, having the meaning of a field or larger district characterized by some kind of grass or rushes.

A sequence of events can now be envisaged. A Norse administrative district apparently retained an older name 'Marown'. When a church was set up around 950 it would be called 'Marown Church'. A century or more later, the church had to be taken into a diocese, and the need was felt at that time to have a patron saint, so the church became 'Church of St Runa'. Meanwhile, the parish continued to be called Marown.

12.4 Parish of Onchan

Certain pieces of basic information are available. When the church at Onchan was granted to the Nunnery of Douglas in 1511, the parish was mentioned as *Parochia Sancti Conchani*. The parish has the Manx name *Skyll Connaghyn* (11). This is said to derive from a certain Saint Connigen or Connaghyn (7).

The earliest reference to this saint seems to be in the `Traditionary Ballad', which dates from the 16th century. While so-called Manx names should be treated with caution, in this case the form *Connaghyn* is likely to be the primitive form of the name, while *Conchanus* is taken to be a latinized version thereof. If this is so, examination of names of the form of `Conchan' will be pointless. Even so, some of the efforts that have been made in this direction are now reviewed. Mr J.J.Kneen offered the following opinions (11):

'The patronal saint of this parish was St.Christopher, but he was better known in Ireland under his Gaelic name Conchenn, meaning `dog-head'... Under April 28th in the calendar of Oengus we find the following reference to St.Christopher: `Christopher, a pious dog-head was he ...' It is very remarkable that there are three cross-slabs in the churchyard of Conchan on which are depicted dog-like monsters.'

These opinions are open to criticism under several headings. Onwards from the 16th century or earlier, records speak of the church of Saint Conchanus. When it was rebuilt in 1833, it was given a new dedication to St Peter. No evidence has been presented that Christopher was the patron saint of Onchan Church at any time.

St Christopher was a martyr in Lycia in Asia Minor. Two legends grew up around his name. One made him a member of a tribe of dog-headed people, and another had him to be a giant who carried the infant Christ across a river. In Bede's calendar of saints, Christopher had his festival day on April 28. This information was available in eighth-century Ireland. The Martyrology of Oengus, written around 800, simply had an entry for `Cristofer' under April 28.

Kathleen Hughes has pointed out that the marginal notes on the manuscript of Oengus were added in the 15th century (13). The marginal note in Old Irish is translated: `Christopher, i.e. a dog-head'. The writer of the note was saying that according to his knowledge of the legend, Christopher was a dog-headed saint. He was not saying that in Ireland, Christopher passed under the name of Conchenn.

The carved figures that might be taken to be dog-headed monsters appear most clearly on a fine wheel-headed cross (No.92) of 10th century date. However, Mr.A.M.Cubbon favoured the simpler explanation that the artist wished to give a representation of lions (14). Dr Trench-Jellicoe held the opinion that none of the monuments at Onchan Church could be given a pre-Viking date (15). It must be concluded that these monuments do not indicate any link with St Christopher.

One of the older explanations is that given by Thwaites, who wrote in 1863 (16):

'It is to St Maughold that we owe the present division of the island into parishes, for each of which he caused a church to be erected. His death happening in 518, according to tradition, St Lonanus, a nephew of St Patrick succeeded him. After him came St Rooney and subsequently St Conanus or Conchan, who, on account of his great learning, had the education of the three sons of Eugenius the fourth king of Scotland. St Conanus died on the 26th January, 648, and was succeeded by St Contentus, Baldus (or Baldinus) and St Malcus, of whom, besides their names, we are are ignorant '.

This account is fictional. These names arise from the desperate efforts of Scottish historians to fill a gap of five centuries in their list of `Bishops of the Isles', as pointed out by Burton (17). The names Conan, Contentus, Bladus and Malcus can be traced back to Keith's `Catalogue of the Scottish Bishops', dated 1755 and cited by Forbes (2). The date of death of Conanus given above is that of the Scottish saint Conan, whose proper field of activity was in Breadalbane.

Further attention is now given to the name of St Connaghan. A similar name is that of the female saint Coningen, reputed to have her church near Arklow, her festival day being April 29. However, there is no indication that she came to the attention of Norse settlers in this district. In a detailed study of the name `Connaghan', Basil Megaw dismissed the idea that this was the name of an Irish St Christopher and suggested that the name may have been that of a local saint (18). In discussing patron saints, this option is always open, but is an unlikely one.

There is a further possibility that the parish name has arisen from a place-name. The Common Gaelic word meaning firewood is *connadh*. Mr Kneen has given an example, `Conocan', this being a farm at the north end of the parish of Arbory, interpreted as `a place of firewood' (11).

This discussion can now be concluded. The name `Conchanus' is taken to be a clumsy latinization of `Connaghyn', a supposed saint. Evidence for the existence of a saint of this name is weak. This leaves open the possibility that a previously existing place-name became accepted as being the name of a saint.

12.5 Parish of Lonan

Evidence from the site of Lonan Old Church is first considered. An alternative name for the church was given by Gill as *Keeill ny traie*, `Church of the shore', from its situation near a swamp (19). The name of a well near the church is not known with certainty. Dr Trench-Jellicoe has examined a cross slab (Manx Museum No.76) found near the church and he assigned it to the monastic phase of the early Manx church (15).

A further monument is a heavy wheel-headed cross (No.73). It has interlacing ornament carved in low relief showing Northumbrian influence (14). Formerly, this cross was assigned to the 9th century, but a more recent opinion has been given by Basil and Eleanor Megaw who said (20): "It is indeed very doubtful whether any of the wheel-headed crosses are earlier than the Viking age and most are certainly no older than the tenth century". So it appears that this cross was set up by a Norseman who had taken over a Celtic keeill.

146

Records of the parish name are now reviewed. The Manorial Roll of 1417-18 gives `Kyrkelonan'(8). The Manorial Roll of 1511 gives *Parochia Sancti Lonani*. On Speed's map of 1605 the parish is marked Kirk Lennon, but on Morden's map of 1695 it is marked S.Lomon (9). Perhaps these names on maps can be regarded as mis-spellings. Elsewhere, the parish name was often spelt `Lonnon' or `Lonnan' up to 1800, but since that time the accepted spelling has been `Lonan'. The present pronounciation has emphasis on the short `o'.

Through the nineteenth century the favoured derivation of the parish name was from St Lomanus, bishop of Trim in Meath. The story of how Patrick and Lomman arrived at Trim was originally told in the *Additamenta* of Tirechan (21). Loman was not subsequently mentioned in the Irish annals. In Jocelin's `Life of Patrick', the saint is mentioned as Lumanus, son of Tygridia, said to be one of the three holy sisters of St Patrick. There seems to be no justification for bringing Lomman into a Manx context, unless as part of the Patrick legend.

A number of saints called Lonan appeared in early Irish lists. Lonan son of Talmach was a bishop in Meath and died around 590. Lonan mac Laisre had his fair day of August 2, but nothing more is known of him. There were further saints in Ireland called Lonan but it is not easy to see the relevance of any of them to the Isle of Man.

A more recent suggestion is that the parish name of Lonan is derived from that of Adamnan, abbot of Iona. He was canonised as St Adamnanus, but the name was never pronounced like this. In Scotland the name was written `Aunan' or `Eonan', pronounced `Yawnan'. For example, it is acknowledged that a parish called Killeonan near Campbeltown in Kintyre was named after Adamnan (4). From a church name such as this, the belief might arise that the saint's name was Leonan, pronounced something like `Lawnan'. Mr Kneen did not favour such a derivation of the name `Lonan', for the reason that `Lonan' has a short first vowel (11).

Some information about names similar to Lonan is available from

Scotland. First, the statement of Forbes is noted (2): "The church of Stornoway in the island of Lewis is dedicated to S.Lennan. Dr.Reeves thinks that this name may be a corruption of Adamnan". This church was built around 1620 and was recorded by Martin in 1716 but has now been demolished (22). At a different place, on the island of Islay, the Kilennan Burn flows westward past the reputed site of the chapel of Kilennan. Mackenzie suggested that the chapel of Kilennan may have been named after a saint called Finan, and Watson agreed with this (4).

These places in Scotland suggest the following proposition. A Norseman in the Isle of Man became acquainted with a saint in the Hebrides called Lennan. Early in the 10th century, he took over an old keeill and gave it a name which later became `Kirk Lennan'. Hence the parish came to be called Lennan or Lonnan.

Some further place-names from Gaelic-speaking districts could now be mentioned. The River Lonan in Argyll flows westward from Loch Lonan through Glen Lonan past Clenmacrie to Loch Nell, three miles south-east of Oban. In a another country, the River Lennon, Leannan or Lenan in Donegal flows eastward from Gartan Lough past Kilmacrenan to Lough Swilly. Turning now to the Isle of Man, a river flows through the middle of the present parish of Lonan, but any Gaelic name possessed by this river has been lost. Perhaps a hypothetical *River Lonnan* transmitted its name to the surrounding district before the river name became lost. At present, the river has the Norse name of Laxey, `salmon river'.

In conclusion, it is seen that there are arguments for taking the parish name of Lonan to be derived either from a distorted saint's name or from a topographical name, but further study of this question is needed.

12.6 Hebridean Connections

The first chapel considered here is Keeill Abban at Baldwin in the north of the parish of Braddan. On this site, the chapel of St Luke was built in 1836. Previously, a keeill stood there having inside dimensions 18 by 12 feet (23).

The earliest available record in the Statute Laws of 1429 mentioned "the last Tynwald holden at *Killabane* before John Walton, Lieutennant of Mann". No further record seems to be available until that quoted by Mr Kneen as "Court Document, 1735", which called the chapel *Kell Abban*. A further reference occurs in the Dictionary of Dr John Kelly, written about 1790. His description of the ceremony of "Hunt the Wren" at Baldwin is taken from Paton's book (24):

... 'but in Baaltin the body of the naked Wren is deposited with much solemnity in Kil-Ammon and the evening concludes with a variety of games on the open ground which adjoins '.

As John Kelly was born at Algare, Baldwin, it might be expected that he was speaking from personal knowledge, but unfortunately his spellings of place-names appear to be distorted and useless. We note that the keeill was already a ruin. There are no local traditions about Abban (24).

Some biographical details of Abban are now given. The name Abban moccu Cormaic indicates that he belonged to the Corbmaic family which was one of the ruling families of the Laigin tribes of Leinster. Abban had two main churches, one at Moyarney near New Ross in Co. Wexford, another further north at Killabban near Stradbally in Laois. He also had two festival days, on March 16 and October 27. Information about Abban comes from a 'Life' which, according to Kenney, may have been written around 800 at Moyarney (25). Plummer's opinion was that Abban belonged to the later 6th century and that his biographer prolonged his life backwards (26). In this way, Abban was made a pupil of Bishop Ibar who died in 499.

Here, the opportunity is taken to mention two adjacent sites in Scotland which may or may not be associated with Abban. The disused church of Knapdale parish is a substantial 12th century building near Keillmore on the peninsula between Loch Sween and the Sound of Jura. Monuments at this site include the elaborately carved Keills Cross, otherwise St Carmaig's Cross, dated around 800. At various times the name of this church has been recorded as *Chillmacdachormes* (1224), *Kilmachermat* (1294) and *Kilvicocharmick* (1677), as reported by the Royal Commission (21).

Three miles to the south, at the mouth of Loch Sween is the island of Eilean Mor. This was noted by John of Fordun who wrote in 1363 and mentioned "The island of Helant MaCarmyk where there is also a sanctuary". According to a tradition recorded in 1797, a tomb on this island was called the tomb of St Macoharmaig (21).

A possible interpretation of the above information is that a founder-saint had the name *Cormac, Ma-Cormac* or *Da-Cormac*. From the 13th century onwards, some writers, but not all of them, wrote down the name as *Mac-Chormaic,* which generated the variants given above. An alternative interpretation favoured by the Royal Commission is that these names were generated from the name of Abban moccu Cormaic (21). This interpretation does not appear to be very convincing.

Whatever happened in the Western Isles, the saint's name arrived in the Isle of Man in the form of Abban, or so one must suppose. His name was bestowed on a temple-replacement chapel at the Thing-field at Baldwin. Abban was known as a guardian of seafarers by reason of his special powers over waters, and his aristocratic lineage would also appeal to the Norsemen.

It is possible that this saint came to the attention of the Norsemen in Ireland, but there seem to be no parallel dedications in Dublin, Wexford or Waterford. Another possibility is that Abban's name was carried to the Isle of Man by Culdees, but the name is not found in the liturgical productions of Tallaght. There is the further possibility that Abban`s name came to the Isle of Man from the West of Scotland, but it has been seen that this is doubtful. A final possibility is that the earliest recorded name of `Killabane' may have a topographical meaning. This discussion has to be left off without reaching a positive conclusion.

The second keeill to be considered here is situated at Ballaconley in

Jurby East. From this site a Norse cross slab (No.119) has been recovered, illustrating scenes from the Sigurd Saga and dated around 1000 (23). Plots called Particles adjacent to the keeill were re-possessed by Lord Stanley in 1429, but a plot continued as part of the glebe of the vicar of Jurby through the 19th century. Nothing is now left of the building.

The quarterland of Ballaconley received its name from the Connelly family who owned and occupied it until 1751. At times, this keeill has been called Keeill Coonlagh after the owner, this being the name used by Kermode (23). David Craine used the name *Kirk Ooslan* without giving further explanation (27). The name of the keeill has been discussed by W.W.Gill, who said (19):

'In pronounciation, "Cunlagh" is sometimes disguised by a metathetical shuffle, as "Cughlan" and "Cuthlan", but its kinship with *Conghalaigh*, the Irish prototype of "Conoly" is clear enough.'

The most likely saint that can be associated with this keeill is Constantine, who was an evangelist in Scotland until he was murdered in Kintyre around the year 600. He had a church of Kilchousland just north of Campbeltown, also at Kildusclan near the Crinan Canal in Knapdale and a church of St Cowstan or St Cowslan at Garrabost near Stornoway. However, this argument is not pursued in detail here for two reasons. There is no good documentary record of the name `Cowslan' at Jurby. Also, it has been seen that Mr Gill has expressed doubt about whether the keeil name contains an authentic saint's name.

12.7 The Columban Church in the Isle of Man

Following repeated Viking raids, the abbot of Iona found it advisable, in 814, to move articles of value to the Columban Church at Kells, County Meath. Although a community continued at Iona, their former position of influence had been lost. The religious life of the community at Iona had only a precarious continuity for four centuries, until Benedictine monks were installed there in 1203. Through most of this very long period, the cemetery at Iona continued to serve as the burial place of the kings of Scotland. This monastic community was not equipped or inspired to embark on missionary enterprises.

Mr A.W.Moore envisaged that Christianity was implanted in the Isle of Man through the agency of three saints, Ninian, Patrick and Columba. Of the last of these, he said (7):

'Let us now briefly investigate the names of the Columban monks in Man. Columba himself has given his name to a parish (Arbory) and also to a keeill; but perhaps an even more significant proof of what his influence was in Man is the fact that his name is still considered an effective charm against the fairies... Of the various Moluas, Molipas, Malius and Maluocs from whom the parish of Malew may have taken its name, the most likely to have been connected with Man is the Moluoc who founded a monastery in Lismore in Columba's time .... St Ronan, too though he lived after Columba's time, belonged to his church and is commemorated in Man in the parish of Marown... The name of Donnan of Eig... perhaps occurs in Ardonan, "Donnan' Height". Such is the evidence which certainly tends to show that there was a Columban Church in Man '.

However, it is not correct to say that any of these saints was an agent of the Columban Church, except, of course, Columba himself. This point has been clarified in the books of W.D.Simpson and others (28).

An entry in the `Annals of Ulster', under the year 979 gave: "Mughron, comarb of Colum-Cille both in Ireland and Alba ended life happily". The same event was reported in the `Annals of the Four Masters', where Mughron was called "sage of the three divisions". Charles Plummer took this to mean the divisions of the Columban Church in Scotland, Ireland and Man (29). Whatever divisions were intended by the annalist, Plummer's suggestion that one of them was Man seems to be a guess, and this suggestion has not been repeated by other writers. In specialized monographs on the Columban Church such as that of Maire Herbert, no mention is made of any property held by this Church in the Isle of Man (30).

Columba was well known to the Norsemen of the Northern and Western Isles. One of the tales in the Orkneyingers Saga tells of a war-band that "fared as far west as the Scilly Isles, and won a great victory in Mary Haven on Columba's Mass", that is, on the 9th of June. Many Norsemen had the personal name of Gilcolum, as, for example, the chief in Somerled's war-band who fell foul of St Maughold. The above two stories date from about 1150. There was a church of St Colum Cille in Dublin, with one or two in Cumbria. Columba was, with Patrick and Bridget, one of the three leading saints in Ireland, and it is to be expected that his name and festival day would be well known in places around the Irish Sea.

In connection with stray and unshorn sheep, a jury of 1570 testified that their owners should be given a customary warning:

'First we find that by Virtue of our said Oathes, that the Foster or his Deputy ought to go forth on St.Collumes Eve through the Forest, and to ride to the highest Hill Topp within the Isle of Mann, and there to blow his Horne thrise, the same done then after to range and view the Forrest...'

At this time, the official name of the church at Arbory was the church of St Columba, and it would be common knowledge that the parish fair was held on St Columba's Day, June 9. A traditional Manx-language prayer that has been recorded by David Craine and others is given here in English (27):

> Peace of God and Peace of man,
> Peace of God and of Columb Killey,
> On each window, on each door,
> On each hole admitting moonlight,
> On the four corners of the house,
> On the place where I am lying
> And the peace of God on myself.

A charm is intended to cure an illness. This composition is a prayer and not a charm, though both are intended to calm the mind. It is not particularly directed against fairies. The above examples give confirmation that Columba had an established place in Manx

153

tradition. However, none of this evidence goes any way towards showing that the Columban Church held lands in the Isle of Man or that it engaged in missionary activity there at any time.

12.8 Keeill sites in Kirk Andreas

Keeill sites have to be approached warily, as details about them have been recorded only quite recently and may or may not be reliable. The farm now known as Balleigh is on the Kiondroughad road. People still living know this farm by the alternative name of Ballakilcrump, which was also recorded in the Census of 1881. Kermode gave the site of Keeill Crump as being opposite the entrance of Ballakelly (22). This location is not near the present boundary of Balleigh, being 400 yards to the north-west of this farm. No visible remains have been reported.

In Ireland, the name *cruimthir* was given to a priest in charge of a church. The place-name Kilcrumper, with variants, also appears in Ireland. The name *cruimthear* persisted in Scottish Gaelic up to a couple of centuries ago, but has dropped out of modern Irish and Manx. The name "Church of a Priest" may appear to be a trivial one, unless a distinction was intended between *cruimthir*, a priest belonging to the Celtic Church, and *sagart*, the term normally applied to a priest of later times. So it is possible that the name Keeill Crump goes back to an unreformed chapel of the 12th century.

The quarterland of Ardonan in the treen of Regaby has a field called Cronk Keeill Traie. Up to 1940, a heap of stones could be seen there. The name `Keeill Traie' implies a chapel near the old shore-line of Lough Mallow. Moore suggested that this chapel was associated with the Scottish saint Donnan of Eigg (7). If so, one would expect to see a name such as `Kildonnan', as given to chapels of Donnan in Scotland. Prior to 1750, the quarterland name was written in the parish church registers as `Ardonagh'.

Kneen preferred to derive the name Ardonan from Adamnan of Iona (11). Watson argued that a site may commemorate Adamnan if

154

land was donated to the Columban Church while Adamnan was abbot (4). He mentioned the place called Ardeonaig or Adewnan on the south side of Loch Tay, which had the meaning of `Promomtory of Adomnan'(4). While this may be so, Ardeonaig, pronounced `Ard-yawneg' does not provide a phonetic equivalent to Ardonan or Ardonagh, which are names with a long `o'. Further, -an and *agh* suffices commonly convey either a locative or diminutive meaning. It has to be conceded that to associate the Ardonan keeill with either of the saints Donnan or Adamnan is not very convincing, and that the name Ardonan may have some simple import such as `little brown hill'.

A further site is now considered. Kermode has an entry in his List of Antiquities (22):

'Site of Keeill, Ballagonnell, near the W. end of Ballacolum, Treen of Ballyhamyg. On the N. side of the road from Andreas Village to the Lhen about 100 yards W. of the house. The late Archdeacon Moore thought this had been called St Martin's, but it is mentioned as Keeill Columb, near Ballacolum in *Manx Society, Vol.5* '.

Two sites are confused here. One is at Ballagonnell on the Kiondroughad road and the other is a mile to the north at the mouth of the Lhen Trench on the land of Ballacallum. A relevant report has been transmitted by Ramsey Moore (35):

'Mr Kinrade records that some of the granite used in the tower came from a Keill on the Estate of Ballacullam in all probability by breaking up Celtic and Runic Crosses such as were found at Knock-y-dooney '.

Andreas Church Tower was built 1866-9. The writer, Mr Kinrade was born in 1883 at the Lhen Mooar, where, no doubt, he received his information from older people. At the time in question, a small group of cottages stood at the mouth of the Lhen Trench. While it is possible that there was a keeill at this place, its exact location has never been established.

It is suggested that the name of the supposed keeill is a modern reconstruction based on the assumption that a place called Ballacallum ought to possess a keeill of St Columba. The personal name Gilcalm was used in the 16th century. In the 17th century it became Collum or Columbus, and during that period, this Christian name was used by four or five different families in Kirk Andreas, as revealed by burial records. It seems likely that the estate called Ballacallum received its name from a family of owners who favoured the Christian name of Callum through several generations. Most of the *Balla-* names of quarterlands came from the name of a resident family.

Another keeill site is at Knock-e-dooney in Kirk Andreas, which has been given the name 'Kyrke Asston' on one occasion only, as part of a treen name in the Manorial Roll of 1515.

At the time when a Celtic keeill was built, it was usually given a name relating to the place where it stood. This practice is illustrated by two or three hundred *Cell* names in Irish lists. In the Isle of Man, the name that a keeill is now found to possess, if it has any, may be the original name or a name later bestowed on a ruin, or indeed the name of a recent owner of the ground. Names showing dedication to either a biblical or an Irish saint were almost certainly given in medieval times when certain keeills were rebuilt, as will be considered later.

References for Chapter 12

(1) W.C.Mackenzie, *Scottish Place-Names*, Kegan Paul, Trench & Trubner, London, 1931, pp.235, 232, 101
(2) A.P.Forbes, *Kalendars of the Scottish Saints*, Edmonston and Douglas, Edinburgh, 1872, pp.379, 307, 378, 407
(3) Daphne Brooke, *Kirk-compound Place-names in Galloway and Carrick*, Trans.Dumfr.& Galloway Nat.Hist.& Ant.Soc., NS.Vol.LVIII, 1983, p.56
(4) W.J.Watson, *History of the Celtic Place-names of Scotland*, Wm.Blackwood, Edinburgh, 1926, pp.162, 468, 285, 148-9, 270

(5) Daphne Brooke, *St Ninian and the Southern Picts*, Trans.Dumfr.& Gall.Nat.Hist.& Ant.Soc., Ser.3, Vol.LXIV, 1989, p.21

(6) Owen Chadwick, 'The evidence of Dedications in the Early History of the Welsh Church' in *Studies in Early British History*, Cambridge Univ. Press, 1954, p.176

(7) A.W.Moore, *A History of the Isle of Man*, T.Fisher Unwin, London, 1900, pp.165, 179, 171, 69, 75

(8) Basil Megaw, 'Norseman and Native in the Kingdom of the Isles' in *Man and the Environment in the Isle of Man* (editor: Peter Davey), British Archaeological Reports, British Series, No.54(i), 1978, p.268 (at pp.293, 311)

(9) A.M.Cubbon, *Early Maps of the Isle of Man*, Manx Museum, 1974, pp.25, 28

(10) B.R.S.Megaw, *The Barony of St Trinian's in the Isle of Man*, Trans.Dumfr.& Gall.Nat.Hist.& Ant.Soc., Vol.27, 1950, p.173

(11) J.J.Kneen, *The Place-Names of the Isle of Man*, Manx Soc., Douglas, 1925, pp.151, 602, 209, 73, 242, 577

(12) A.W.Moore, *Manx Ballads and Music*, G.& R.Johnson, Douglas, 1896, p.9

(13) Kathleen Hughes, *Church and Society in Ireland, AD 400-1200*, Variorum Reprints, London, 1987, No.XIII, p.329

(14) A.M.Cubbon, *The Art of the Manx Crosses*, Manx Museum, 1977, p.13, 15

(15) R.Trench-Jellicoe, *A Re-definition and Stylistic Analysis of Manx Scupltured Monuments*, Lancaster Univ. Ph.D. Thesis, 1985

(16) Wm.Thwaites, *Isle of Man*, Sheffield Publ.Co., 1863, p.64

(17) J.H.Burton, *History of Scotland*, Wm.Blackwood, Edinburgh, 1897, Vol.1, p.391

(18) B.R.S.Megaw, *Who was St Conchan ?*, Journ.Manx Museum, Vol.VI, 1957-65, p.187

(19) W.W.Gill, *A Manx Scrapbook, Vol.1*, Arrowsmith, London, 1929, pp.70, 245, 259

(20) Basil and Eleanor Megaw, 'The Norse Heritage in the Isle of Man', in *The Early Cultures of North-West Europe*, (editors: C.Fox & B.Dickens), Cambridge Univ.Press, 1950, p.151

(21) Ludwig Bieler, *The Patrician Texts in the Book of Armagh*, Dublin Institute for Advanced Studies, 1979, p.167

(22) Royal Commision on the Ancient and Historical Monuments of Scotland, *Argyll*, *Vol.7*, HMSO, 1992, p.114, 85, 89, 74

(23) P.M.C.Kermode, *List of Manx Antiquities*, L.G.Meyer, Douglas, 1930, p.62, 29, 33

(24) C.I.Paton, *Manx Calendar Customs*, Wm.Glaisher, London, 1939, pp.39, 102

(25) J.F.Kenney, *Early History of Ireland: Ecclesiastical*, Irish Univ. Press, Dublin, 1929, p.318

(26) C.Plummer, *Vitae Sanctorum Hiberniae*, Clarendon Press, Oxford, 1910, p.xxiii

(27) D. Craine, *Manannan's Isle*, Manx Museum, 1955, pp.30, 233

(28) W.D.Simpson, *The Historical Columba*, Oliver & Boyd, Edinburgh, 1963, p.33

(29) Chas. Plummer, *Irish Litanies*, Henry Bradshaw Soc., London, 1925, pp.65, xxi

(30) Maire Herbert, *Iona, Kells and Derry*, Four Courts Press, Dublin, 1996, p.82

(31) Ramsey B.Moore, *Kirk Andreas*, Manx Museum, 1958, p.6

Chapter 13
BISHOPS AND THE CATHEDRAL

From around the year 1100, it might be expected that documents would offer better assistance, but they are still not very plentiful. Further, it is necessary to distinguish between factual reports and imaginative story-telling. A very useful document is the *Chronicon Manniae*. It was started by the monks of Rushen Abbey in 1249 and attempted to record events over the previous two centuries, while a later portion continued up to 1376.

Some uniformity can now be seen in ecclesiastical trends throughout Western Europe coinciding with the growing authority of the Pope. Although the diocese of the Sudreys was attached to Nidaros in Norway, it kept in step with what was happening in countries nearer home.

13.1 Christ-Churches at Lezayre and Rushen

During the time that Thorfinn, earl of Orkney held the Isle of Man in the name of the king of Norway, one of his bishops was Throlf or Roolwer. The Chronicon reported that when Roolwer died, he was interred at Maughold, and while no date was given, this was probably around 1060. Young suggested that he was not interred at Christ Church, Lezayre for the reason that this church had not yet been established (1).

Thorfinn's deputy was Sitric Reginaldson, who was followed in 1065 by his son Godred Sitricson. During Godred' reign the bishop was William, an Englishman. As Godred was no longer bound by arrangements made by the Earl of Orkney, his bishop may have been consecrated by Lanfranc, Archbishop of Canterbury. This would be in parallel with the practice followed in Dublin. Most likely, Godred Sitricson and Bishop William resided at Peel Island.

The next king was Godred Crovan. His father was Harald the Black of Islay who was a grandson of Eric Bloodaxe, one-time king of

Norway. Godred's wife Ragnhild was a daughter of Harald Hardrada, king of Norway. Godred Crovan fought with the army of Harald Hardrada at Stamford Bridge in 1066. Subsequently, he made attempts to take over the Isle of Man, and accomplished this at the battle of Sky Hill in 1079. Some writers maintain that Godred took possession of all land in the manner of a feudal lord, but others have disagreed.

Godred Crovan's bishop was Hamond son of Jole, a Manxman. He was probably consecrated at Canterbury. Godred Crovan, who was remembered as King Orry, introduced new legislation, which may have included a closer definition of the parishes, as suggested by Young (1). Many have held the opinion that Godred Crovan lived near Ramsey, and it has been supposed that the Christ-Church at Lezayre was set up as the personal church of Bishop Hamond. There was no Norse cemetery on this site that might indicate that a previous church stood there. The previous Norse church in Lezayre, if there was one, must have been elswhere.

Godred Crovan died in 1095. His heir Olaf Kleining was still a child and spent some time at the court of Henry I of England. Olaf supposedly became king in 1105 but he may not have been well established until about 1113. He resided at the fort of Cronk Howe Mooar near Port Erin. Hamond continued as bishop, but the exact date of his death is not known. The site of the parish church of Rushen has not yielded any Norse cross-slabs. Young believed that it was built as the church of Olaf's bishop, and that it then received the name Christ Church (1). A direct road leads from the fort to the church, a distance of about half a mile.

The previous church of Rushen may have stood at Ballaqueeney, half a mile south of the present church. This site has produced one of Gaut's sculptures dated about 960. Also, graves have yielded coins of the Saxon kings Edmund, Eadred and Edwy, whose reigns spanned the period 939 to 957. This church may have become disused when Kirk Christ Rushen was built. The name of this church has been lost and nothing is now left of it.

A notable event in Olaf's reign was the arrangement he made in

160

1134 with Thurstan, archbishop of York and with Ivo, the abbot of Furness Abbey, resulting in the founding of Rushen Abbey. An agreement was made that the abbot of Furness should have the right to nominate the bishop of the Sudreyan diocese. The first bishop to be appointed under this arrangement was Wimund. According to the writings of William of Newburgh, Wimund was taken into Furness Abbey as a boy. Later he was sent to the Isle of Man where he became so popular that the people asked that he should be made their bishop (2).

When he was appointed, Wimund took up residence on the island of Skye, but exactly where he lived there is uncertain. Wimund interested himself in political intrigues in Scotland. As a result, he was imprisoned in 1151, as stated by Skene, and did not return to his duties as bishop (3). It is seen that the latter part of Olaf's reign, there was no resident bishop in the Isle of Man.

13.2 Nidaros and Bishops of the Sudreys

In 1152, King Olaf Kleining of the Sudreys, as a gesture of loyalty, sent his son Godred Olafson on a visit to King Inge of Norway. In the same year, Olaf was murdered by his nephew Reginald. Also in 1152, Cardinal Nicholas Breakspear was sent by the Pope to organize an archdiocese for Norway at Nidaros, later called Drontheim. The new province, established in 1153, consisted of ten dioceses, including those of the Orkneys and of the Sudreys, the first archbishop being John Birgisson.

Archbishop John at Nidaros then appointed a Norwegian called Ragnald as bishop of the Sudreys. Simultaneously, Archbishop Roger of York, acting on an agreement with the late Olaf Kleining, appointed Gamaliel. However, Gamaliel did not take up office. At the end of the year 1154, the situation was that Godred Olafson had returned to take possession of the Isle of Man. He was accompanied by his bishop Ragnald, who stayed for four years before returning to Norway. According to the Chronicon, Ragnald made a ruling that one third of the income from the parishes should be made over to the bishop. This implies that eccesiastical parishes

161

already existed.

Somerled of Argyll arrived in 1158 and took possession of the Isle of Man, after driving out Godred Olafson. He then installed Christian of Argyll as bishop. On the return of Godred Olafson in 1164, Christian remained as bishop. Christian may have retired in 1188, and on his death, he was buried at Bangor Abbey, County Down. When King Godred Olafson died in 1187 he was followed by his son Reginald Godredson whose long reign extended to 1226. During this time, three bishops appeared (see Figure 6).

Bishop Michael, a Manxman, had been a monk at Rushen Abbey. In Mr Young's opinion, he was consecrated by the Archbishop of York in 1191. He died around 1203 and was buried at Fountains Abbey, Yorkshire. The next bishop was Nicholas of Argyll. He may have been consecrated by the archbishop of York, but may have been consecrated again at Nidaros in 1210. When he died in 1217 he was buried at Bangor in Ulster.

Reginald became the next bishop of the Sudreys. He was a nephew of King Reginald Godredson, who appointed him, and he was probably consecrated at York. During his episcopate, two puppet bishops of the Sudreys were also appointed, possibly by the archbishop of York, these being Nicholas of Meaux and John MacIver, otherwise John son of Harfare. When Bishop Reginald died in 1225 he was buried at Rushen Abbey.

In 1226, Reginald Godredson was displaced as king of the Sudreys by his younger brother Olaf the Black. It is known that Olaf lived at Peel Island, as his ships were burnt there during an attack made by his brother Reginald in 1228. This sets the scene for a review of the literature relating to the Cathedral.

13.3 Jocelin's writings

For a long time, the work of Jocelin of Furness was accepted as a cornerstone of history, so an outline of his career is now given. A new bishop arrived in Glasgow in 1175. He started to build the

162

cathedral which still stands there, and he wished to have a new biography of St Kentigern, the patron saint. He sought the help of Jocelin, a monk from the Cistercian monastery of Furness in Lancashire. Jocelin examined available documents, which perhaps included some that have since been lost, and wrote his `Life of St Kentigern' in 1180.

We turn now to events in Ulster. One of the Normans that arrived there was John de Courcy. From 1177, he proceeded to subjugate County Down. In 1180, he married Affreca, daughter of Godred Olafson, king of the Sudreys, and in the same year he decided to rebuild a monastery at Inch, a mile or so from Downpatrick. To assist in this project, he brought Cistercian monks from Furness Abbey, one of whom was Jocelin. A little later, in 1183, he brought Benedictine monks from St Werburgh's Abbey in Chester to re-found the church at Downpatrick. Relics of Saints Patrick, Bridget and Columba were acquired in 1185 (4).

Jocelin was asked to write a book that would add to the prestige of the new abbeys at Inch and Downpatrick. In this literary venture, he received encouragement from Thomas O'Connor, archbishop of Armagh. Jocelin's book `Life of Patrick' was finished in 1186. The culmination of these plans came when the relics were installed in Downpatrick Abbey in the presence of the Archbishop and of Cardinal Vivian, the papal legate. After being rebuilt, this church still exists as Downpatrick Cathedral.

Present-day students of St Patrick do not find Jocelin's work to be very useful, as he had no sources in addition to those available today. Attention is now given to this book, particularly the passage relating to Peel Island. Swift's translation of 1809 is used here (5):

The Saint (Patrick), beholding in Hibernia that the harvest was great but the labourers few, passed over into Britain to obtain assistants in the field of the Lord. And forasmuch as the pest of the Pelagian heresy and the Arian faithlessness had in many places defiled that country, he by his preaching and working miracles recalled the people to the way of truth. And many are the places therein which even to this day bear witness to his miracles and are

163

imbued with his sanctity. And he brought away with him many learned and religious men, thirty of whom he afterwards advanced unto Episcopal Office '.

'Returning to Hibernia, he touched on the islands of the sea, one whereof, Eubonia, that is Mannia, at that time subject unto Britain, he by his miracles and preaching converted to Christ... And the Saint placed as Bishop over the new church of this nation a wise and holy man named Germanus who placed his Episcopal Seat in a certain promontory unto this day called St Patrick's Island, for the Saint had there some time abided. And the other islands being converted to the faith, he placed over them Bishops from among his disciples ... and then he returned to Hibernia '.

In the light of present-day knowledge, this account is seen to contain much that is fantastic. Although the date of consecration of the Cathedral at Peel is not known with any precision, it must have been dedicated to Germanus at the time when Jocelin was writing. So Jocelin's narrative was developed from two starting points, the name of St Patrick's Isle and the name of Germanus. It appears that Jocelin was acquainted with Bede's `Ecclesiastical History'. Bede had much to say about the heresy of Arianism. However, this heresy had ceased to be an issue before the lifetime of Germanus of Auxerre. On the other hand, Germanus was deeply concerned with the heresy of Pelagianism.

Three steps can be distinguished in the construction of Jocelin's story. First, he transferred the anti-Pelagian activities of Germanus to Patrick. In fact, the writings of Patrick do not reveal that he had any awareness of this controversy. Jocelin threw in Arianism for good measure. Secondly, Jocelin made Germanus an assistant of Patrick. Jocelin did not say explicitly where Germanus came from, but his account implies that Germanus was one of the helpers whom Patrick had recruited in Britain. British assistants did, indeed, accompany Patrick on his mission, but Patrick did not return to Britain to fetch them, and none of them was recorded as having the name of Germanus.

Thirdly, Jocelin brought Patrick and Germanus together in the Isle of Man. One might make the comment that after the historical Patrick reached Ireland, he stayed there for the rest of his life, and, of course, the historical Germanus of Auxerre never came near the Isle of Man. The reference to "the other islands" appears to mean that Patrick also installed bishops in the Western Isles of Scotland, in places where Columba and others worked at a later time. This claim is, of course, unfounded.

It appears that Jocelin had access to a biography of Patrick, very likely in the form of the 'Tripartite Life of Patrick' which was written soon after 900 and which incorporated Muirchu's memoir. Earlier in his book, Jocelin described how Patrick, during his voyage to Ireland, visited St Patrick's Island near Skerries, north of Dublin, and this information can be found in Murchu's account (6). Therefore, Jocelin did not confuse this island with St Patrick's Isle in the Isle of Man. So his remark that Patrick once lived on St Patrick's Isle in the Isle of Man must be seen as a reckless attempt to explain the name of this island.

However, it might be that this explanation was not devised by Jocelin himself. In the passage quoted above, the assertion is made that after Patrick had passed over into Britain and had preached there, he was remembered in many places. This may be an allusion to churches of Norse origin in Lancashire and Cumbria which were dedicated to St Patrick and which had already existed for at least two centuries. The chapel at Heysham is an example. At these places, fables may have already been in circulation claiming that Patrick had paid a personal visit. Perhaps a similar fable told of Patrick's visit to the Isle of Man.

Jocelin certainly did not say that Germanus was an Irishman. Nevertheless, many subsequent writers have searched diligently for him in Irish records. There is no reference to a person called Germanus in any biography of Patrick that existed before Jocelin's time. Jocelin's account of the arrival of Germanus at Peel is not confirmed by any other source. The character whom Jocelin described under the name of Germanus is quite unreal.

165

13.4 Traditional Bishops

At this point it may be useful to reconsider the passage in Jocelin's book relating to the arrival of a person whom he called Machaldus (5).

'And in Ulydia (County Down) was Magiul, a Heathen, who was called Machaldus... he committed himself to the waves and was borne by them unto the Island Eubonia, which is named Mannia. And therein were two Bishops named Conindrius and Romulus, whom Patrick himself had consecrated and appointed to rule over the people of that island and to instruct them in the faith of Christ after the death of Germanus the first Bishop '.

This passage may be compared with Muirchu's account of the arrival of Mac Cuill, as given by Hood (6):

'And he found there two most admirable men ... who were the first to teach the Word of God and baptism in Evonia, and the islanders were converted by their teaching to the catholic faith; their names are Conindri and Rumili... He (Mac Cuill) trained body and soul in accordance with their rule... until he was made their successor in the episcopate '.

Jocelin reproduced the names of the two bishops, but modified Muirchu's account in various ways. Muirchu clearly stated that these two bishops were the first to preach in the Isle of Man, so they did not come after Germanus or anyone else. Further, Muirchu did not claim that the two bishops had been consecrated by Patrick. It was Jocelin's idea that the reformed robber Mac Cuill should be identified with Machaldus, or possibly he had heard a story to this effect. No one called Machaldus was mentioned by Muirchu, and this identification has not been confirmed elsewhere.

According to Jocelin, the sequence of bishops in the Isle of Man started with the British Germanus who had been left by Patrick. Next came Conindrus and Romulus, who were followed by the Irish Maughaldus. Jocelin must have been able to convey his views to the monks of Rushen Abbey when he joined their community around 1188. They were ready to accept certain parts of Jocelin's account, but not all of it. Some years later in 1249, they wrote in the *Chronicon Manniae*:

'The first bishop that is known before the reign of Godred Crovan is Bishop Roolwer, who lies in the church of St Machaldus. Many bishops have existed since the time of the Blessed St Patrick who first brought and preached the catholic faith to the Manx in Man, but the memory of these bishops has perished. Suffice it to say that who or what bishops existed before, we know not, because they have not been transmitted to us in writing nor by the traditions of our fathers '.

We see that the Cistercian monks endorsed the tradition that Patrick preached in the Isle of Man, but they pointedly omitted to mention Germanus. They must have been aware that the Germanus to whom the Cathedral was dedicated was Germanus of Auxerre, and not Patrick's assistant.

The 'Ballad of Mannanan Beg Mac y Leirr', usually called the 'Traditionary Ballad', was set down in Manx by an unknown writer at some date thought to have been around 1523, and was printed in Douglas in 1778 (7). Short extracts given here are from a translation by J.J.Kneen, reproduced by William Cubbon (8):

'Then came Patrick the gentle... And he drove Manannan on the wave... That is how the first faith came to Man, by Holy Patrick brought to us... Patrick blessed Holy German, and left him Bishop in it... And he (German) built all the Chapels. In each Treen Balley he raised one, for the people to come and pray; he built German's Church also, which is still a-sitting in Peel '.

Thomson confirmed that the Traditionary Ballad was written in language that belonged to the 17th century, but he conceded that it may have been written during the 16th century (9). It can be seen that the writer of the Traditionary Ballad used the story of Patrick's preaching that had been approved in the 'Chronicon', and also the story of the arrival of Germanus as supplied by Jocelin.

167

Some notice may be taken here of places in the vicinity of Peel that are connected with the name of St Patrick. There were Stafflands of St Patrick near Peel, but it is likely that they gained this name as endowments of the church of St Patrick on Peel Island. Further, the Barony of Bangor and Sabhal consisted of six quarterlands in the parish of Patrick. While the date of this grant is not known, this must have been after 1125, when the monasteries at Bangor and Sabhal were refounded by Malachy. The grant was probably made by Godred Olafson in the late 12th century when his daughter Affreca married John de Courcy. There is no solid evidence that St Patrick had been heard of in the Isle of Man before the building of St Patrick's Church in the tenth century.

13.5 Origin of the name `German'

The first reliable information seems to come from the *Chronicon Manniae*, written around 1250, where the name of the Cathedral is clearly given as *Ecclesia Germani*. The Manx name of the parish has been given by Kneen and others as *Skyll Charmane* (10). According to Kneen, the festival of *Laa'l Carmane* was held on July 13 (Old Calendar). In the Traditionary Ballad, the name `German' was written `Karmane' (11). These names will have to be considered in detail, but first, some background information is required.

When Germanus of Auxerre visited Britain in 429 he did not travel so far west as Wales, but he became known there as a patriarchal figure under the name of Garmon. Stories took hold that the early Welsh saints such as Illtud and Paulinus were pupils of Garmon. Legends about him were developed by Nennius, the monk from Bangor in Caernarvon, who wrote his *Historia Brittonum* around 830. He claimed that the dynasty of Powys in Wales had received the special blessing of Germanus (12). This approbation would be transferred to Merfyn Frych of Gwynedd when he married Nest, the heiress of Powys around 840. However, Merfyn had left the Isle of Man twenty years previously. The idea that the Welsh princes set up a church named after Garmon in the Isle of Man is too unlikely.

168

A revival of the veneration of Germanus might be noted here. A new church was erected in 859 at Auxerre to hold the shrine of Germanus. Charles the Bald, who became king of France in 875, had a son Lothair, who was abbot of Auxerre. Lothair commissioned his assistant Heiric to write a new biography of Germanus with the design of attracting pilgrims to the shrine.

Out of a dozen churches in the British Isles dedicated to Germanus, three may be briefly mentioned. The oldest is in the village of St Germans in Cornwall, just west of Saltash. A British monastery there called Lanalet possessed relics of Germanus of Auxerre. When King Athelstan wished to inaugurate the diocese of Bodmin in 936, the bishop he appointed resided at St Germans, where a fine priory church was built later.

The following two establishments were set up in Norman times. A church at Selby, Yorkshire was founded by Benedict, a monk from Auxerre. The story goes that he arrived in 1069 carrying a relic of Germanus. He dedicated his church to St Germain, and this church developed into Selby Abbey. At Tranent in East Lothian, the hospital of St German or St Germayne was built around 1170 by monks of the Bethlehemite order. These monks had their headquarters at Clemency within the diocese of Auxerre, which would be the reason why they named their Scottish hospital after Germanus.

In the calendars of most English churches, from the 11th century through to the Reformation, there were entries for Germanus of Auxerre, on July 31 and also for Germanus, Bishop of Paris, on May 28. At the time when the Cathedral was first consecrated, which is taken to be around 1180, it is inconceivable that the dedication would be to an obscure Celtic saint, and it must be accepted that the dedication was to a recognized saint of the Roman Church. It can be assumed that this saint was Germanus of Auxerre, on the grounds that no church in the British Isles was dedicated to any other Germanus. It would be expected that the festival day of Germanus of Auxerre would be observed with some ceremony in the Cathedral, but no record of this has survived.

In the Cathedral, the Latin name `Germanus' would be used, but otherwise, in ecclesiastical circles, the saint would be known by his Norman-French name of Saint Germain, with accent on the second syllable. This name would be taken into Gaelic with a hard `G', and would become Garmane or Carmane, with accent also on the second syllable. This hypothesis might appear to be adequate for explaining the Manx form of the name, and was accepted by Kneen (10). The construction *Laa'l* is a contraction of *Laa feaill*, meaning `festival day', as in *Laa'l Carmane*. The initial letter of the saint's name is not usually aspirated. On the other hand, the parish name often has the saint's name in aspirated form, as *Skyll Charmane*, with gutteral `Ch'.

While these local usages persisted, the parish took its official name from the parish church, which was the Cathedral. In the Manorial Roll of 1515, the parish was named *Parochia Sancti Germani* and in the Statute Laws of 1595 the modern name of Kirk German may be seen.

At the Reformation, celebration of festivals of patron saints was disallowed in all churches. A spectacle was provided at Peel Fair in 1713 when Katherine Kinred was punished for her misdeeds by being dragged in the harbour behind a boat, as mentioned by Canon Kermode (13). This occurred on St German's Day, July 13. At this time, the old festival of St German on July 31 had been discontinued for more than a century. It seems that a new date for Peel Fair had been fixed at July 13, which then became St German's Day. It is noted that an Act of Tynwald of 1610 laid down that herring fishing should not start before July 16. By fixing the new date of Peel Fair just before the opening of the fishing season, the urgent business of hiring boat crews would be facilitated.

In the above discussion, it has been accepted that the popular name `Saint Carmane' was derived from the name of St German. This is not completely satisfactory, as it leaves unanswered the question of why Germanus was selected as the patron saint. As Jocelin made use of the name `Germanus' in 1186, it must have already been applied to the Cathedral.

170

The name 'Germanus' may have been selected because a saint called Carmane had a prior association with the site of the cathedral. A church may have previously stood on the cathedral site, as suggested by Moore (14). Although nothing is known with certainty about this church, it may have been named after Saint Carmane, so that the name Carmane would become adapted to 'Germain' when a canonized saint was required for dedication of the Cathedral. A possible origin of the name 'Carmane' is now investigated.

Recent excavations on Peel Island reported by Dr Freke have revealed graves assigned to the 10th century Viking period by reason of dated grave-goods (15). These graves overlaid earler graves dated to the 7th or 8th century. The early graves are seen as evidence for the presence of a Celtic church or monastery.

Peel Island provides an excellent natural setting for a fort. The excavation of a large pit for storing corn lends weight to the theory that the site was occupied as an Iron Age fort, as suggested by Dr Freke. It is conjectured that this fort may have had some name such as *Cathir Mane*. The name 'Mane' has not been directly corroborated, except perhaps in the concluding sentence of the Mac Cuill story in Muirchu's memoir, as previously mentioned. It may be further conjectured that a name 'Carmane' was transferred to a church on Peel Island and eventually gave rise to an imagined founder-saint of this name.

13.6 Background to the Cathedral

King Olaf Kleining, during his long reign, did not live at Peel, but at Cronk Howe Mooar, near Port Erin. His son Godred Olafson then came to live at Peel Island in 1154 and continued there all his life, except for a break of six years. According to the 'Chronicon' he died there in 1187 and was interred at Iona.

Some writers have supposed that the cathedral of St German was located on Peel Island because of the long-standing sanctity of this place, but a more practical reason may be that king was living there at the time when the foundations were laid. Mr Young expressed the opinion (1): "The building of the Church of St.German... seems to have been commenced during Godred's reign".

It was formerly believed that the existing chancel of the cathedral was the oldest part, but the more recent opinion is that the nave is the oldest part of the structure that now exists. The arches of the nave aisle have been classified as "Transitional", a style of the 12th century (16). This earlier building may have been finished during the time of Bishop Michael and stood through the time of the next two bishops, who were Nicholas of Argyll and Reginald. Dates of kings and bishops are shown in Figure 6.

Olaf the Black arrived as king in 1226, and in the same year, the abbot of Furness nominated the new bishop. He was Simon, a native of Argyll who had been a monk at the Benedictine monastery at Iona. Simon was consecrated at Bergen in Norway in 1226. He held a synod at Kirk Braddan in 1229, when a number of regulations were laid down concerning tithes and fees.

The Cathedral was rebuilt by Bishop Simon. The chancel was extended eastwards and the new east gable is that which can be seen today. The windows in this wall are in the Early English style, which came into use in England from 1220 onwards. Olaf the Black had his residence on Peel Island and died there in 1237. So it may be expected that he would take a personal interest in the rebuilding of the Cathedral.

Bishop Simon died at Bishopscourt, Kirk Michael in 1248. The *Chronicon Manniae* stated that he was buried in the church of St German *quam ipse aedificare ceperat,* `which he himself had undertaken to build'.

At this point, some remarks may be made about the organisation of the diocese. In Scotland, the reign of David (1124-53) is associated with a vigorous campaign to appoint new diocesan bishops and to replace Culdees with priests trained in the observances of the Roman Church. In the kingdom of the Sudreys, a step in this direction was taken when Olaf Kleining established Rushen Abbey

172

in 1134. However, reform of the ecclesiastical system may have proceeded slowly on account of the absence of an effective bishop in the last decades of Olaf's reign. Subsequently, the growing influence of the Roman Church is revealed by examples of direct papal intervention. Some of these examples are now mentioned.

During the reign of Olaf's son Godred, it became known that Godred had not been regularly married to his wife Princess Finola. Cardinal Vivian came to the Isle of Man in 1177 to ensure that the marriage was made lawful. Some years later, Godred's son Reginald found that he was expected to pay homage to the king of England while he still had to pay tribute to the king of Norway, as explained by Young (1). When Reginald was in London in 1219, he made the gesture of presenting his kingdom to Pope Honorius as a gift. The kingdom was returned to Reginald by papal legate Pandolph on condition that he paid an annual fee to Furness Abbey. Soon afterwards in 1223, Pope Honorius sent Reginald a letter requesting that each church in the kingdom of the Sudreys should be endowed with sufficient land for the building of a house for the clergyman.

It is suggested that reform of the ecclesiastical organisation in the kingdom of the Sudreys took place within the fifty years 1150 to 1200, and within this period, the Cathedral was laid down. By the latter date, parish churches were already being served by priests who conformed to the practices of the Roman Church. Steps were also being taken to refurbish a number of rural chapels. These chapels had a history of their own, to be considered in more detail in the next chapter.

References for Chapter 13

(1) G.V.C.Young, *The History of the Isle of Man under the Norse*, Mansk Svenska, Peel, 1981, pp.58, 84-87, 105, 112-116
(2) G.T.Stokes, *Ireland and the Anglo-Norman Church*, Hodder & Stoughton, London, 1889, p.200
(3) W.F.Skene, *John of Fordun's Chronicle*, Edmonston & Douglas, Edinburgh, 1872, p.428. (there is a Llanerch reprint)

(4) A.Gwynn and R.N.Hadcock, *Medieval Religious Houses: Ireland*, Longman, 1970, pp.135, 105

(5) Edmund L.Swift, *Jocelin's "Life of Patrick"*, Hibernia Press, Dublin, 1809, p.129

(6) A.B.E.Hood, *St Patrick: His Writings and Muirchu's Life*, Phillimore, London, 1978, p.87

(7) W.Cubbon, *A Bibliographical Account of Works relating to the Isle of Man*, Oxford Univ. Press, 1939, p.799

(8) W.Cubbon, *Island Heritage*, Geo.Faulkner, Manchester, 1953, p.11

(9) R.L.Thomson, *The Date of the Traditionary Ballad*, Journ. Manx Museum, Vol,VI, 1957-65, p.53

(10) J.J.Kneen, *The Place Names of the Isle of Man*, Manx Soc., Douglas, 1925, p.373

(11) A.W.Moore, *Manx Ballads and Music*, G.and R.Johnson, Douglas, 1896, p.7

(12) John Morris, *Nennius: British History and Welsh Annals*, Phillimore, London, 1980, p.28

(13) R.D.Kermode, *The Annals of Kirk Christ Lezayre*, Norris Modern Press, Douglas, 1954, p.106

(14) A.W.Moore, *A History of the Isle of Man*, 1900, reprinted by the Manx Museum, 1977, p.172

(15) D.Freke, *The Peel Castle Dig*, Manx Museum, 1995, p.11

(16) Robert A. Curphey, *Peel Castle*, Manx National Heritage, Douglas, p.10 13

Chapter 14
RURAL CHAPELS

Previous chapters have followed the affairs of kings and bishops without giving adequate attention to the way of life of the ordinary people. Although a point was reached when the Norse proprietors decided to set up district churches, some further time elapsed before accommodation could be provided for everyone. Rural chapels appeared in the later period of Norse rule and these promoted a distinctive set of cultural values. One of the questions to be investigated is the relationship between these chapels and the pattern of land settlement.

14.1 Pattern of Norse Settlement

The typical farm that supported a family was the quarterland, of about a hundred acres. These farms are found to be in groups called treens. Often, but not always, there were four quarterlands in a treen. Definitive treen boundaries were given in the atlas prepared in 1867 by James Woods (1). With only minor changes, his treen names correspond with those listed in the Manorial Rolls of 1511 and 1515.

The name 'treen' is peculiar to the Isle of Man, but is cognate with the Hebridean *tir-uinge*, meaning 'ounce-land', that is, a parcel of land attracting an overlord's tax of one ounce of silver annually. It might be supposed that in each treen a head-man collected rents and procured services. A scheme like this operated until recently in the bishop's lands in the parish of Jurby, where a particular tenant was nominated 'Serjeant of the Northern Barony'. However, in the Manorial Rolls mentioned above, the Lord's Rent had already been specified for each quarterland. For some further period, tasks such as repairing churchyard walls and pinfolds may have been allotted to treens, but alternative arrangements were made in 1660, as mentioned by Moore (2). So treen divisions ceased to have legal significance, except for defining plots of ground.

Treen boundaries sometimes followed topographical features such as a stream or a road, but often the boundary was an arbitrary one, apparently enclosing land that had been allotted to a settler. The present boundaries of civil parishes are now such that they enclose whole treens, and presumably this has always been so.

It is envisaged that in the process of land-taking, a Norseman selected an estate and cleared the original occupants off it. He removed hedges belonging to crofts to create larger fields. His original residence can often be recognised as the principal quarterland of a treen, often carrying the same name as the treen, and such a farm is still colloquially called a treen farm. An analogous situation in the Hebridean island of Coll was mentioned by Anne Johnston (3). There, Norse settlement resulted in the formation of ten ouncelands, each of which became subdivided into secondary settlements, usually four in number.

As an example of a configuration of treens in the Isle of Man, a portion of the parish of Andreas has been selected from Woods' Atlas as shown in Figure 7. This district takes in treens named Smeal, Braust and Leodest. Mr Kneen has interpreted these Norse names as *Smidabol*, `Portion of the Smiths', *Brusastadr*, `Brusi's Farm' and *Ljotsstadr*, `Leot's Farm'(4). These are now considered in more detail.

The treen of Smeal consists of the principal quarterland of Smeal (170 acres), with three further quarterlands. The treen of Smeal-beg consists of the central quarterland of Johneoies flanked by quarterlands of Knock-e-Nean, Dhowin and Ballaquane. The treen of Smeal-beg may have come into existence by partition of an original large treen of Smeal, but there are no good grounds for making this assumption.

The Dhowin quarterland was divided up into a dozen crofts of about ten acres each, and these continued to support families up to around 1890. It seems quite reasonable to project this configuration back to Norse times. When the Norse proprietor came into possession of the treen of Smeal-beg, he did not wish to clear the previous inhabitants off all of his land, but permitted some to remain as rent-

176

paying crofters and hired workers, a view supported by Canon Kermode (5). Braust is a smaller treen of only two or three quarterlands.

Leodest presents an unusual situation. The primary treen has been partitioned to form the treens of Leodest and Alia Leodest. It might be expected that the principal quarterland now called Leodest would have remained in the treen of Leodest, but instead, this quarterland is now found to belong to the treen of Alia Leodest. The treen now designated as Leodest is comprised of three peripheral quarterlands named Ballacunner, Balleigh and Ballakelly. These quarterland names are recent ones, probably given by occupiers in the 15th century. Canon Kermode suggested that 'Alia' partitions were made when lands were granted to monastic houses in order to maintain the number of rent-paying treens (5).

Lowland treens contained only arable land. Poor or wet land was known as 'intack'. This conveys the meaning of land that was never attached to any particular treen. If this land was of some small value, its rent was calculated separately from rents of treen land, so the rent collector saw it as land that had been 'taken in'. Between the treens of Leodest and Smeal-beg, there is a strip of land adjacent to water-courses. This was divided into intacks with names such as Rheast, Curragh Cowle, Laagagh, Ballalough, Larivane and Poyll. Although these names may not be of any great antiquity, they are Gaelic names having the meaning of poor or swampy ground. This suggests that in the land-taking, the natives were not hounded out of the country, but were constrained to live on poor ground on the borders of arable treen land.

Due to parcels of land being bought and sold, one cannot be sure that quarterland boundaries have remained fixed. For example, in 1860, the treen of Alia Leodest included the quarterlands of Leodest-e-Kee and Leodest-e-Cowle. Soon after this date, these quarterlands were merged to form the present farm of Leodest. Further examples can be found where old quarterlands have become dismembered. Nevertheless, many quarterlands still have boundaries that may have changed very little since Norse times. This possibility has been discussed by Basil Megaw (6). He

177

suggested that some division resembling a treen may have originated in pre-Norse times as a combination of four quarterlands carrying a tax sufficient for supporting one soldier. Apparently, the average treen, of about five hundred acres, was of a convenient size for carrying this level of taxation.

However, it is argued here that treens were not arbitrary combinations of quarterlands, for the reason that many treens have a principal quarterland which was evidently the nucleus of an estate. Of course, it is possible that some of these estates may have belonged to pre-Norse owners who were dispossessed, but in any case, the new owner usually gave his estate a new name that continues in use to the present day. The primary Norse treens must have been defined during the the land-taking, that is around 830, as the need would then arise for allocating the tax payable to the overlord. Barbara Crawford suggested that the farms called *stadr* were probably established at this early date (7).

14.2 Treens and Keeills

William Cubbon has provided a convenient source of information on treens in his maps published in Kneen's `Place-names' (4). All the treens in the Isle of Man that were known around 1500 may be added up to obtain a total of about 175. Considerable grants of land were made to ecclesiastical bodies from 1100 onwards. This land would have been previously divided into treens, but the names and boundaries of such treens have become lost. This land amounted to the equivalent of at least 35 treens. Mr Megaw has estimated that with this additional number, the total for the Isle of Man may have been as high as 220 (6). Some of the treens partitioned into `Alia' and `Beg' portions and some of the very small treens may have been formed at a relatively late date, but no documentary evidence is available.

Basic information on keeills was provided in the Archaeological Survey carried out by P.M.C.Kermode and summarized in his `List of Manx Antiquities' of 1930 (8). Some of these entries have not been accepted, and there have been a few more recent discoveries, leading to a total of about 175 keeills. A notable attempt was made by Professor Carl Marstrander in 1937 to associate keeills with treens. He used information from the sources mentioned above and came to the conclusion that most of the treens once possessed a keeill.

A difficulty with this generalization is that neither historical accounts nor local traditions confirm that any particular keeill served any particular treen, with one or two possible exceptions. Each treen and keeill has had its own complex history. Some comments on Marstrander's theories have recently been given by Christopher Morris in his report on the excavation of Keeill Vael at Druidale, and also by Christopher Lowe in an addendum to this report (9).

14.3 Classification of Keeills

A church or keeill is obviously a building reserved for religious purposes. Its site usually has features such as a graveyard. Keeills were built or rebuilt over the millenium between the fifth and fifteenth centuries, so any discussion of them can only make sense if the period of use can be narrowed down a little. A simple classification is:

(1) Pre-Norse (Celtic) chapels not subsequently used
(2) Parish churches and temple replacements
(3) Rural chapels rebuilt for communal or private use

The last of these categories will be examined here in an attempt to establish its historical context. A keeill might be included in this category if some substantial stone-work has been reported, or if the keeill was known to be named after a recognisable saint.

It has already been proposed that Norse churches were set up soon after 930 within districts that correspond, more or less, with the later parishes. As a starting point, we may take the time when Bishop

179

Roolwer was sent by Earl Thorfinn around 1060. Regional churches had existed for a century or more. They did not belong to the king or to the bishop, but to local landowners. Tithes were not yet collected and parish boundaries were not yet clearly defined, but landowners collected a toll for supporting the priests that they employed.

It is suggested that Bishop Roolwer found the regional churches to be serving a landowning aristocracy, while little consideration had been given to the lower social classes. Very likely, he requested that the use of highly ornate memorial slabs should be discontinued. However, he may not have been able to bring about any further reforms for the reason that no central organisation existed for putting these reforms into effect.

An analogy has often been drawn between the Manx keeills and the ounceland chapels of the Orkney Isles. These buildings were erected at a similar time for a similar purpose, the purpose being to bring church facilities within reach of the people. However, the social structure was rather different in the Orkney Isles, as there the population was more homogeneously Norwegian. When Earl Thorfinn died in 1065, or possibly before this time, the Isle of Man came under the influence of Dublin, and Bishop William was appointed to the Sudreys. Again it is not clear that he was in a position to bring about significant changes.

It seems that no traditions speak of any land associated with recorded keeill sites, apart from an occasional small cemetery. This can be understood if endowments of land were appropriated at a very early stage of Norse colonisation. This land was not restored later, because there was no need for endowments at a later time, as the keeills then functioned as chapels attached to existing regional churches.

During the centuries since the keeills fell into disuse, it can be imagined that many farmers would drive their ploughs close to the keeill sites. A sad story is told in Kermode's `List of Antiquities'. The foundations of perhaps a dozen keeills that could be remembered by local people at the time of the Ordnance Survey of

1871 could no longer be found by 1930. Since then, the last traces of many more have disappeared.

In trying to isolate the keeills that were functional in medieval times, the overall list can be whittled down to some extent. Parish churches can be excluded and keeills of hermits in remote places are not relevant. The keeills standing on artificial platforms were certainly very old. Some of these were rebuilt and some were not, but many of the rebuilt keeills stood on pre-Norse foundations.

As an example of the material available for study, the list of keeills for the parish of Marown is reproduced from Kermode's list (8). The table below shows the present-day farm on which each is located, with the name of the keeill, if known, and the internal dimensions (to the nearest foot

Rheyn		
Eyreton	Keeill Vreeshey	16 x 9
Ballafreer	Keeill Pharick	15 x 9
Glenloch	Cabbal Druiagh	
Ballaquinney		
Ballingen	Keeill Ingan	13 x 10
Ballachrink		10 x 6
Ballanicholas		

All these keeils show evidence of having been laid down in pre-Norse times. Where any stonework is still left, this is drystone walling. These keeills were fairly uniformly distributed over the populated districts of Marown, as shown in Figure 8, but it cannot be assumed that all of them were in use simultaneously. Two treens each have two keeill sites while two more have none. Possibly the chapel at the Rheyn was originally a private one, as a runic stone bearing the name `Thurbiaurn' was found nearby. `Cabbal Druiaght' is a modern name applied to a ruin, and the name `Keeill Ingan' is not considered to be fully reliable.

Information for other parishes is not so plentiful. In Kirk Andreas,

181

which is one of the more fertile parishes, and which contains sixteen treens, only five keeills have been recorded. No trace now remains of any of these except one, and this has been reduced to an outline of the walls at ground level. It is highly likely that others once existed, but they have had their foundations uprooted before any record could be made of them. Possibly, names of sites have also been lost. Quarterland names of the `Balla-(Family name)' type continued to be formed up to about 1600. Instances are known where these names became replacements for older names of the `Ballakil-(Saint)' type. Undoubtedly, there were other instances where an older name once existed, but has now been lost.

14.4 Dedications of Keeills

The names given to keeills may prove useful in any attempt to reconstruct their history. About fifty had recorded names. Some of these names are modern or unreliable and some are incomprehensible, but some show dedication to a recognizable saint. The table below gives names of Manx keeills, the saint after whom each was named and the approximate number of keeills so named.

Keeill Woirrey	Virgin Mary	8
Keeill Pherick	Patrick	6
Keeill Vael	Michael	3
Keeill Pharlane	Bartholomew	2
Keeill Vian	Matthew	2
Keeill Vartyn	Martin	2
Keeill Vreeshey	Bridget	1
Keeill Catreeney	Catherine	1
Cabbal Niglus	Nicholas	1
St Keyll's Chapel	Cecilia	1

In this list, the saints can be clearly recognised. This rules out the possibility that the keeill names came from the Celtic Church, which did not dedicate churches to saints.

Anglo-Saxon England had a few churches dedicated to the Virgin Mary, but her cult was reinforced in the British Isles during the 12th century when the Continental monastic orders arrived. For example, no churches in Ireland were dedicated to the Virgin Mary until this time (10). Although the Cistercian monks normally took no part in pastoral work, their presence at Rushen Abbey and the increasing influence of the Roman Church would be reflected in the naming of the rebuilt chapels.

The runic stone at Keeill Woirrey in Maughold shows that Juan the Priest officiated there as a priest of the Roman Church. This stone, dated around 1200, does not confirm that the chapel was named Keeill Woirrey at that time, though there is no reason to doubt it. Further, one might expect that the writings of Jocelin would promote the popularity of St Patrick from 1200 onwards.

Names of keeills were written down during the Ordnance Survey of 1866-71, and only two or three were recorded earlier. The saints in the above list can be recognised as belonging to the church calendar of medieval England. Their names have been translated into Gaelic. Grammatically, the possessive case aspirates the initial letter of the saint's name (M to V, etc.). Michael was written `Mial' in Bishop Phillips' Prayer Book of 1610, while `Mail', `Maayl' and `Mael' are more recent spellings. `Mian' is the Manx form of Matthew, as used in the Manx Bible of 1763. `Parlane', standing for Bartholomew, resembles the popular Scottish Gaelic name `Parlan'. Martin could be regarded as a Roman saint here.

Saint Nicholas of Myra in Lycia (Asia Minor) was not known in Western Europe until about 1050. From that time he came to be known as a patron saint of seafarers and children and was celebrated on December 6. Dedications in England can be dated from 1150 onwards. Catherine of Alexandria has her festival on November 25. Possibly, her name was brought to England during the reign of Henry II (1154 to 1189), from lands that he held in France. Early dedications to Catherine can be traced in England from about 1150, but she did not become a popular saint until the following century.

On the basis of dedications, it seems likely that keeils named after the Virgin Mary, Michael, Patrick and Bridget may have been re-established during the century 1150 to 1250. However, dedications to Nicholas, Catherine and Cecilia appear to fall into a later period, possibly 1200 to 1350. St Keyll's Chapel at Jurby West is named after St Cecilia (her day November 22). Architecturally, this building belongs to the 14th century, but was renovated as a school-room in 1749, as noted by Kneen (4).

Apart from names, it may be helpful to consider the building technique. Some keeills can now be selected for which the dedication is known and for which internal dimensions are also known from existing stonework. The following table shows selected keeills, their locations and internal dimensions (feet).

Keeill Woirrey	Cornaa, Maughold	14 x 10
Keeill Vartyn	Ballakilmartin, Onchan	18 x 9
Keeill Vreeshey	Eyreton, Marown	16 x 10
Keeill Pherick	Ballafreer, Marown	16 x 9
Keeill Woirrey	Glen Mooar, Patrick	17 x 7
Keeill Pherick-a-Droma	Corvalley, German	18 x 9

These keeills were of substantial drystone construction, and typically had a doorway in the west gable, and a window in the east gable. It is generally admitted that dating of these buildings is difficult, due to the absence of distinctive architectural features. Even so, by reason of dedication to a recognisable saint, and by reason of similarity in size, it is suggested that the keeills in the above list form a homogeneous group.

For building dwelling houses, lime mortar was not much used in the Isle of Man until the late 18th century. Previously, clay bonding was used, and it is still easy to find ruined buildings of this kind. Therefore, it is surprising that many of the keeills did not use clay bonding. They were of primitive drystone construction, often with stone facing on the inside and outside of walls about three feet thick, the walls having a filling of earth and small loose stones.

The primitive construction of many keeills argues for an early dating, possibly to the 8th or 9th century. On the other hand it is not possible that keeills should have been named after a set of saints of the Roman Church at this time. The explanation may be that a selected number of chapels which had already stood for some time were renovated by building up their existing walls and were then given new names. This must have occurred rather late in the 12th century or early in the 13th century. No records of these names are available from this early time, and it has to be assumed that the names then given to them were the same as those they are found to possess in later times.

14.5 Utilization of Rebuilt Keeills

Possibly, some people hesitated to attend the regional churches because there was no room for them. However, it can be perceived that some chapels served a fairly well-defined district situated at a considerable distance from the parish church. For example, Keeill Woirrey in Maughold is four miles from the parish church and served farms in the valley of Upper Cornaa. Also, Keeill Pherick-a-Droma is a similar distance from the church of the parish of German and is in a district of upland farms. An entry in the *Chronicon Manniae* dated 1373 refers to *Capella Sancti Nicholai* at Laxey, which was three miles from Lonan parish church. The six keeills listed in the above table can only represent a small sample of the total number brought into use during the period considered, as information concerning most of them is lacking. The total number may have been forty or fifty.

It appears that a programme of keeill building was put in hand as a step towards providing adequate church accommodation. However, considerations of convenience for remote communities may have extended the useful life of some of the keeills even after adequate parish churches had been built. At a synod held by Bishop Russell at Kirk Michael in 1350, penalties were laid down for non-attendance (2). However, it is likely that church attendance had already been compulsory for at least a century.

Not all of the reconstructed chapels served communities in remote places, as some are found quite near to the parish church and may have been private chapels attached to the estate of a prominent person. An example is the keeill at Ballakillingan, Lezayre, of which nothing is now left.

We can now look again at the `Traditionary Ballad' of the 16th century, which has coloured the thinking of so many writers:

> And he (German) built all the chapels,
> In each Treen Balley he raised one,
> For the people to come and pray.

The person who wrote this knew that a large number of chapels were scattered around the countryside. Most of these were ancient ruins but some were still in use at the time when he was writing. He also knew that each parish was divided into about a dozen treens. In an imaginative reconstruction, he supposed that in some former age, all these chapels were simultaneously in use and were associated with the treens.

Ascertainable facts do not give any strong support to this idea. Where a keeill stood on a platform, the platform probably formed part of a pre-Christian ceremonial site, and this site would bear no relationship to the boundaries of the later Norse treens. If Earl Thorfinn ordered the construction of chapels on every treen, it is uncertain whether any progress was made with his scheme in the Isle of Man. What can now be assessed with some degree of confidence is that at a rather later date, a selected number of chapels became dedicated to medieval saints and became integrated into the diocese.

Some light is thrown on the state of the diocese by the letter written in 1223 by Pope Honorius III to King Reginald Godredson, requesting that his churches should be given land for the clergyman's house (11). It appears that while little money was available for ecclesiastical buildings, the people could be ordered to build up the walls of some of the old chapels.

14.6 Churches in the Western Isles

The places considered here include Arran, Bute, Kintyre, Islay and Mull. It is remarkable that churches to the number of well over a hundred all had names of the 'Kil-(Saint)' type, without any 'Kirk-(Saint)' names as used in the north of England. By the time these churches were taken into a diocesan organisation, the inhabitants of mixed Scots and Norse descent already spoke Gaelic.

Two chapels of drystone construction on the island of Colonsay can now be considered (12). Cill Mhoire is located at Upper Kilchattan. This had inside measurements 7 x 4 m (23 x 13 feet). Cill Chaitriona stood within a mile of the northern extremity of Colonsay, having measurements 7.1 x 3.5 m (23 x 12 feet). These chapels are distinctly larger than the above-mentioned chapels in the Isle of Man.

A serious problem arises here. The technique of drystone construction is primitive, dating back to the 9th century or earlier. However, dedication to the Virgin Mary and Catherine reveals the influence of the Roman church and suggests that the names were given at a time no earlier than the mid-12th century. Churches named Cill Mhoire have also been recorded in Islay and Oronsay, just as there were several called Keeill Woirrey in the Isle of Man. Although these Scottish islands were taken over by Somerled in 1156, their churches appear to have run a parallel course of development to those in the Isle of Man.

The Celtic Church did not have any strong tradition of congregational worship. A chapel was primarily for the use of the priest, and the people may have entered in groups to receive the sacrament. With the coming of Roman practice in the twelfth century, the need arose for improving church accommodation. On many sites, the Celtic chapel was demolished to make room for a new building. However, some chapels were retained and renovated by restoring the drystone walls that already stood on old

187

foundations, thus continuing a tradition of building that was out of date by some centuries. Such renovated chapels received a new name that was out of keeping with the archaic style of the building.

The transition from Celtic chapel to parish church is illustrated by the archaeological work carried out at St Ronan's Church at Iona by O'Sullivan (13). Here, an older building of internal dimensions 4.5 by 3.3 m (15 by 11 feet) had been taken down and replaced by a church of dimensions 11.5 by 4.7 m (39 by 16 feet), the date of this rebuilding being around 1200. Many parish churches of this date can be found in a ruined condition in the Western Isles of Scotland. In the Isle of Man, most of the parish church buildings of the late 12th century have disappeared, but a few buildings may still contain masonry of this date, such as the church at Maughold and the old churches at Lonan and Marown.

14.7 Religion and language

As religion has to be conveyed through the medium of language, an outline is now given of some recent discussions on how language developed in the Isle of Man during the period of Norse rule. Grave monuments of the period 950 to 1050 form a homogeneous group carrying inscriptions in the Old Norse language written in the runic alphabet. This prompted Kneen to assert (4):

'When the Norsemen settled in Man, the Gaelic language was replaced by a Scandinavian dialect; the runic monuments conclusively prove this. The earlier Gaelic population was either wiped out or absorbed... No doubt there were small isolated communities of Gaels here and there, but Gael and Scandinavian were eventually fused into one race, known to the Irish as Gall-Gael, or `Stranger-Gael'.

This statement has to be reconsidered. Monuments had runic inscriptions because they were erected by the wealthier members of the community, these being the landowners of Norse descent or others who wished to emulate them. This point was accepted by Megaw (6). Runic writing was the recognised medium of communication at that time among the Norsemen in Dublin and the north of England. It is not reasonable to deduce from these inscriptions that the Gaelic population of the Isle of Man either disappeared or ceased to speak Gaelic. Kneen proceeded to say (4):

'About the middle of the 13th century the kingdom of `Man and the Isles' came under the domination of the King of Scots... It is probable that many Gaelic immigrants from Galloway and Ireland now took up their abode in Man and as a direct result of this immigration the Gall-Gaelic dialect was eventually superseded by a purer Gaelic idiom '.

It need not be disputed that Scottish influence was felt at this time. However, it is not easy to accept that a mixed language reverted to Gaelic at this time, or that such a mixed language ever existed. Megaw has given arguments in favour of continuity of Gaelic culture from the 8th century. He said (6):

'The (Norse) settlers had become Christian within a century, at most, of their arrival: this alone reveals the effective influence of native culture on the incomers '.

There is some difficulty about this assertion. It has been argued in this book that parish churches were established within a political environment that was totally dominated by Norse settlers. Establishment of churches was activated by circumstances external to the Isle of Man. Much the same course would have been followed if the Celtic Church had never existed. Some have claimed that the native Celts converted the Norse invaders to Christianity, but it is not obvious that this could occur spontaneously. Outside of the restricted question of conversion of the Norsemen, it is possible to accept that there was some degree of cultural continuity. Megaw proceeded to say (6):

'A true estimate of conditions in Man, I suggest, has to balance substantial evidence of a powerful and persistent Scandinavian element in the ruling circle and the chief landownwers against a background of native continuity, presumably with widespread bilingual ability in much of the population. On conditions in the

189

ninth century the absence of Norse women's graves amongst those of the settlers argues for continuity on the distaff side at the crucial settlement-stage '.

In the Isle of Man, the picture presented by place-name studies is that Norsemen took possession of all the useful land. However, the crucial factor seems to be that most of these adventurers were unmarried when they arrived. Although the Gaelic-speaking inhabitants were dispossessed, they were not annihilated, and survived to intermarry with the newcomers. This is confirmed a century later when many names recorded on gravestones are seen to be Gaelic names.

These considerations need not cast doubt on the assumption that the Norse invasion inflicted a crippling degree of damage on the pre-Norse ecclesiastical system. This point was appreciated by A.W.Moore (2). Former priests were reduced to the status of mendicants and had no means of training successors. Even so, it must be supposed that the less privileged people continued to use the burial grounds of the Celtic keeills for two or three centuries. During this time they would only be able to call upon the services of itinerant or self-appointed clerics.

14.8 Cultural Impact of the Rural Chapels

One can search through books such as Cyril Paton's `Manx Calendar Customs' without finding any genuine traditions of the Celtic Church that have had continuity in the Isle of Man from Celtic times (14). As a possible exception, one might examine the Manx name *Laa'l Chibbyrt Ushtey*, the Festival of the Water Well, this being the name for Epiphany on January 6. As such a name could not have been introduced by the Roman Church, it is possibly a relic left by Culdee priests (15).

A more specific meaning can now be given to the notice erected by Juan at Keeill Woirrey, when he declared that he was `Shepherd of all the sheep in Cornaa-dale'. It might be envisaged that this chapel had been recently refurbished and dedicated to the Virgin Mary.

190

Juan, a priest of the Roman Church, was saying that he alone could provide pastoral services, to the exclusion of irregular priests. He may have used the Norse language in order to assert his authority.

The flourishing of rural chapels from the late 12th century onwards is not to be taken as an indication of the survival of Celtic ethnic groups. By this time, the population consisted of the descendants of Norse settlers who had arrived three centuries earlier and who had intermarried with the pre-Norse inhabitants. The social stratification that arose during the land-taking, based on race, language and religion had already dissolved. Even though the people lived in a land that still possessed the Norse place-names given during the land-taking, they now spoke Gaelic. This point has been discussed by Megaw (6). From this time, the lives of the people revolved around a calendar of church festivals and associated fairs. However, this calendar was that of the English Church and owed nothing to the Celtic Church, apart from the festivals of Patrick, Bridget and Columba which had been introduced by Norsemen.

As the thirteenth century progressed, more capacious parish churches were built. These were of mortared masonry, the inside dimensions being around 55 by 18 feet. When such buildings were provided, the need for the small chapels of drystone construction would be less urgent. They probably became disused at the Reformation, but chapel graveyards may have continued in use a little longer.

In olden times, there was a special celebration at each chapel on the feast day of the patron saint. This was disallowed at the Reformation, but in many places, a fair continued to be held on the saint's day near the site of the chapel. A blow was struck at this practice when the Gregorian Calendar was introduced in England in 1751 and extended to the Isle of Man by an Act of Tynwald in 1753. The same provision was made for Scotland and Wales.

An unfortunate clause in this legislation required that fairs should be held eleven days after their previous and proper dates. This deprived fair days of their old association with saint's days. Thus,

191

Tynwald Fair Day, previously held on the day of St John the Baptist, June 24, was henceforth held on July 5. A further blow was struck in 1834 when many fairs were discontinued by a Government order, on the grounds that they had become disorderly or unnecessary.

It is an interesting literary exercise to try to relate recorded fair days with the festival of the saint who was supposedly associated with the chapel. There are only a few recorded dates of fairs before the change of calendar, and none earlier than 1710. For example, St Catherine's fair was held through the nineteenth century near the site of St Catherine's Chapel at Colby. The fair was held on December 6, eleven days after Catherine's feast day of November 25. Catherine's feast day appears in the calendar of the Anglican Church for all to see, but when the saint was not so favoured, the outcome of such investigations may not be completely satisfactory.

References for Chapter 14

(1) James Woods, *A New Atlas & Gazetteer of the Isle of Man*, London, 1867
(2) A.W.Moore, *A History of the Isle of Man*, T.Fisher Unwin, London, 1900, pp.371, 200, 79
(3) Anne Johnston, `Norse Settlement Patterns in Coll and Tiree', in *Scandinavian Settlement in Northern Britain*, (editor: B.E.Crawford), Leicester Univ.Press, 1995, p.108
(4) J.J.Kneen, *The Place-names of the Isle of Man*, The Manx Soc., Douglas, 1925, pp.585-605, 488, xvi
(5) R.D.Kermode, *The Annals of Kirk Christ Lezayre*, Norris Modern Press, Douglas, 1954, pp.16-17
(6) Basil Megaw, *Norsemen and Natives in the Kingdom of the Isles*, British Archaeological Reports, British Series No.54(i), 1978, p.265 (see pp.279-80, 270, 288)
(7) Barbara E.Crawford, *Scandinavian Scotland*, Leicester Univ.Press, 1987, p.108
(8) P.M.C.Kermode, *List of Manx Antiquities*, Louis G.Meyer, Douglas, 1930

(9) C.D.Morris, 'The Survey and Excavations at Keeill Vael, Druidale, in their context', in *The Viking Age in the Isle of Man* (editors: C.Fell *et al.*), Viking Soc. for Northern Research, Univ.Coll.London, 1983, p.107

(10) J.M.Mackinlay, *Ancient Church Dedications in Scotland: Scriptural Dedications*, David Douglas, Edinburgh, 1910, p.70

(11) G.V.C.Young, *The History of the Isle of Man under the Norse*, Mansk-Svenska Publ. Co., Peel, 1981, p.116

(12) Royal Commission on the Ancient and Historical Monuments of Scotland, *Argyll: Vol.5*, HMSO, 1984, pp.157-184

(13) Jerry O'Sullivan, *Excavation of an early church and women's cemetery at St Ronan's medieval parish church, Iona*, Proc.Soc.Antiquaries of Scotland, Vol.124, 1994, p.327

(14) C.I.Paton, *Manx Calendar Customs*, Wm.Glaisher, London, 1939, p.31

(15) D.S.Dugdale, *Manx Church Festivals*, Andreas Parish Church, 1983

Chapter 15
PARISH CHURCHES AS THEY NOW STAND

Much of this book has been concerned with making the best use of meagre scraps of information. After the Reformation, more continuous records give information such as the succession of parish priests. Manorial Rolls of 1511-5 and 1643 give only a restricted view of farmsteads and occupiers but registers kept in most parish churches from 1650 onwards provide a new contemporary record of people and places. As many churches were rebuilt from 1700 onwards, records can be found relating to most of them. However, it is beyond the bounds of this book to describe church buildings in any detail.

15.1 Matters of Organisation

Marown must have existed as a parish at the time when King Olaf Kleining granted Marown Church with its tithes to Whithorn Priory. A little later, during the 13th century, Marown was subdivided to form the parish of Santan, bringing the total number of parishes in the Isle of Man to seventeen. By an Act of Tynwald of 1796, the parishes of Onchan and Marown were transferred to different sheadings, as shown in Figure 9.

The owner of a church was also its patron, that is, the person who nominated the minister or confirmed his appointment. The parishes of Kirk Andreas, Kirk Bride and Ballaugh continued as rectories belonging to the Lord of Man. The churches of German, Patrick, Braddan and Jurby belonged to the Bishop. The remaining churches with their tithes were granted at various times to Rushen Abbey and the Nunnery of Douglas and to various abbeys in the North of England and Northern Ireland. Such monastic houses appointed a vicar to a church that belonged to them. The parishes are now followed in a clockwise direction starting with the Sheading of Ayre.

15.2 Andreas, Bride and Lezayre

It is not now certain where the sheading centre for Ayre was located but there are indications that it may have been at the site of Kirk Andreas Church. Here, a rearrangement of the road system occurred, probably in 1650 when a new rectory house was built. Previous to this time, the main access to the church was from a north-south road passing to the west of the church, a road of which only slight traces now remain. West of the line of this road is a glebe field now called the Round Allan which, in a record of 1644, was designated a `Meeting Place'(1).

When the church tower was being built at Andreas, coins were dug up that had been issued by Edwy and Edgar, who ruled in England 955 to 975. So it is likely that the cemetery was being used at this time. A number of Norse cross-slabs testify that a church existed from around 950. The first building about which anything is known was that which stood at the highest point of the churchyard, and which may have been built in the 12th century. It had inside dimensions 54 by 18 feet (2).

It is known that Laurence was the archdeacon in 1247 and it been assumed that he was also rector of Andreas. John Litherland, who was John Stanley's governor, held a court at the church of `Kirkandras' in 1417. This may be the earliest reliable reference to the church or parish. There seems to be no hard evidence to show that the church was dedicated to St Andrew in Norse times, but there is no good reason to doubt this.

Arrangements for building a new church were made by an Act of Tynwald of 1800, and this church was probably finished around 1806. The old church was demolished, and no trace of it now remains. Later, the church was given a new roof of steeper pitch by Archdeacon Joseph Moore, and his bell-tower was finished in 1869.

At the church at Kirk Bride, a primitive cross-slab may indicate that there was an ancient keeill on this site, but it cannot be assumed that this keeill was associated with St Bridget. Two Norse crosses have been found here. The elaborate Thor Cross (No.97) belongs to the

11th century.

The church was granted in 1328 to the Priory of Whithorn. This grant was confirmed by Robert, king of Scotland, in a document written in Edinburgh in 1451. The text, as given by Gill, shows the name of the church as *Ecclesia S.Brigide in Lair in Manne* (3). Apparently, this grant did not take effect, as a Statute of Tynwald of 1408 mentioned `Kyrkebride' as a rectory, which it still is. Bridget's Manx name is *Brede*, the parish is *Skyll Vreeshey*, and the saint's day is *Laa'l Breeshey*, February 1.

The former church at Kirk Bride was of red sandstone, having dimensions 54 by 16 feet. An `Adam and Eve' stone of twelfth century date was set over the chancel door and is still preserved. A drawing of the old church is given in the book by William and Constance Radcliffe (4). A new church was built just north of the old one, which was demolished. The new church was finished in 1872 and the tower in 1876.

Property near Lezayre Church was the subject of a document written in 1257 by Magnus, King of Man, in which he mentioned `the village of Kellcrast near Ramsa'(5). In 1285, King Alexander of Scotland granted to Whithorn Priory the *Ecclesia sancte Trinitatis apud Ramsaych in Mannia* (4). Subsequently, an entry in the *Chronicon Manniae* under the year 1376 mentioned `Kyrkcrist'. Through the next century the church is mentioned as *Ecclesia Sancti Trinitatis in Leayre*, that is, `in the Ayre'. The modern form of the parish name appeared in the Manorial Roll of 1515, which gave *Parochia Sancti Trinitatis in Lezayre*.

The medieval church at Lezayre was rebuilt by Bishop Wilson in 1704. A chancel was added in 1723 to give internal dimensions 84 by 20 feet (5). Part of a wall of this church can still be seen at the east end of the churchyard. When the present church came to be built, a new plot from the estate of Ballakillingan was donated, and the church was consecrated in 1835 in the time of Bishop Ward.

15.3 Maughold and Lonan

The name *Ecclesia Sancti Maughaldi* appeared in the *Chronicon Manniae* when this was originally written in 1249. When this manuscript was revised by a later contributor around 1376, the name `Maughaldus' was deleted and replaced by `Machutus', as pointed out by Ralegh Radford (6). Machutus, otherwise Maclovius or Malo was born in Monmouthshire, and was associated with the monastery of Llancarvan. He afterwards went to Brittany and became bishop at the place now called St Malo. His death has been variously dated 565 to 627. In fact, he had no connection with the northern parts of the British Isles, although stories dating from around 870 made him the companion of St Brendan on voyages of discovery.

Two dedications in Scotland may be mentioned. The church at Lesmahagow in Lanarkshire was already dedicated to Machutus in 1144, as revealed by a charter of King David of Scotland (7). Here, Machutus almost certainly replaced the name of an earlier Celtic saint. At Wigtown, the church was dedicated to Machutus after it was rebuilt in the twelfth century, though its previous name is not known. The church became disused at the Reformation, but its ruin can still be seen.

It is likely that the churches at Lesmahagow, Wigtown and Maughold were dedicated to Machutus for the reason that at each place, the need was felt to adopt a canonised saint of the Roman Church. No connection existed between these churches, though it is possible that the church at Maughold followed the example of the Scottish churches. A likely timing for the dedication of the church at Maughold to Machutus would be when the church was granted to Furness Abbey in 1299.

Naturally, in places where Machutus became the patron saint, his feast day would be observed. English church calendars showed the festival of Machutus on November 15. This fair day was called *Laa'l Maghal Geuree*, the winter feast day, to distinguish it from St Maughold's chief fair day, *Laa'l Maghal Toshee*, which was on July 31.

197

Maughold Church is considered to be the oldest church building still in regular use in the Isle of Man. Stone mouldings that can be seen in the arch over the doorway are in the Irish Romanesque style, dated around 1150, but the masonry in which they are now set is more recent. The width of the twelfth-century church was probably the same as it is at present, that is, 17 feet. The church was extended eastwards at some time prior to 1660, to bring the church to its present length of 72 feet (8). The north and south walls were extensively rebuilt in 1860.

Lonan Old Church is on the quarterland of Ballakilley in the south-east corner of the parish. One report says that the church remained a rectory until 1350, when it was acquired by Rushen Abbey. This church had inside measurements 54 by 18 feet.

In Bishop Wilson's time, an Act of Tynwald of 1733 provided for the building of a larger church nearer the centre of the parish of Lonan at a place named `Bolliee Veen'. By this Act, parishioners retained the right of interment in the old churchyard. This new church was again rebuilt in its present form by Bishop Ward in 1834. At this time, the Anglican Church did not approve of dedication to local saints, so the church was dedicated to All Saints.

When the New Church at Lonan was first built, the builders were permitted to demolish the Old Church at Ballakilley. Fortunately they did not do this. Canon John Quine, when he became vicar of Lonan in 1895, was able to restore the eastern end of the Old Church. The stonework of this part is therefore modern, while the walls of the roofless western part are possibly of 12th century date.

15.4 Onchan, Braddan and Santan

These parishes now make up the sheading of Middle. The old church at Onchan stood in the lower part of the present churchyard. From around 1300, it belonged to the Nunnery of Douglas. John Feltham gave the dimensions 56 by 15 feet. The parish was referred to in the Manorial Roll of 1511 as *Parochia St Conchani*. After about 1800, the parish name `Kirk Conchan' was more usually written as `Kirk Onchan'. A new church was built by Bishop Ward in 1833 and received the dedication to St Peter which it still has.

Churches at Kirk Braddan are now considered. The Irish saint Brendan was known in Scotland as Brandon, and the Norsemen also knew him by this name. In the writing of medieval Latin manuscripts, the letter `n' was sometimes indicated by a contraction line or bar over the preceding vowel, the letter `n' itself being dropped. This bar eventually came to be misunderstood and omitted, so that `Brandon' became `Bradon'. The parish name was written as `Kirk Bradan' up to about 1650 and afterwards as `Kirk Braddan'.

Braddan Old Church still stands, and a description of it was given by Thwaites (2):

The church is a small ancient building erected on the site of a former structure in 1773... The building measures 71 feet in length by 21 feet broad. It contains a long low roof, tall and narrow doors and narrow windows. The arches of the windows of the nave are of herring bone work. At the western end is a square battlemented tower... On the eastern side of the tower is the date 1774 '.

The previous church was possibly of 12th century date. During the reconstruction in the time of Bishop Hildesley, this early church was increased in length but parts of its walls were retained. Stone mouldings were re-used but a new tower was built. Some distance away from the old church, a new church was built in the English Style in 1876, on ground donated by Lady Buchan.

The site of Santan Church has no Norse monuments. The name of an early parish priest appeared in the *Rotuli Scotiae* of 1291, this being during the time of Scottish rule (9):

'Odo of Kinconcaithe has letters of presentation to the *Ecclesiam Sancti Santani* in Man, vacant and in the gift of the king, on account of the land of Man being in the King's hands, and letters are directed to the Bishop of Sodor. Witness, the King, at Berwick on Tweed '.

199

The king was Edward I of England, who had, in that same year, taken control of Scotland. Santan had, by this time, attained parochial status as a rectory. The church was later acquired by Rushen Abbey, to which it belonged at the Reformation.

As far back as records go, the parish name has been spelt indifferently as Santan or Santon. From about 1650, it was believed in some quarters that the church was dedicated to St Anne, the mother of the Virgin Mary, and the parish was occasionally called Kirk St Anne in official records. The church was enlarged in 1725 but this structure was taken down and rebuilt in 1773, to give the building its present form. From 1891 the original dedication to St Sanctan was restored, very likely as a result of recent studies.

15.5 Malew, Arbory and Rushen

Rushen is a place-name, not a saint's name, and relates to some feature of the coast-line. Originally, the name may have been applied to a land division corresponding with the modern sheading of Rushen. This sheading became subdivided into the parishes of Malew, Arbory and Rushen. The town of Castletown was formerly called 'Russin', and Castle Rushen is situated there, but both Castletown and Rushen Abbey are in the parish of Malew.

Malew church was dedicated to St Lupus, who probably replaced an earlier saint at some unknown date. As early as 1428, the parish name was written as 'Kirkmalew' (10). Since about 1600, Statutes and other records have given the parish name as Malew. The church belonged to Rushen Abbey. The nave, of width 18 feet, appears to be a very old part, to which a chancel and transept have been added.

We turn now to the parish of Arbory. A directive in *Rotuli Scotiae* dated 1291 reads:

'Alan of Wygeton has letters of presentation to the vacant *Ecclesia Santi Carber* in Man, in the gift of the King, on account of the lands of Man being in the King's hands '.

200

This shows that the church was dedicated to a saint called Carber. Now we pass to the supposed Bull of Pope Gregory IX which mentioned "the land of St Columba called Herbery". Basil Megaw suggested that this spurious document can be assigned to the episcopate of John Donegan (1374 to 1395). In fact, a slightly earlier document can be invoked. This described the grant of land by Sir William le Scrope to Franciscan monks in 1373. This land was situated "in the village of St Columba", as mentioned by Canon Stenning (11). From these documents it can be seen that the new dedication to Columba must have taken place at some date between 1291 and 1373.

It is further noted that within the period 1275 to 1348, there was a sequence of five bishops, namely: Mark, Alan of Galloway, Gilbert Maclellan, Bernard de Linton and Thomas of Dunkeld, all of them Scotsmen. Probably the new dedication was proposed by one of these bishops. This name continued in use in official circles, and the Manorial Roll of 1511 gave *Parochia St Columba*. However, it is unlikely that this name was ever in general use, as the earlier Garrison Roll of 1428 gave the parish name as `Kirkarbory' (10).

The medieval church at Arbory belonged to Rushen Abbey, and was renovated around 1530. In Bishop Hildesley's time an Act of Tynwald dated 1757 called for a new church to be built on the north side of the old one, the old one to be taken down. This was done.

We now look at Kirk Christ Rushen. The church may have been built on a new site early in the reign of Olaf Kleining. At some time before the Reformation, the church passed into the hands of Rushen Abbey. A new church was built on the old foundations in 1775 and an apse was added in 1872.

15.6 Marown, Patrick and German

These parishes make up the present sheading of Glenfaba. Marown Old Church stands on the quarterland of Ballakilley. Parts of the existing building possibly date from the twelfth century, and at that time, the church was granted to Whithorn Priory. In 1754 the

201

church was enlarged by building an extension of fifteen feet on the west end to give internal dimensions 60 by 18 feet. After 1850, the Old Church was no longer required. The eastern half of it was demolished and a new east gable was built, but the foundations of the demolished part can still be seen. Eventually, the Old Church was closed, but was again opened for occasional use in 1959. The new church, built in 1850, stands by the Douglas-to-Peel road, and now serves as the parish church. Like the old one, it is dedicated to St Ronan or St Runius.

The original church of the parish of Patrick was on St Patrick's Isle, although, during the 14th century, the people of the parish may not have had free access to it. During the 17th century, this church was still in a sound state, and had a twin bell-turret on the west gable. However, the building then fell into disrepair and became roofless. Local people made use of the church of St Peter in Peel.

Bishop Wilson, in 1710, obtained an Act of Tynwald for building a new church, when it was stated that "The Inhabitants of the Parish of Patrick have for some Ages past been destitute of a place of publick Worship". Land was donated by Captain Silvester Radcliff of `Knock-Aly-Moor'. The new church was built near the ancient Keeill Croo and was finished in 1714. For the construction of this church, Bishop Wilson did not strip lead off the cathedral roof as some people have alleged, but used lead that had been assigned to the cathedral, as stated in the Act of Tynwald.

In the course of time, the parish church at Knockaloe became delapidated. A new one was built in 1881 adjacent to the old one, which was taken down completely. Through the nineteenth century, rebuilt churches were dedicated to saints that appeared in the calendar of the Church of England, but St Patrick was not one of these. So the new church was dedicated to the Holy Trinity.

In the parish of German, the Cathedral served as the parish church. It was substantially finished during Simon's episcopate, but additions were still being made as late as 1291. After 1333, Peel Island was fortified, and the Cathedral became inaccessible for a time. Governor William le Scrope repaired the cathedral in 1392, when battlements were added to the towers. By the time when Bishop Rutter was interred there in 1661, part of the roof was off (10). It was never completely restored, though occasional services were held in the chancel up to 1799.

Meanwhile, the people of the parish of German used St Peter's Church in Peel. The fabric of St Peter's Church incorporated pre-Reformation features, and the date of its erection has been estimated at 1550. The tower of St Peter's was built much later, around 1850, and although the church has now been demolished, its tower still remains. In 1884, Bishop Rowley Hill supervised the erection of the new church of St German in the town of Peel. Henceforth, this church served the parish of German, which includes the town of Peel.

15.7 Michael, Ballaugh and Jurby

A major cemetery was located at Kirk Michael, as shown by a number of Norse memorial slabs. The church was mentioned in the *Chronicon Manniae* in 1250 as *Eccl.Sti.Michaelis*. In 1299, Bishop Mark agreed that the church should be granted to Furness Abbey. The Manx name of the parish, `Skyll Michal', shows the pronounciation (as in Michaelmas) that prevailed until recently. The chancel of the old church was rebuilt by Bishop Wilson's son Thomas in 1776. Alongside this church, a new one was built on a cruciform plan in 1835, during Bishop Ward's time. The old church was then demolished, though a small piece of its masonry can still be seen.

The site of Ballaugh Old Church at Ballaugh Cronk has provided one of Gaut's Norse cross-slabs. Around 1500, the name was *Ecclesia Sanctae Mariae de Balylagh*, but from about 1600 the parish name has been written as `Ballaugh'. Parish registers still exist from 1598. The old church of St Mary was rebuilt by Bishop Wilson in 1717. It retains some of the features of the previous medieval building and is still used occasionally. As it was situated in one corner of the parish, a new church, also dedicated to the Virgin Mary, was built in what is now Ballaugh Village, and was consecrated by Bishop Ward in 1832.

At the parish church of Jurby, dedicated to St Patrick, several Norse cross-slabs have been found. There is a tradition that a stone church was built in 1213 (12). One of the earliest written records of this church is preserved in the *Rotuli Scotiae* of the Scottish Parliament, dated 1291 (1):

'Roland, chaplain, has letters of presentation from the King to the *Ecclesia Sancti Patricii de Dureby*, vacant, and in the King's gift '.

The old church stood in the middle of the churchyard. An Act of Tynwald of 1813 required the old church to be taken down and a new church built on the south side of the churchyard. This building, as seen today, was finished in 1829.

15.8 Time goes by

A few events of more recent times are outlined here. This is a postscript, and is in no sense a coherent account of church affairs. We recall that the diocese of the Sudreys became attached to the Norwegian province of Nidaros, Drontheim or Trondheim in 1154. In 1266 the Isle of Man came into the possession of King Alexander of Scotland, but the diocese continued to be attached to Norway. It was called `Sodor', or alternatively, `The Isles', and included the Western Isles of Scotland.

Mark of Galloway, a very capable agent of King Alexander was appointed bishop in 1275 and retained this position until his death in 1303. Within this period, it has been seen that at least three Scotsmen were installed as parish priests, at Santan, Arbory and Jurby. Following Bishop Mark, the next four bishops covering the period up to 1348 were also Scotsmen, and went to Norway for consecration. During this long period, it would not be surprising if the Scottish bishops and their assistants moulded the Manx Church according to the ideas they brought with them, but it is not certain that they spent much of their time in the Isle of Man.

204

William Russell, a Manxman, was abbot of Rushen Abbey when he was made bishop in 1348. One of the last of the bishops of 'Man and The Isles' was John Donegan, another Manxman who had previously been archdeacon of Down in Ulster. He was bishop 1374 to 1392.

After the Stanleys arrived as proprietors of the Isle of Man, separate bishops were appointed for Man and for The Isles. The first bishop to be appointed for the Isle of Man was Richard Pulley, who came in 1410. The diocese continued to be attached to Drontheim until 1458, when it became attached to York.

The Act of Uniformity, confirmed in 1558 during Queen Elizabeth's reign, constituted the Church of England as the only lawful church. The Reformation had few immediate effects in the Isle of Man, but from this time, the succession of priests in each parish is fairly well known, whereas little is known of their predecessors. For a long time after the Reformation, the erection of gravestones was discouraged, and gravestones in Manx churchyards dated prior to 1750 are quite scarce.

The Welshman John Phillips, appointed bishop in 1604, is notable as being the first person to commit the Manx Gaelic language to writing, but his Prayer Book of 1610 was not printed at that time. At the Restoration in 1662, a revised Anglican Prayer Book appeared, and this served in an unchanged form until 1928.

Thomas Wilson was bishop 1698 to 1755. Here, it must suffice to say that he worked resolutely for the welfare of his diocese. Mark Hildesley, bishop 1755 to 1772, is remembered for the encouragement he gave to the translation of the Bible into the Manx language. It is remarkable that he was able to obtain contributions from clergymen in every parish, to complete the work in 1775.

William Ward, bishop 1827 to 1838, made his mark by raising funds for rebuilding churches. These were needed, as the rural population increased to a maximum around 1840.

References for Chapter 15

(1) P.M.C.Kermode, *List of Manx Antiquities*, L.G.Meyer, Douglas, 1930, p.32

(2) W.Thwaites, *Isle of Man*, Sheffield Publishing Co.,1863, pp.306, 384, 371

(3) W.W.Gill, *A Manx Scrapbook*, Vol.1, Arrowsmith, London, 1929, p.220

(4) William and Constance Radcliffe, *Kirk Bride: A Miscellany*, Nelson Press, Douglas, 1982, p.116

(5) R.D.Kermode, *Annals of Kirk Christ Lezayre*, Norris Modern Press, Douglas, 1954, pp.206, 25, 32, 53, 207

(6) C.A.Ralegh Radford, *Excavations at Whithorn*, Trans.Dumfr.& Gall.Nat.Hist.& Ant.Soc., Vol.27, p.85 (at p.101)

(7) A.C.Lawrie, *Early Scottish Charters*, James MacLehose, Glasgow, 1905, pp.135, 397

(8) J.W. & C.K.Radcliffe, *History of Kirk Maughold*, Manx Museum, 1979, p.42

(9) J.Stevenson, *Documents: History of Scotland*, Vol.1, H.M.General Register House, Edinburgh, 1870, p.215

(10) Basil Megaw, `Norsemanm and Native in the Kingdom of the Isles', in *Man and the Environment in the Isle of Man*, (editor: Peter Davey), British Archaeological Reports, British Series 54(i), 1978, p.265 (see p.312).

(11) E.H.Stenning, *Portrait of the Isle of Man*, Robt.Hale, London, 1958, pp.89, 91

(12) David Craine, *Manannan's Isle*, Manx Museum, 1955, p.23895

INDEX

Mythical Saints 113-4, 138
Mytum, H. 21

Narberth 10
Nechtansmere, Battle of 54, 57
Nendrum 18, 102
Nennius 11, 50, 168
Nicholas, Bishop 162, 172
Nicholas, St 88, 183
Nidaros 68, 72, 130, 159, 161, 204
Ninian, St 13-15, 152
Norn 69
Norse monuments 93-4, 116, 126, 129, 143, 188, 195, 203
Norse settlement 65, 69, 72-3, 93, 175-8
Northumbria 52-5, 59, 62, 88-91
Norway 65, 67-8, 94, 160-1

Oengus, Martyrology of 131, 134, 144
Ogham 19, 20, 23, 120
Olaf Cuaran 81, 90, 91, 98
Olaf Godredson of Dublin 90
Olaf Kleinig 103, 134, 140, 142, 160-1, 171-2, 194, 201
Olaf, St 67-8, 115
Olaf the Black, king of Sudreys, 142, 162, 172
Olaf Trygvason of Norway 67
Olrik, A. 66
Onchan 143, 194, 198
Oram, R.D. 58, 97
Ordnance Survey 180, 183
Orkneyingers' Saga 70, 153
Orkney Isles 65, 69-72, 180
Orlyg 111
Osred of Northumbria 55
O'Sullivan, J. 188
Oswald, king of Northumbria 52
Oswy, king of Northumbria 53-6
Ouncelands 69, 71, 175, 180

Pagan worship 8, 11, 19, 43, 65-6, 75-

6, 125
Palladius, bishop 17
Parishes, formation of 160-1, 179
Paton, C.I. 149, 190
Patrick, parish 63, 168, 202
Patrick, St 14-17, 20-2, 45-8, 78-9, 84, 115, 163-8, 183, 191
Paul the Hermit 60-1
Paulinus, bishop 52
Pearce, S,M. 26, 49, 63, 101
Pechthelm, bishop 57
Pembrokeshire 19, 30
Penda of Mercia 52, 87
Penmachno 23
Penrith 89, 91-2
Phillips, Bishop 205
Picts 32-3, 57, 60-1, 69, 70
Plummer, C. 33, 63, 149, 152

Quarterlands 175-8, 182
Quine, J. 198

Radcliffe, W. & C. 49, 123, 196, 206
Radford, C.A.R. 14, 57-8, 63, 72, 97-8, 101, 103, 106, 111, 197
Ramsey 196
Ragnald, Bishop of Sudreys 161
Ragnald Ivarson 79, 89
Reeves, W. 112
Reformation 89, 115, 118, 122, 169, 191, 194, 205
Reginald, bishop of Sudreys 162, 172
Reginald Godredson of Sudreys 120, 162, 173, 186
Reginald Kolson 72
Relics 118, 121, 169
Rheged 54-8
Rhiainfellt 56
Rhys, J. 24
Richter, M. 26
Ripon 53
Rollason, D. 100, 123

212

****

214